Key Readings in Addiction Psychiatry

Edited by
American Academy of Addiction Psychiatry

Sevarino   *Treatment of Substance Use Disorders*
Rosenthal   *Dual Diagnosis*

Board of Directors of
the American Academy of
Addiction Psychiatry

DUAL DIAGNOSIS

Edited by
Richard N. Rosenthal, M.D.

BRUNNER-ROUTLEDGE
New York • London

Published in 2003 by
Brunner-Routledge
29 West 35th Street
New York, NY 10001
www.brunner-routledge.com

Published in Great Britain by
Brunner-Routledge
27 Church Road
Hove, East Sussex
BN3 2FA
www.brunner-routledge.com.uk

Brunner-Routledge is an imprint of the Taylor & Francis Group.
Printed in the United States of America on acid-free paper.

10 9 8 7 6 5 4 3 2 1

Library of Congress Cataloging-in-Publication Data
Dual diagnosis / edited by Richard N. Rosenthal.
    p. ; cm. — (Key readings in addiction psychiatry)
  Includes bibliographical references and index.
    ISBN 0–415–94436–8 (pbk.)
  1. Dual diagnosis.
    [DNLM: 1. Diagnosis, Dual (Psychiatry)—methods. 2. Mental Disorders—
  diagnosis. 3. Substance-Related Disorders—diagnosis. WM 141 D8118 2003]
  I. Rosenthal, Richard N. II. American Academy of Addiction Psychiatry
  III. Series.

  RC564. 68D697 2003
  616.86—dc21
                                                              2002155073

Contents

Introduction to the Key Readings in Addiction Psychiatry Series

The American Academy of Addiction Psychiatry is pleased to announce a new book series entitled "Key Readings in Addiction Psychiatry." Substance abuse adversely affects a very large portion of the world's population, causing more deaths, illnesses, and disabilities than any other preventable health condition. According to Dr. Alan I. Leshner, Former Director of the National Institute on Drug Abuse, "addiction has so many dimensions and disrupts so many aspects of an individual's life, treatment for this illness is never simple." [1] Scientific advances are occurring at an increasingly rapid rate, leading to an array of effective pharmacologic and behavioral treatment approaches. These new advances are stimulating a new level of scientific curiosity and research and accelerating the application of scientific findings in the clinical setting.

Through the compilations of up-to-date articles on various aspects of substance use disorders, the American Academy of Addiction Psychiatry, through the "Key Readings" series, seeks to:

- advance the knowledge of those committed to the treatment of substance abuse
- introduce those new to the field of addictions to recent advances in substance use disorders
- inspire those without knowledge of substance use disorders and reinvigorate those with anihilistic view of their treatment to work to advance the field addiction medicine beyond its current knowledge base.

Each book will serve as a quick guide to research studies and treatment approaches in the addiction field. They will serve as reference tools, edited by

---

1. Leshner, A. I. (1999). Principles of Drug Addiction Treatment. National Institute on Drug Abuse, Bethesda, MD.

an expert in the field, keeping today's busy professional informed of timely, critical, and interesting research and clinical treatment issues. Each book within the series will present outstanding articles from leading clinical journals of relevance to the addiction psychiatrist whether in clinical, research, administrative, or academic roles. The "Key Readings in Addiction Psychiatry" series will be presented in several volumes focused on treatment, dual diagnosis, and psychosocial therapies.

A new book in the series will be published annually, providing a continuous flow of new information in a handy, easily accessible form. This compilation of key readings in one source will be an excellent supplement to textbooks and can be used not only to keep up with rapid change in our field but also in preparation for the certification or recertification examinations in addiction psychiatry.

Stephen L. Dilts, M.D., Ph.D.
Past President
American Academy of Addiction Psychiatry

Introduction—
Key Readings in Addiction Psychiatry: Dual Diagnosis

This second volume in the *Key Readings in Addiction Psychiatry* series offers current reviews from journals that have published work focusing on the identification and treatment of co-occurring substance use and mental disorders.

Because of the dramatic negative clinical impact of under-identification of substance use disorders in mental health settings and mental disorders in addiction treatment settings, this compilation begins with four articles on vulnerability, screening, and differential diagnosis of substance use and comorbid mental disorders. The first article, *Illicit psychoactive substance use, heavy use, abuse, and dependence in a U.S. population-based sample of male twins* by Kendler et al., is a population epidemiologic study of male twins that examines the genetic and familial-environmental influences on risk for substance use. Genetic factors appear to account for most of the twin resemblance and heritability of heavy substance use, abuse, and dependence in men. The next two articles are from treatment-seeking samples that focus upon the etiology of psychiatric symptoms in the context of substance abuse. Toneatto et al. find in *Diagnostic subgroups within a sample of comorbid substance abusers: correlates and characteristics* that patients with substance-induced disorders and Axis II disorders tend to have more severe addiction histories. Compton et al. in *Psychiatric disorders among drug dependent subjects: are they primary or secondary?* confirm the high lifetime prevalence of co-occurring mental disorders among drug-dependent patients and importantly distinguish that the order of onset of these disorders varies depending upon the type of mental disorder, gender, and race. The last article in this group, *Reliability and validity of screening instruments for drug and alcohol abuse in adults seeking evalu-*

ation for attention-deficit/hyperactivity disorder by McCann et al., finds the DAST and AUDIT adequate for addiction screening among adults seeking treatment for ADHD. Because of the negative impact of substance use disorders on mental health outcomes, screening should maximize sensitivity with low cut-off scores on the scales to avoid false negatives.

The next group of articles focuses upon current clinical issues in dual-diagnosis treatment. Critical components of effective programs and strategic changes for optimizing systems of care for co-occurring severe mental illness and substance abuse are reviewed in *Implementing dual-diagnosis services for clients with severe mental illness* by Drake et al. However, because effective treatment interventions for this population are not necessarily complex, Martino and colleagues demonstrate how even one pre-admission session of *Motivational interviewing with psychiatrically ill substance abusing patients* can positively impact treatment retention and exposure.

Subsequent articles focus upon particular diagnosis of mood, anxiety, and psychotic disorders among substance abusers. In *Current concepts in the treatment of depression in alcohol-dependent patients,* McGrath, Nunes, and Quitkin provide the latest in etiologic theory and treatment for depressed alcoholics. Psychosocial treatments are beneficial in bipolar disorder, and it is striking that, in *Utilization of psychosocial treatment by patients diagnosed with bipolar disorder and substance dependence* by Weiss et al., patients typically show decreasing engagement in self-help and specific psychotherapeutic support over time. Because appropriate timing is important in screening for the anxiety and mood disorders so prevalent in substance dependent patients undergoing detoxification, we next present *Screening and diagnosis of anxiety and mood disorders in substance abuse patients* by Franken and Hendriks. PTSD and substance use disorders have a high rate of comorbidity. In *Substance use disorders in patients with posttraumatic stress disorder: a review of the literature*, Jacobsen et al. describe neurobiological factors potentially common to PTSD and withdrawal and make a case for why both pathological arousal and withdrawal symptoms should be aggressively managed in these patients. Even without a substance diagnosis, the detrimental effects of using substances in schizophrenia are elucidated in *Social functioning, psychopathology, and medication side effects in relation to substance use and abuse in schizophrenia* by Salyers and Mueser. Finally, because primary prevention will necessitate identifying those at high risk, *Personality and substance use disorders: a prospective study* by Sher et al. educates the reader about the important role of personality in predicting the risk for substance use disorders in young adults.

It is hoped that this compendium of articles will update the reader with timely information about co-occurring substance use and mental disorders among a broad continuum of diagnoses, and stimulate further interest in identifying and treating patients with these disorders.

Richard N. Rosenthal, M.D.
Professor of Clinical Psychiatry
Columbia University College of Physicians and Surgeons
Chairman, Department of Psychiatry
St. Luke's-Roosevelt Hospital Center, New York, NY

President,
American Academy of Addiction Psychiatry

Illicit Psychoactive Substance Use, Heavy Use, Abuse, and Dependence in a U.S. Population-Based Sample of Male Twins

Kenneth S. Kendler, M.D.
Laura M. Karkowski, Ph.D.
Michael C. Neale, Ph.D.
Carol A. Prescott, Ph.D.

Illicit psychoactive substance use, abuse, and dependence are major public health problems. To develop informed approaches to prevention and treatment, we need to understand the sources of individual differences in risk. Substantial evidence suggests that the liability to psychoactive substance use disorder (PSUD) aggregates in families.[1-6] Both twin[7-10] and adoption[11-13] studies suggest that part of this familial aggregation is due to genetic factors.

In the first phase of a comprehensive study of PSUD in a U.S. population-based twin population, we examined cannabis, cocaine, hallucinogen, opiate, sedative, and stimulant use, abuse, and dependence in personally interviewed members

Accepted for publication December 1, 1999.

This work was supported by grants MH/DA-49492 and DA-11287 from the National Institutes of Health and by Research Scientist Award MH-01277 from the National Institute of Mental Health (Dr. Kendler), Bethesda, MD. The Virginia Twin Registry, established by W. Nance, M.D., Ph.D., and maintained by L. Corey, Ph.D., is supported by grants HD-26746 and NS-31564 from the National Institutes of Health.

Reprints: Kenneth S. Kendler, M.D., Department of Psychiatry, Medical College of Virginia, Virginia Commonwealth University, Box 980126, Richmond, VA 23298–0126.

of more than 800 female–female twin pairs.[14–16] In a separate and recently completed study, we have interviewed personally, with the same assessment instrument, both members of 1,193 male–male (MM) pairs ascertained from the same twin registry. In this chapter, therefore, we examine the results for the use, heavy use, and abuse of and dependence on these categories of psychoactive substances in these MM pairs.

SUBJECTS AND METHODS

Subjects

This report is based on data collected in the second wave of interviews in a new study of adult twins from the Virginia Twin Registry (now part of the Mid-Atlantic Twin Registry). The Virginia registry was formed by a systematic search of all Virginia birth certificates since 1918. Subjects from multiple births are matched by names and birth dates from state records to obtain addresses and telephone numbers. Twins were eligible for participation in this study if one or both twins were successfully matched, were members of a multiple birth that included at least 1 male, were white, and were born between 1940 and 1974. Of 9,417 individuals eligible for the first wave, 6,814 (72.4%) had completed interviews, 1,163 (12.4%) refused, 33 (0.4%) had incomplete interviews, 388 (4.1%) did not agree within the study time limit, 862 (9.1%) could not be located, and 157 (1.7%) were deceased or too ill to be interviewed. At least 1 year after the completion of the first-wave interview (performed by telephone in most instances), we contacted the twins again and attempted to schedule a second-wave interview. The number of subjects eligible for wave-2 interviews included the 6,814 with complete wave-1 interviews as well as 3 subjects interviewed at wave 2 who were eligible at wave 1 but from whom completed wave-1 interviews were not obtained. Whenever possible, this interview was completed face-to-face (79.4% of sample). Of the 6,817 individuals eligible for the wave-2 interview, 5,629 (82.6%) were successfully interviewed while 852 (12.5%) refused, 22 (0.3%) had incomplete interviews, 237 (3.5%) did not agree within the study time limit, 51 (0.7%) could not be located, and 26 (0.4%) were deceased or too ill to be interviewed. To assess the test-retest reliability of our assessments, 131 members of MM twins were reinterviewed 4.4 ± 1.1 months (mean ± *SEM*) after their initial interview.

The current report is based on 1,198 MM pairs with complete data on PSUD from the wave-2 interview. There were 1,184 male–male twins, with 12 pairs from 4 all-male triplet births and 1 pair each from a male–male–female triplet birth and a male–male–female–female quadruplet birth. In addition, this sample includes 534 subjects whose cotwins did not complete a wave-2 interview, of whom 247 came from monozygotic (MZ) and 287 from dizygotic (DZ) pairs.

At the time of second-wave interviews (1994–1998), subjects were 20 to 58 years old (mean [*SD*], 36.8 [9.1]) and had a mean of 13.4 years of education (*SD*,

2.6). Interviewers had a master's degree in a mental health–related field or a bachelor's degree in this area plus 2 years of clinical experience. They received 40 hours of classroom training plus regular individual and group review sessions. Two senior staff reviewed each interview for completeness and consistency. Members of a twin pair were interviewed by different interviewers who were blind to clinical information about the cotwin.

Zygosity Diagnosis

We began assessing zygosity by genotyping 227 twin pairs with 8 or more highly polymorphic DNA markers. Using these pairs, we developed a Fisher discriminant function with PROC DISCRIM in SAS[17] using height, weight, six standard zygosity questions, and the twins' history of any blood tests. Using this discriminant function, we could confidently assign zygosity to all of the remaining sample (operationalized as an estimated probability of monozygosity of $\leq 10\%$ or $\geq 90\%$) except for 97 pairs. Of these, we had usable DNA from both members of 65 pairs, from which we obtained zygosities. All available information on the remaining 32 cases, including photographs, was reviewed by two of us (K.S.K. and C.A.P.), who assigned final zygosities. Assignment of zygosity for twins without an interviewed cotwin was done using the discriminant function analysis. These analyses were based on 708 complete MZ pairs and 490 complete DZ pairs.

Measures

Lifetime use, heavy use, abuse, and dependence were assessed separately for seven categories of substances using an adaptation of the Structured Clinical Interview for *DSM-III-R*.[18] With illustrative specific forms, these categories were cannabis (marijuana and hashish); sedatives (quaalude, Seconal, and Valium); stimulants (speed, ecstasy, and Ritalin); cocaine (intranasal, freebase, and crack); opiates (heroin, Demerol [meperidine hydrochloride], and morphine); hallucinogens (lysergic acid diethylamide, mescaline, and phencyclidine); and "other," including inhalants (glue and nitrous oxide), over-the-counter medications (diet and sleeping pills), and miscellaneous (steroids and poppers). For those substances that could be legally obtained, we told respondents that we were interested solely in nonmedical use, defined as use (1) without a physician's prescription; (2) in greater amounts than prescribed; (3) more often than prescribed; or (4) for any other reason than that a physician said they should be taken. Heavy use was defined as ever using the substance more than 10 times per month.

Drug abuse and dependence were diagnosed using *DSM-IV* criteria,[19] except that we ignored criterion B for substance abuse, which rules out abuse in the presence of dependence. Thus, we diagnosed abuse and dependence nonhierarchically. Use and misuse of the *other* category were too rare to usefully analyze separately, but the *other* category was added to the category of *any* PSUD.

Statistical Analysis

We assess twin resemblance in three ways. First, proband concordance is the proportion of affected individuals among cotwins of affected twins. This statistic ignores information from pairs in which both twins are unaffected. Second, the odds ratio (OR) reflects the risk of being affected (or using a substance) among cotwins of affected twins compared with the risk of being affected among cotwins of unaffected twins.

Third, we use a liability threshold model to estimate the genetic and environmental contributions to twin resemblance for substance use, abuse, and dependence. For categorical characteristics, such as lifetime use or dependence, the estimates reflect resemblance in twins pairs for their liability to develop the disorder.[20] Liability is assumed to be continuous and normally distributed in the population, with individuals who exceed a theoretical threshold expressing the disorder.

Individual differences in liability are assumed to arise from three sources: (1) additive genetic (A), from genes with allelic effects that combine additively; (2) common environment (C), which includes all sources shared by members of a twin pair, including family environment, social class, and schools; and (3) specific environment (E), which includes all remaining environmental factors not shared within a twin pair plus measurement error. Monozygotic twins within a pair resemble one another because they share all of their A and C components, while DZ pairs share (on average) half of their A and all of their C components. It is possible to include nonadditive genetic effects, such as dominance or epistasis, but these have not been implicated in prior studies of PSUD and their inclusion did not improve the fit of our models, so we did not consider them further.

Our model also assumes independence and additivity of the three components and the equality of shared environmental effects. The equal environment assumption requires that MZ and DZ pairs be equally similar in the etiologically relevant aspects of their shared environments. To test this assumption, we assessed twin similarity for environmental exposure in childhood using standard questions.[21] Similarity of their adult environment is assessed by measures of current frequency of contact. We examine whether, when controlling for zygosity, pairs with greater environmental similarity are more similar for substance use, heavy use, abuse, or dependence.

Since drug use, abuse, and dependence are correlated in twin pairs, twin studies provide a method for detecting cooperation bias. If, for example, drug use predicts noncooperation, then drug use in one twin should predict a decreased probability that the cotwin would be successfully interviewed.

Traditional twin modeling examines only pairs concordant for assessment. However, information about diagnostic thresholds is contained in twins whose cotwin was not interviewed. Using a recently developed option in the software package Mx,[22] we fit models including single twins by the method of maximum likelihood. During optimization, trial values of the parameters were used to generate an overall predicted covariance matrix and an overall matrix of thresholds.

For any particular observation, the overall matrix was filtered to create a submatrix matching those observations that were present. Likewise, the corresponding subset of the matrix of thresholds is created. These matrices are then used to compute the log likelihood of the observation in question. The log likelihoods of all cases were summed to obtain the log-likelihood of the sample, which was maximized using numerical optimization software.

Maximum likelihood analysis of raw ordinal data does not directly provide an overall test of goodness of fit of the model. However, it is possible to perform such a test by comparing the fit of the model being used with the sum of the fits of models (MZ and DZ fitted separately) in which every correlation and every threshold are estimated as free parameters. Twice the difference in log likelihood between this saturated model and the model being tested yields a statistic that is (under certain regularity conditions) asymptotically distributed as chi-square values with degrees of freedom equal to the difference in the number of parameters in the two models. Tests between alternative models may be carried out the same way.

Alternative models are evaluated by comparing the difference in their chi-square values relative to the difference in their degrees of freedom, according to the principle of parsimony—models with fewer parameters are preferable if they do not provide a significantly worse fit. We operationalize parsimony by using the Akaike information criterion (AIC) statistic,[23] calculated as $\chi^2 - 2$ df, where df indicates degrees of freedom.

RESULTS

Potential Biases

Noncooperation of the cotwin predicted an increased risk for psychoactive substance use, heavy use, abuse, and dependence in the twin in 10 of 56 analyses. For MZ twins, it predicted sedative use; sedative, stimulant, and opiate heavy use; cocaine abuse; and cocaine and opiate dependence. For DZ twins, it predicted sedative use and marijuana and sedative dependence. Although the findings were replicated across zygosity groups only once (for sedative use), these many significant findings—all in the same direction—were unlikely to occur by chance ($p = .005$).[24]

Controlling for zygosity, the similarity of childhood and adult environments significantly predicted twin resemblance 7 out of 56 times: (1) For childhood environment, it predicted stimulant and hallucinogen use, cannabis, and any heavy use. (2) For adult environment, it predicted cocaine heavy use, hallucinogen abuse, and sedative dependence. Although there was no replication across substances or levels of use or misuse, this number of significant findings would occur by chance approximately 2% of the time,[24] and all the significant effects were in the predicted direction.

For most drug use categories, rates were higher in DZ than MZ twins. Although these differences were usually modest, they reached significance for cannabis use and abuse; sedative abuse; opiate heavy use; hallucinogen use; and any use, heavy use, and abuse.

Test-Retest Reliability

Drug use was assessed with excellent reliability ($\kappa > .70$ and $r > .90$ for all), as was heavy use except with sedatives (Table 1.1). The test-retest reliabilities for drug abuse and dependence (where available) were in the fair to good range (most κ values between .50 and .70 and most r values > .80).

Prevalences and Patterns of Twin Resemblance

For MZ and DZ twins, Table 1.2 presents the prevalence, probandwise concordance, OR, and difference in ORs between zygosities for the use, heavy use, and abuse of and dependence on any illicit substance and for the six specific classes of illicit substances. The following results are noteworthy: (1) Prevalences of the various drug use categories differ widely. Rates for cannabis are consistently the highest and opiates among the lowest. (2) Across the various substances, abuse is usually more frequently reported than heavy use, while dependence is substantially rarer. (3) In MZ twins, ORs were significantly greater than 1 for all categories of use; all categories of heavy use and abuse except opiates; and all categories of dependence except sedatives, opiates, and hallucinogens. For DZ twins, ORs significantly exceeded unity for all forms of use except opiates; for cannabis, stimulant, and cocaine heavy use; for cannabis and cocaine abuse; and for cocaine dependence. (4) In MZ twins, higher ORs were consistently seen for heavy use and abuse than for use. This trend was less clear in DZ twins. (5) Odds ratios were

TABLE 1.1. Test-Retest Reliability of Psychoactive Substance Use, Heavy Use, Abuse, and Dependence ($n = 131$)

Substance	Use		Heavy Use		Abuse		Dependence	
	κ	r	κ	r	κ	r	κ	r
Cannabis	+0.91	0.99	+0.84	0.98	+0.67	0.89	+0.60	0.89
Sedatives	+0.79	0.97	+0.39	0.79	+0.51	0.82	—	—
Stimulants	+0.72	0.92	+0.72	0.95	+0.60	0.92	+0.66	0.94
Cocaine	+0.93	0.99	+0.72	0.95	+0.68	0.92	+0.47	0.80
Opiates	+0.74	0.96	+0.66	0.94	+0.49	0.86	—	—
Hallucinogens	+0.88	0.99	—	—	+0.59	0.91	—	—
Any	+0.89	0.99	+0.74	0.93	+0.65	0.89	+0.63	0.92

Note. Dashes indicate that fewer than four individuals met the criteria on either occasion of measurement.

TABLE 1.2. Prevalence, Probandwise Concordance, and Odds Ratios for Illicit Psychoactive Substance Use, Heavy Use, Abuse, and Dependence in Monozygotic (MZ) and Dizygotic (DZ) Twins

Substance	Prevalence ± SE		Probandwise Concordance ± SE		Odds Ratio (95% CI)		Difference in Odds Ratios	
	MZ	DZ	MZ	DZ	MZ	DZ	χ^2 (df = 1)	p
				Use				
Cannabis	50.4 ± 1.3	55.9 ± 1.8	0.73 ± 0.01	0.71 ± 0.02	7.5[a] (5.4–10.5)	4.2[a] (2.9–6.2)	0.95	.33
Sedatives	10.1 ± 0.8	11.5 ± 1.0	0.44 ± 0.03	0.25 ± 0.03	11.7[a] (6.7–20.6)	3.1[a] (1.6–6.3)	8.57	.003
Stimulants	17.7 ± 1.0	19.8 ± 1.3	0.52 ± 0.03	0.40 ± 0.03	9.5[a] (6.1–14.9)	3.9[a] (2.4–6.4)	7.00	.008
Cocaine	16.0 ± 1.0	18.2 ± 1.2	0.52 ± 0.03	0.36 ± 0.03	11.0[a] (6.9–17.5)	3.4[a] (2.0–5.7)	11.22	.001
Opiates	5.9 ± 0.6	6.0 ± 0.8	0.29 ± 0.04	0.07 ± 0.02	8.9[a] (4.1–19.2)	1.2 (0.3–5.1)	6.78	.009
Hallucinogens	12.9 ± 0.9	16.4 ± 1.2	0.62 ± 0.03	0.45 ± 0.03	26.7[a] (15.5–46.0)	6.7[a] (3.9–11.5)	12.62	.001
Any	52.6 ± 1.3	59.0 ± 1.6	0.74 ± 0.01	0.73 ± 0.02	6.8[a] (4.9–9.4)	4.2[a] (2.8–6.1)	3.55	.06
				Heavy Use				
Cannabis	14.5 ± 0.9	17.2 ± 1.2	0.63 ± 0.03	0.41 ± 0.03	26.2[a] (15.5–44.2)	5.2[a] (3.0–6.7)	18.87	<.001
Sedatives	1.1 ± 0.3	2.0 ± 0.5	0.13[b] ± 0.06	0.00[b]	15.4[a] (1.6–145.5)	—	2.60	.11
Stimulants	4.0 ± 0.5	5.6 ± 0.7	0.36 ± 0.05	0.15 ± 0.04	20.7[a] (8.3–51.2)	3.2[c] (1.0–10.0)	6.96	.008
Cocaine	3.0 ± 0.5	3.7 ± 0.6	0.42 ± 0.06	0.22 ± 0.05	40.4[a] (14.4–113.9)	9.4[a] (2.7–32.0)	3.32	.07
Opiates	0.8 ± 0.2	2.0 ± 0.5	0.00[b]	0.00[b]				
Hallucinogens	0.8 ± 0.2	1.5 ± 0.4	0.18[d] ± 0.09	0.00[b]	38.8[c] (3.5–428.1)	—	3.22	.07
Any	16.3 ± 1.0	19.8 ± 1.3	0.63 ± 0.03	0.43 ± 0.04	22.5[a] (13.7–36.8)	4.7[a] (2.9–7.7)	19.76	<.001

Continued

7

TABLE 1.2. Continued

Substance	Prevalence ± SE		Probandwise Concordance ± SE		Odds Ratio (95% CI)		Difference in Odds Ratios	
	MZ	DZ	MZ	DZ	MZ	DZ	χ^2 (df = 1)	p
Abuse								
Cannabis	16.6 ± 1.0	20.1 ± 1.3	0.58 ± 0.03	0.38 ± 0.03	15.0[a] (9.4–24.0)	3.2[a] (2.0–5.3)	20.23	.001
Sedatives	2.3 ± 0.5	4.3 ± 0.7	0.24 ± 0.06	0.05 ± 0.02	18.1[a] (5.1–64.3)	1.2 (0.2–9.0)	7.01	.008
Stimulants	7.1 ± 0.7	8.7 ± 0.9	0.40 ± 0.04	0.16 ± 0.03	14.8[a] (7.4–29.3)	2.3 (1.0–5.6)	11.49	.001
Cocaine	4.6 ± 0.6	5.7 ± 0.7	0.31 ± 0.04	0.25 ± 0.04	13.4[a] (5.7–31.9)	7.1[a] (2.7–18.5)	0.96	.33
Opiates	1.5 ± 0.3	2.3 ± 0.5	0.00	0.00				
Hallucinogens	3.3 ± 0.5	3.5 ± 0.6	0.34 ± 0.05	0.00	24.3[a] (8.8–67.0)		9.37	.002
Any	19.8 ± 1.1	23.6 ± 1.4	0.61 ± 0.02	0.42 ± 0.03	14.5[a] (9.3–22.5)	3.2[a] (2.1–5.1)	22.02	<.001
Dependence								
Cannabis	4.1 ± 0.5	4.4 ± 0.7	0.28 ± 0.04	0.09 ± 0.03	12.4[a] (4.9–31.4)	2.4 (0.5–11.1)	3.56	.06
Sedatives	0.4 ± 0.2	0.8 ± 0.3	0.38[e] ± 0.15	0.00[e]			3.38	.07
Stimulants	2.1 ± 0.4	2.1 ± 0.5	0.13 ± 0.04	0.10[b] ± 0.05	3.5[e] (1.7–42.0)	5.6 (0.6–49.1)	0.09	.76
Cocaine	2.8 ± 0.4	3.1 ± 0.6	0.41 ± 0.06	0.13 ± 0.04	41.0[a] (14.0–120.2)	5.6[c] (1.1–27.5)	4.56	.03
Opiates	0.4 ± 0.2	1.0 ± 0.3	0.00[d]	0.00[d]				
Hallucinogens	0.5 ± 0.2	1.0 ± 0.3	0.29[d] ± 0.13	0.00[d]		—	4.27	.04
Any	6.9 ± 0.7	8.6 ± 0.9	0.41 ± 0.04	0.24 ± 0.04	15.5[a] (7.8–30.8)	4.2[a] (1.9–9.4)	6.10	.01

Note. Dashes indicate that the value was not calcuated; CI indicates confidence interval.
[a] p < .001.
[b] n ≤ 20.
[c] p < .05.
[d] n ≤ 10.
[e] p < .01.

estimable in both MZ and DZ twins in 20 substance category combinations. The OR was greater in MZ twins in all 20 categories and this difference was significant in 18. The 2 categories in which MZ resemblance did not significantly exceed DZ resemblance were cannabis use and cocaine abuse.

Tetrachoric Correlations

As with the ORs, the tetrachoric correlations were consistently higher in MZ than in DZ twins (Table 1.3). With two exceptions (sedative heavy use and stimulant dependence), tetrachoric correlations in MZ twins exceeded .55, indicating a high degree of twin resemblance. Tetrachoric correlations in DZ twins were more variable, ranging from nearly zero for opiate use and sedative abuse to greater than .40 for stimulant use, marijuana heavy use, and cocaine heavy use and abuse.

Model-Fitting Results

Use

For model fitting, we will describe the results in each category for cannabis, as it is the most commonly used substance and therefore provides the greatest statistical power. We comment more briefly on results for other substances. For use, the full or ACE model fits moderately well for cannabis ($\chi^2_3 = 7.40$, $p = .06$). Compared with this model, by the χ^2 difference test we could reject the AE ($\chi^2_1 = 7.43$, $p = .006$), CE ($\chi^2_1 = 5.41$, $p = .02$), and E-only models ($\chi^2_2 = 218.67$, $p < .001$). The best-fit ACE model, which produced the lowest AIC value, suggested that one-third of the variance in liability to cannabis use was due to additive genetic factors, one-third to family environment, and one-third to unique environment.

Similar results were found for any substance use and hallucinogen use. For both these categories, the AE and CE models could be rejected at or nearly at the .05 level and the E-only model could be rejected at the .0001 level. From the best-fit ACE model, family environment was seen to account for approximately 35% of the variance in liability, while genetic factors were considerably more important for hallucinogens than for any drug use.

For sedative, stimulant, cocaine, and opiate use, however, the best-fit model was the simple AE model, with the heritability of liability to use being estimated in the range of 50% to 70%. Against the ACE model, the CE models could be rejected at the .05 level and the E-only models at the .0001 level for all these substances. It is noteworthy that in models containing both A and C, the positive correlation of these parameter estimates produces quite large confidence intervals (CIs). That is, when there is evidence of an effect of both genes and family environment for a dichotomous trait such as substance use, even with relatively large sample sizes, parameter estimates for these two factors are known with little precision. In AE models, by contrast, the CIs are narrower.

TABLE 1.3. Tetrachoric Correlations, Model Fitting, and Parameter Estimates of Best-Fit Model for Illicit Psychoactive Substance Use, Heavy Use, Abuse, and Dependence in Monozygotic (MZ) and Dizygotic (DZ) Twins

Substance	Tetrachoric Correlations		Model Fit in c^2 Units				F, B	Parameter Estimates for Full and Best-Fit Models (95% CI)		
	MZ	DZ	AGE^a	AE^b	CE^b	E^c		a^2	c^2	e^2
Use										
Cannabis	0.67	0.51	7.4^d	14.8	12.8	226.1	F, B	0.33 (0.05–0.60)	0.34 (0.10–0.58)	0.33 (0.26–0.40)
Sedatives	0.67	0.34	3.4	3.4^d	12.8	80.3	F	0.68 (0.25–0.77)	0.00 (0.00–0.38)	0.32 (0.24–0.45)
							B	0.68 (0.55–0.78)		0.32 (0.22–0.45)
Stimulants	0.67	0.45	4.9	6.5^d	11.9	133.9	F	0.47 (0.12–0.75)	0.21 (0.00–0.50)	0.33 (0.24–0.43)
							B	0.69 (0.60–0.77)		0.31 (0.23–0.40)
Cocaine	0.69	0.40	3.3	3.6^d	14.5	127.3	F	0.61 (0.25–0.77)	0.09 (0.00–0.40)	0.30 (0.22–0.40)
							B	0.70 (0.61–0.78)		0.30 (0.22–0.39)
Opiates	0.55	0.03	3.5	3.5^d	8.9	26.1	F	0.52 (0.11–0.69)	0.00 (0.00–0.33)	0.48 (0.32–0.69)
							B	0.52 (0.31–0.68)		0.48 (0.32–0.69)
Hallucinogens	0.82	0.58	5.4^d	9.3	18.1	205.8	F,B	0.53 (0.23–0.85)	0.30 (0.00–0.57)	0.17 (0.11–0.17)
Any	0.64	0.51	6.9^d	15.1	10.6	199.3	F, B	0.27 (0.00–0.55)	0.38 (0.12–0.46)	0.36 (0.29–0.44)
Heavy Use										
Cannabis	0.83	0.51	5.8	7.1^d	24.6	209.7	F	0.66 (0.35–0.89)	0.18 (0.00–0.46)	0.17 (0.11–0.24)
							B	0.84 (0.77–0.89)		0.17 (0.11–0.23)
Sedatives	0.49	0.00	2.8	2.8^d	5.3	5.3	F	0.45 (0.00–0.82)	0.00 (0.00–0.40)	0.55 (0.18–0.98)
							B	0.45 (0.00–0.82)		0.55 (0.18–0.98)
Stimulants	0.69	0.28	1.7	1.7^d	8.3	38.4	F	0.70 (0.20–0.84)	0.00 (0.00–0.42)	0.30 (0.16–0.49)
							B	0.70 (0.51–0.84)		0.30 (0.16–0.49)
Cocaine	0.78	0.51	0.3	0.8^d	3.5	48.1	F	0.55 (0.00–0.90)	0.23 (0.00–0.74)	0.22 (0.10–0.41)
							B	0.80 (0.62–0.90)		0.20 (0.10–0.38)
Hallucinogens	0.63	0.00	4.0	4.0^d	5.7	8.1	F	0.62 (0.00–0.91)	0.00 (0.00–0.65)	0.38 (0.09–0.98)
							B	0.62 (0.02–0.91)		0.38 (0.09–0.98)
Any	0.81	0.50	4.9	6.1^d	24.6	215.3	F	0.65 (0.36–0.88)	0.17 (0.14–0.44)	0.18 (0.12–0.25)
							B	0.83 (0.76–0.88)		0.17 (0.12–0.24)

Abuse

Drug							Model	A	C	E
Cannabis	0.75	0.39	5.4	5.4[d]	25.6	164.0	F	0.76 (0.42–0.82)	0.01 (0.00–0.31)	0.23 (0.17–0.33)
							B	0.76 (0.68–0.83)		0.24 (0.17–0.32)
Sedatives	0.61	0.03	10.8	10.8[d]	15.3	23.0	F	0.59 (0.06–0.81)	0.00 (0.00–0.37)	0.41 (0.20–0.73)
							B	0.59 (0.27–0.80)		0.41 (0.20–0.73)
Stimulants	0.68	0.22	5.0	5.0[d]	15.1	57.6	F	0.66 (0.30–0.77)	0.00 (0.00–0.29)	0.34 (0.22–0.50)
							B	0.66 (0.50–0.78)		0.34 (0.22–0.50)
Cocaine	0.61	0.49	2.6	4.1	3.5[d]	41.7	F	0.32 (0.00–0.78)	0.32 (0.00–0.68)	0.37 (0.37–0.37)
							B		0.57 (0.40–0.70)	0.43 (0.30–0.60)
Hallucinogens	0.70	0.00	8.0	8.0[d]	14.9	32.3	F	0.65 (0.24–0.82)	0.00 (0.00–0.34)	0.35 (0.19–0.58)
							B	0.65 (0.41–0.82)		0.35 (0.18–0.59)
Any	0.76	0.40	4.6	4.6[d]	26.6	186.6	F	0.74 (0.42–0.83)	0.03 (0.02–0.31)	0.23 (0.17–0.31)
							B	0.77 (0.69–0.83)		0.23 (0.17–0.31)

Dependence

Drug							Model	A	C	E
Cannabis	0.59	0.20	4.0	4.0[d]	7.4	25.5	F	0.58 (0.00–0.75)	0.00 (0.00–0.02)	0.42 (0.42–0.65)
							B	0.58 (0.35–0.75)		0.42 (0.26–0.66)
Sedatives	0.83	0.00	4.5	4.5[d]	7.3	12.2	F	0.87 (0.00–0.99)	0.00 (0.00–0.80)	0.13 (0.01–0.68)
							B	0.87 (0.32–0.99)		0.13 (0.01–0.67)
Stimulants	0.43	0.34	1.9	2.1	2.0[d]	7.9	F	0.22 (0.00–0.72)	0.21 (0.00–0.62)	0.57 (0.28–0.92)
							B		0.39 (0.08–0.64)	0.61 (0.36–0.92)
Cocaine	0.77	0.37	1.1	1.1[d]	6.0	39.8	F	0.79 (0.09–0.90)	0.00 (0.00–0.62)	0.21 (0.17–0.28)
							B	0.79 (0.59–0.90)		0.21 (0.10–0.42)
Hallucinogens	0.80	0.00	4.1	4.1[d]	6.5	10.4	F	0.79 (0.00–0.90)	0.00 (0.00–0.73)	0.21 (0.03–0.80)
							B	0.79 (0.20–0.97)		0.21 (0.04–0.80)
Any	0.69	0.39	4.1	4.2[d]	10.8	68.2	F	0.65 (0.16–0.81)	0.05 (0.00–0.48)	0.29 (0.18–0.44)
							B	0.71 (0.57–0.82)		0.29 (0.18–0.43)

Note. A indicates additive genes; C, common or familial environment; E, individual specific environment; CI, confidence interval; F, full model; B, best-fit model by Akaike information criteria. Results could not be estimated for opiate heavy use, abuse, or dependence because of the absence of concordant pairs.

[a] Using 3 *df*.
[b] Using 4 *df*.
[c] Using 5 *df*.
[d] Best-fit model using Akaike information criteria.

Heavy Use

The results for heavy use of cannabis differed substantially from those for use. The full model fit well ($\chi^2_3 = 5.81$, $p = .12$). Against the ACE model, the AE model could not be rejected ($\chi^2_1 = 1.26$, $p = .26$), but both the CE ($\chi^2_1 = 18.79$, $p < .001$) and E-only ($\chi^2_2 = 203.87$, $p < .001$) models could be strongly rejected. The best-fit model was AE, with an estimated heritability of liability to cannabis heavy use of 84%. The absence of twin pairs concordant for opiate heavy use, abuse, or dependence made model fitting impossible. For heavy use of all other substances and any substance, the AE model provided the best fit, with estimated heritabilities that ranged from 45% for sedatives to 83% for any substance. The CE model could be rejected against the ACE model at the .05 level only for stimulant and any substance. The E-only model could be rejected for stimulants, cocaine, and any substance. The low prevalence of sedative and hallucinogen heavy use resulted in heritability estimates with wide CIs.

Abuse

Results for cannabis abuse resembled those seen for heavy use. While the AE model gave the same fit as the ACE model, the CE ($\chi^2_1 = 20.22$, $p < .001$) and E-only ($\chi^2_2 = 158.64$, $p < .001$) models could be rejected with high levels of statistical confidence. The heritability estimated from the best-fit AE model was high (76%), with a relatively narrow CI. Qualitatively similar results were obtained with abuse of any substance, as well as abuse of sedatives, stimulants, and hallucinogens. For all of the categories, both the CE and E-only models could be rejected against the ACE model by the χ^2 difference test. The rarer the rates of abuse, the broader were the CIs around the parameter estimates of the best-fit models.

However, cocaine abuse was an exception to this pattern. Here, the tetrachoric correlation was only modestly greater in MZ than DZ twins (+0.61 vs. +0.49). The full-model estimates of a^2, c^2, and e^2 were 32%, 32%, and 37%, respectively. The E-only model could be confidently rejected against the ACE model ($\chi^2_2 = 39.12$, $p < .001$), but neither the AE nor the CE model could be rejected ($\chi^2_1 = 1.51$, $p = .22$; and $\chi^2_1 = 0.94$, $p = .33$; respectively). Although the CE model produced the best fit by AIC, the fact that the fits of the AE and CE models were within .57 χ^2 units of each other suggested that we had little power to determine the contribution of genetic versus environmental factors to the familial resemblance for cocaine abuse.

Dependence

The findings for cannabis dependence resembled those obtained for cannabis heavy use and abuse. Against the ACE model, the E-only model could be confidently rejected ($\chi^2_1 = 21.47$, $p < .001$) and the CE model could be rejected at marginal levels of significance ($\chi^2_1 = 3.42$, $p = .06$). By AIC, the AE model produced the best fit, with an estimated heritability of 58%. Because of its greater rarity, the CIs on heritability estimates for cannabis dependence are considerably larger than those seen for cannabis abuse.

For both any cocaine use and cocaine dependence, the pattern of results was similar and the CE models could be rejected at the .05 level against the ACE models ($\chi^2_1 = 6.68$, $p = .01$; and $\chi^2_1 = 4.90$, $p = .03$; respectively). Estimates of heritability were high (71% and 79%, respectively). Results were less certain for sedative, stimulant, and hallucinogen dependence. For all three substances, the E-only model could be rejected ($\chi^2_2 = 7.73$, $p = .02$; $\chi^2_2 = 5.98$, $p = .05$; and $\chi^2_2 = 6.34$, $p = .04$; respectively), supporting the evidence of aggregation of risk within twin pairs. For both sedative and hallucinogen dependence, c^2 was estimated at zero in the ACE model, but the deterioration in fit from the ACE to CE models was modest ($\chi^2_1 = 2.76$, $p = .10$; and $\chi^2_1 = 2.36$, $p = .12$; respectively). For stimulant dependence, the full model produced estimates of a^2, c^2, and e^2 of 0.22, 0.21, and 0.57, respectively. The CE model produced the best fit by AIC, but the fact that the fits of the ACE, AE, and CE models were within 0.18 χ^2 units of one another indicated that we have little power to determine the source of familial resemblance for stimulant dependence.

COMMENTS

The goal of this chapter was to determine the sources of individual differences in risk for the use, heavy use, and abuse of and dependence on illicit psychoactive substances in men from a U.S. population-based twin sample.

How representative of U.S. men were the twins assessed in this study? In 1996, during the data-collection phase of this study, the National Household Survey on Drug Abuse assessed lifetime psychoactive substance use in more than 18,000 individuals.[25] Using the age categories for non-Hispanic white males in their report (reweighted to approximate the age distribution of our sample), the predicted lifetime rates for the three categories of drug use in which our data were most comparable were cannabis, 41.2%; cocaine, 14.7%; and hallucinogens, 13.5%. Weighted estimates for lifetime use and dependence in U.S. males are also available from the National Comorbidity Survey, conducted from 1990 through 1992. This survey reported lifetime use (dependence) rates for categories similar to five of our six categories: cannabis, 51.7% (6.2%); sedatives, 14.0% (1.0%); stimulants, 18.4% (1.8%); cocaine, 19.5% (3.5%); and hallucinogens, 14.1% (0.7%). The rates found in our twin sample (Table 1.2) were nearly all within the range found in these two comparable epidemiologic studies. Consistent with other studies, which showed that twins do not differ from the general population in rates of psychopathologic conditions,[26-28] these results suggest that our sample is likely to be broadly representative of U.S. men.

Two large-scale general population twin studies of psychoactive substance use and misuse are particularly comparable with this study: the male Vietnam Era

Twin Registry[8] and female–female twin pairs previously studied from the Virginia Twin Registry.[14–16] Results from the Vietnam Era Twin Registry were reported for a category closest to our definition of abuse.[8] Uniformly, across substance categories, the Vietnam era sample produced lower levels of heritability and more evidence for family environment than found in our sample. For the comparable categories of any substance, cannabis, and hallucinogen abuse, the heritability values reported from the Vietnam era study were below the lower 95% CIs of our estimates. Although these differences could be caused by many factors, the two cohorts differed substantially in mode of ascertainment (birth certificates vs both members inducted into the armed services). Furthermore, the Vietnam era sample may have had a unique historical experience of drug exposure.

Our results were more similar to those found in adult female–female twin pairs from the Virginia Twin Registry.[14–16] For example, in women, the best-fit models for cannabis use and abuse produced estimates of a^2, c^2, and e^2 of 0.40, 0.35, and 0.25 and 0.72, 0.0, and 0.28, respectively, which are close to the estimates for men (Table 1.3). Some differences were noteworthy. In women, we found strong evidence that family environment affected risk for cocaine and stimulant use.[15,16] In men, by contrast, the evidence, while present for both cocaine and stimulant use (i.e., DZ correlations greater than half the MZ correlations), was slight, and the AE model fit best for both substances.

Our findings are relatively similar to those reported from a treated sample of U.S. twins. van den Bree et al.[9] also found more evidence in men for familial-environmental effects on use than on abuse/dependence; heritability estimates for abuse and/or dependence were mostly in the range of .60 to .80. As in our study, an investigation of adolescent Virginia twins reports that family environment substantially influences the risk for use of marijuana or any illicit substance.[29]

The results of this study should be interpreted in the light of six potential methodologic limitations. First, although our sample size was large, the numbers of twins with certain forms of heavy use, abuse, and especially dependence were small. As reflected by the large CIs of our model-fitting results, this sample was insufficient to determine with high precision the magnitude of the genetic and environmental effects for a number of subtypes of PSUD.

Second, as this sample was restricted to whites, it is not possible to extrapolate these results to other ethnic groups. Third, although our sample was derived from a population-based twin registry and our prevalences were in the range of those reported elsewhere, results suggested that for several categories of drug use and misuse the final study sample was unlikely to be completely representative of the original twin population. This is consistent with prior evidence that individuals with substance abuse are somewhat less likely to cooperate in general population surveys.[30,31] The impact of differential cooperation on the results from twin studies is complex and not entirely predictable,[32,33] but underestimation of heritability is probably more likely than overestimation.[32] Furthermore, our analyses using Mx software[22] included twins whose cotwins were not interviewed, which eliminates some of the bias. Essentially, we used information on potential differences in the prevalence of PSUD in those twins with versus without a cotwin participating to obtain a better estimate of the prevalence of PSUD in the population. The method is a binary data maximum likelihood application of the "missing-at-random" principle expounded by Little and Rubin.[34]

Fourth, we found higher rates of substance use and misuse in DZ versus MZ twins. This pattern of findings could result from "true" differences (e.g., higher average cotwin social support in MZ vs DZ twins) and/or methodologic factors (higher MZ correlations for noncooperativity leading to more effective screening of MZ versus DZ pairs[32]). From whatever cause, the differences were modest and unlikely to substantially influence the results obtained.

Fifth, we assessed PSUD in this sample with a single structured interview. In this design, unreliability is confounded with individual-specific environment[35] and produces a downward bias in estimates of heritability. We can roughly assess the magnitude of this problem by examining the tetrachoric correlations from our test-retest reliability study (Table 1.1). These correlations suggest that with the possible exceptions of sedative heavy use and abuse and cocaine dependence, the magnitude of diagnostic error was insufficient to produce large downward biases in our parameter estimates. However, some of the estimates reported here for individual-specific environment undoubtedly reflect diagnostic unreliability.

Finally, the human twin study is a quasiexperimental method that cannot approach the methodologic rigor possible in controlled genetic experiments.[35] With a phenotype such as illicit substance use and misuse, which is strongly correlated with a range of social factors,[36,37] it is a particular concern that excess environmental resemblance of MZ versus DZ twins might upwardly bias heritability estimates.[35] We found modest evidence for such an effect using standard measures of the correlated childhood and adult environments. To further evaluate this possible bias, we fitted structural equation models designed to detect and correct for the effects of the equal environment assumption[38] to the seven conditions in which we found evidence for its violation. For sedative dependence, too few affected twins were available to permit stable model estimation. For the remaining six conditions, the proportion of variance in liability in the full model accounted for by the correlated environment averaged 7%. However, in all but one of these models, this correlated environmental factor could be set to zero with an improvement in the model AIC. The one exception was frequency of adult contact and heavy cocaine use, for which, with the inclusion of a parameter reflecting equal environment assumption violations, the heritability of liability declined from 80% to 60%. It is unlikely that the overall results of this investigation were substantially biased by violations of the equal environment assumption.

These results reinforce a growing body of family,[1-6] twin,[7-10,14-16,39,40] and adoption studies[11-13] that suggest the risk for psychoactive substance use and misuse is substantially influenced by genetic factors. Our results also support the hypothesis that family environment is important at the stage of substance initiation. The magnitude of genetic influences on PSUD is striking and exceeds that seen in our sample for common psychiatric disorders, such as major depression,[41,42] panic disorder,[43] and phobias.[44]

The demonstration of genetic variance in risk is only the beginning rather than the conclusion of a research program. Of the many questions that can now be asked, four are noteworthy: (1) What are the pathways from genes to substance misuse and to what extent do they involve personality, psychopathologic processes, variations in metabolism, target receptors, and/or postreceptor mechanisms? (2) What is the relationship between the genetic and environmental factors that influence initiation versus subsequent misuse?[45] (3) How specific are genetic risks for the use and misuse of individual psychoactive substances?[10] (4) What are the chromosomal locations of susceptibility genes for PSUD?[46]

REFERENCES

1. Croughan JL. The contributions of family studies to understanding drug abuse. In: Robins LN, ed. *Studying Drug Abuse.* New Brunswick, NJ: Rutgers University Press; 1985:240–264.
2. Mirin SM, Weiss RD, Sollogub A, Michael J. Psychopathology in families of drug abusers. In: Mirin SM, ed. *Substance Abuse and Psychopathology.* Washington, DC: American Psychiatric Association Press; 1984:79–106.
3. Rounsaville BJ, Kosten TR, Weissman MM, Prusoff R, Pauls D, Anton SF, Merikangas K. Psychiatric disorders in relatives of probands with opiate addiction. *Arch Gen Psychiatry* 1991;48:33–42.
4. Dinwiddie SH, Reich T. Genetic and family studies in psychiatric illness and alcohol and drug dependence. *J Addict Dis* 1993;12:17–27.
5. Merikangas K, Stolar M, Stevens DE, Goulet J, Preisig MA, Fenton B, Zhang H, O'Malley SS, Rounsaville BJ. Familial transmission of substance use disorders. *Arch Gen Psychiatry* 1998;55:973–979.
6. Bierut LJ, Dinwiddie SH, Begleiter H, Crowe RR, Hesselbrock V, Nurnberger JI Jr, Porjesz B, Schuckit MA, Reich T. Familial transmission of substance dependence: alcohol, marijuana, cocaine, and habitual smoking: a report from the Collaborative Study on the Genetics of Alcoholism. *Arch Gen Psychiatry* 1998;55:982–988.
7. Grove WM, Eckert ED, Heston L, Bouchard TJ Jr, Segal N, Lykken DT. Heritability of substance abuse and antisocial behavior: a study of monozygotic twins reared apart. *Biol Psychiatry* 1990;27:1293–1304.
8. Tsuang MT, Lyons MJ, Eisen SA, Goldberg J, True W, Meyer JM, Eaves LJ. Genetic influences on abuse of illicit drugs: a study of 3,297 twin pairs. *Am J Med Genet* 1996;67:473–477.
9. van den Bree MB, Johnson EO, Neale MC, Pickens RW. Genetic and environmental influences on drug use and abuse/dependence in male and female twins. *Drug Alcohol Depend* 1998;52:231–241.
10. Tsuang MT, Lyons MJ, Meyer JM, Doyle T, Eisen SA, Goldberg J, True W, Lin N, Toomey R, Eaves L. Co-occurence of abuse of different drugs in men: the role of drug-specific and shared vulnerabilities. *Arch Gen Psychiatry* 1998;55:967–972.
11. Cadoret RJ, Troughton E, O'Gorman TW, Heywood E. An adoption study of genetic and environmental factors in drug abuse. *Arch Gen Psychiatry* 1986;43:1131–1136.
12. Cadoret RJ, Yates WR, Troughton E, Woodworth G, Stewart MA. Adoption study

demonstrating two genetic pathways to drug abuse. *Arch Gen Psychiatry* 1995; 52:42–52.

13. Cadoret RJ, Yates WR, Troughton E, Woodworth G, Stewart MA. An adoption study of drug abuse/dependency in females. *Compr Psychiatry* 1996;37:88–94.

14. Kendler KS, Prescott CA. Cannabis use, abuse and dependence in a population-based sample of female twins. *Am J Psychiatry* 1998;155:1016–1022.

15. Kendler KS, Prescott CA. Cocaine use, abuse and dependence in a population-based sample of female twins. *Br J Psychiatry* 1998;173:345–350.

16. Kendler KS, Karkowski LM, Prescott CA. Hallucinogen, opiate, sedative and stimulant use and abuse in a population-based sample of female twins. *Acta Psychiatr Scand* 1999;99:368–376.

17. SAS Institute. *SAS/STAT User's Guide, Version 6, Fourth Edition, Vols 1 and 2*. Cary, NC: SAS Institute Inc; 1990.

18. Spitzer RL, Williams JB, Gibbon J. *Structured Clinical Interview for DSM-III-R-Patient Version*. New York: New York State Psychiatric Institute; 1987.

19. American Psychiatric Association. *Diagnostic and Statistical Manual of Mental Disorders, Fourth Edition*. Washington, DC: American Psychiatric Association; 1994.

20. Falconer DS. The inheritance of liability to certain diseases, estimated from the incidence among relatives. *Ann Hum Genet* 1965;29:51–76.

21. Loehlin JC, Nichols RC. *Heredity, Environment and Personality: A Study of 850 Sets of Twins*. Austin: University of Texas Press; 1976.

22. Neale MC. *Statistical Modelling With Mx*. Richmond: Dept of Psychiatry, Medical College of Virginia, Virginia Commonwealth University; 1991.

23. Akaike H. Factor analysis and AIC. *Psychometrika* 1987;52:317–332.

24. Feild HS, Armenakis AA. On use of multiple tests of significance in psychological research. *Psychol Rep* 1974;35:427–431.

25. *SAMHSA: National Household Survey on Drug Abuse Main Findings 1996*. Rockville, MD: National Clearinghouse for Alcohol and Drug Information; 1998.

26. Kendler KS, Martin NG, Heath AC, Eaves LJ. Self-report psychiatric symptoms in twins and their nontwin relatives: are twins different? *Am J Med Genet* 1995;60:588–591.

27. Rutter M, Redshaw J. Annotation: growing up as a twin: twin-singleton differences in psychological development. *J Child Psychol Psychiatry* 1991;32:885–895.

28. Kendler KS, Pedersen NL, Farahmand BY, Persson PG. The treated incidence of psychotic and affective illness in twins compared to population expectation: a study in the Swedish Twin and Psychiatric Registries. *Psychol Med* 1996;26:1135–1144.

29. Maes HH, Woodard CE, Murrelle L, Meyer JM, Silberg JL, Hewitt JK, Rutter M, Simonoff E, Pickles A, Carbonneau R, Neale MC, Eaves LJ. Tobacco, alcohol and drug use in eight-to-sixteen-year-old twins: the Virginia Twin Study of Adolescent Behavioral Development. *J Stud Alcohol* 1999;60:293–305.

30. Allgulander C. Psychoactive drug use in a general population sample, Sweden: correlates with perceived health, psychiatric diagnoses, and mortality in an automated record-linkage study. *Am J Public Health* 1989;79:1006–1010.

31. Kessler RC, Little RJ, Groves RM. Advances in strategies for minimizing and adjusting for survey nonresponse. *Epidemiol Rev* 1995;17:192–204.

32. Kendler KS, Holm NV. Differential enrollment in twin registries: its effect on prevalence and concordance rates and estimates of genetic parameters. *Acta Genet Med Gemellol (Roma)* 1985;34:125–140.

33. Neale MC, Eaves LJ. Estimating and controlling for the effects of volunteer bias with pairs of relatives. *Behav Genet* 1993;23:271–277.

34. Little RJ, Rubin DB. *Statistical Analysis With Missing Data*. New York: John Wiley & Sons; 1987.

35. Kendler KS. Twin studies of psychiatric illness: current status and future directions. *Arch Gen Psychiatry* 1993;50:905–915.
36. Hawkins JD, Catalano RF, Miller JY. Risk and protective factors for alcohol and other drug problems in adolescence and early adulthood: Implications for substance abuse prevention. *Psychol Bull* 1992;112:64–105.
37. Webster RA, Hunter M, Keats JA. Peer and parental influences on adolescents' substance use: a path analysis. *Int J Addict* 1994;29:647–657.
38. Hettema JM, Neale MC, Kendler KS. Physical similarity and the equal-environment assumption in twin studies of psychiatric disorders. *Behav Genet* 1995;25:327–335.
39. Gynther LM, Carey G, Gottesman II, Vogler GP. A twin study of non-alcohol substance abuse. *Psychiatry Res* 1995;56:213–220.
40. Jang KL, Livesley WJ, Vernon PA. Alcohol and drug problems: a multivariate behavioural genetic analysis of co-morbidity. *Addiction* 1995;90:1213–1221.
41. Kendler KS, Neale MC, Kessler RC, Heath AC, Eaves LJ. A population-based twin study of major depression in women: the impact of varying definitions of illness. *Arch Gen Psychiatry* 1992;49:257–266.
42. Kendler KS, Prescott CA. A population-based twin study of lifetime major depression in men and women. *Arch Gen Psychiatry* 1999;56:39–44.
43. Kendler KS, Neale MC, Kessler RC, Heath AC, Eaves LJ. Panic disorder in women: a population-based twin study. *Psychol Med* 1993;23:397–406.
44. Kendler KS, Neale MC, Kessler RC, Heath AC, Eaves LJ. The genetic epidemiology of phobias in women: the interrelationship of agoraphobia, social phobia, situational phobia, and simple phobia. *Arch Gen Psychiatry* 1992;49:273–281.
45. Kendler KS, Neale MC, Sullivan PF, Corey LA, Gardner CO, Prescott CA. A population-based twin study in women of smoking initiation and nicotine dependence. *Psychol Med* 1999;29:299–308.
46. Straub RE, Sullivan PF, Ma Y, Myakishev MV, Harris-Kerr C, Wormley B, Kadambi B, Sadek H, Silverman MA, Webb BT, Neale MC, Bulik CM, Joyce PR, Kendler KS. Susceptibility genes for nicotine dependence: a genome scan and follow-up in an independent sample suggest that regions on chromosomes 2, 4, 10, 16, 17 and 18 merit further study. *Mol Psychiatry* 1999;4:129–144.

Chapter 2

Diagnostic Subgroups within a Sample of Comorbid Substance Abusers

Correlates and Characteristics

Tony Toneatto, Ph.D.
Juan Carlos Negrete, M.D.
Kim Calderwood, M.S.W.

With the accumulating evidence of considerable psychiatric comorbidity among treatment-seeking substance abusers, there is a need for a better characterization of the phenomenological heterogeneity of this population. Such knowledge may be significant in the assessment of substance use and psychiatric symptoms, planning of treatment, evaluating prognosis, and preventing relapse. Although the research literature has focused primarily on establishing a relationship between psychiatric and substance use disorder,[1,2] relatively less attention has been paid to describing subsets of comorbid populations along clinical, psychosocial, and demographic characteristics. Mowbray et al.[3] have pointed out that insufficient information is gathered about different subtypes of psychiatric comorbidity among substance abusers to effectively plan treatment services. They suggest that more descriptive research is needed on the clinical, demographic, and social adjustment characteristics of comorbid populations in order to portray their heterogeneity and better select treatment strategies.

In a sample of male alcoholics with psychiatric disorders, Penick and colleagues[4] found that a substantial proportion qualified for multiple psychiatric diagnoses. Furthermore, these psychiatric disorders did not cluster randomly. For example, antisocial personality tended to co-occur with drug abuse, while anxiety and mood disorders tended to cluster together. Penick et al.[4] suggest that subtyping alcohol abusers on the basis of psychiatric syndromes may have clinical implications (e.g., comorbidity of antisocial personality and schizophrenia with substance abuse may be prognostic of a poorer clinical course compared to individuals without the additional Axis II disorder). Nace et al.[5] showed that substance abusers with personality disorders differed from those without a personality disorder in patterns of alcohol and drug use, psychiatric symptoms, and overall life satisfaction.

Sloan and Rowe[6] demonstrated that substance abusers who had a history of psychiatric treatment reported greater psychosocial dysfunction (e.g., health problems, unemployment, disability) and more treatment contacts for substance problems than those without a treatment history. Ojehagen et al.[7] found that male alcoholics with more psychiatric symptoms did not differ from those with fewer symptoms on measures of alcohol use, but did so on measures of social functioning. These findings were also reported by several others.[8–10] Alterman et al.[11] found that dual-disorder patients have more problems compared to those who were assigned either a substance abuse or mental illness diagnosis and suggest that the treatment needs of the dually disordered will reflect the type of psychiatric disorder (e.g., Axis I or II), type of substance problem, and other associated life problems.

The purpose of this study was to contribute to our understanding of how subgroups of comorbid substance abusers, defined on the basis of their psychiatric status at the time of treatment, differ from each other. Such data may serve to better differentiate the characteristics and needs of these subgroups and reduce the tendency to view comorbid substance abusers as a homogeneous group. These subgroups were compared with respect to their demographic profile, measures of psychiatric and addictive disorder severity and treatment history, family history of addiction and psychiatric problems, self-rated psychological distress, and alcohol-related psychosocial consequences.

METHOD

Subjects

The sample consisted of patients consecutively seeking treatment at the Addiction Research Foundation (ARF) between July 1992 and November 1994. ARF is an outpatient, provincially funded, clinical and research institute. ARF is centrally located and serves primarily an urban, male, Caucasian population. Patients who were triaged to the Mental Health Unit (MHU) from the Intake Department were eligible for this study ($N = 713$). Triage to MHU was made on the basis of several screening questions assessing the presence of symptoms of the major mood and anxiety disorders. Any indication of suicidal risk or psychosis was also a sufficient reason for a referral to MHU. Referred patients completed an assessment interview surveying past and present substance use and psychiatric history, treatment history, familial history of substance use and psychiatric problems, time-line assessment of alcohol consumption,[12] and alcohol- and drug-related negative consequences. Patients also completed the Symptom-Checklist-90-Revised[13] and were clinically interviewed by a psychiatrist or a clinical psychologist within 2 weeks of their intake assessment. The clinical interview yielded psychiatric diagnoses consistent with the diagnostic criteria defined in the *Diagnostic and Statistical Manual of Mental Disorders, Revised Third Edition (DSM-III-R)*.[14] Comorbidity was defined by the co-occurrence of a nonsubstance psychiatric disorder and a substance use disorder at the time of the psychiatric assessment. Individuals who met criteria only for a current substance use disorder (with or without a history of psychiatric disorder) were considered noncomorbid. Only subjects who completed the MHU assessment form and were clinically interviewed by a psychiatrist or a clinical psychologist were retained for data analysis ($n = 586$). Due to slightly different versions of the MHU assessment form, the data were incomplete for some variables. Both the MHU assessment and psychiatric assessment occurred within 2 weeks of registration at Intake.

RESULTS

Data Analysis

Given the unstructured nature of the psychiatric assessment and the relatively small samples for some of the diagnostic categories, individual psychiatric diagnoses were combined into six classes of psychiatric disorder corresponding to the framework found in *DSM-III-R* (i.e., mood, anxiety, adjustment, organic, psychotic, Axis II) to increase the reliability of the data. *Mood disorders* ($n = 228$) included diagnoses of major depression, dysthymia, and mood disorder NOS. *Anxiety disorders* ($n = 165$) included diagnoses of social phobia, panic disorder with agoraphobia, generalized anxiety disorder, obsessive-compulsive disorder, posttraumatic disorder, and anxiety disorder NOS. *Organic (substance-induced) disorders* ($n = 63$) included diagnoses primarily of organic mood and anxiety disorders. *Psychotic disorders* ($n = 48$) consisted primarily of diagnoses of schizophrenia and psychotic disorder NOS. *Adjustment disorders* ($n = 43$) consisted primarily of adjustment disorder with depressive or mixed features. Finally, *Axis II disorders* ($n = 166$) consisted primarily of Cluster B (59%) and Cluster C (27%). A control group of noncomorbid subjects ($n = 48$) was also formed consisting of individuals referred to MHU who did not meet criteria for any Axis I or II diagnoses at the time of the assessment, but may have in the past.

Groups were compared on demographic, substance use history, alcohol consumption, addiction and psychiatric treatment history (personal and familial), and health care utilization by calculating odds ratios for each of the six classes of psychiatric disorder. The odds ratio is a measure of association especially suited for two-by-two contingency tables in which a ratio is computed comparing the probability of an event or characteristic being present in a diagnostic subgroup to the probability of the event or characteristic being present in those outside of the diagnostic subgroup. An odds ratio of 1 is indicative of no association between an event or characteristic and the diagnostic subgroup.

The likelihood ratio chi-square was used to assess statistical significance. Two-tailed *t* tests were used to measure differences in continuous variables. Due to inflated type I error rates as a result of multiple comparisons, the *p* value was set at .01, although results significant at *p* = .05 are also reported.

Demographic Characteristics

As a whole, the sample was primarily male (75%), in their mid-30s (mean 36.3), nonpartnered (23% married), underemployed (35% working full-time; 29% on government assistance), with almost 12 years of education.

Table 2.1 shows that patients diagnosed with an anxiety disorder were half as likely to be male and twice as likely to be living in stable accommodations (i.e., renting or owning their home or apartment) than patients not given this diagnosis. However, patients diagnosed with an organic or substance-induced disorder were at least two and a half times more likely to be male than those without this diagnosis and significantly less likely to be employed. Patients assigned a psychotic diagnosis were less than half as likely to be living in stable accommodations or working, but twice as likely to be receiving government assistance than those without such a diagnosis. There was little difference in age (means ranging from 35.2 to 37.9 years for all groups) or years of education (ranging from 11.7 to 12.5 years).

Substance Use History

Patients with an anxiety diagnosis were twice as likely to have ever used an anxiolytic, but less likely to have used illicit drugs such as cocaine and heroin, than those without such a diagnosis (see Table 2.2). An Axis II diagnosis was associated with a significantly higher likelihood of lifetime use for most classes of substances, including disulfiram. Mood-diagnosed patients were almost 3 times as likely to have ever been prescribed antidepressants, while the psychotic diagnosed patients were, not surprisingly, almost 14 times as likely to have been prescribed antipsychotics as those without these diagnoses.

Alcohol Use

There were no differences between diagnostic classes on measures of alcohol consumption in the 3 months prior to seeking treatment. Drinks per drinking day ranged between 6.6 standard drinks (noncomorbid) and 10.0 standard drinks (adjustment disorder). Percent days abstinent ranged from 44.2% (anxiety disorder) to 55.6% (adjustment disorder). Years of heavy drinking ranged from 6.3 years

TABLE 2.1. Odds Ratios[a] for Demographic Variables by Type of Psychopathology

Variable	Mood (n = 228)	Anxiety (n = 165)	Adjustment (n = 43)	Organic (n = 63)	Psychotic (n = 48)	Axis II (n = 166)	No Dx[b] (n = 48)
Male	1.02	**0.50[c] 61%/76%**	.72	**2.57[c] 86%/70%**	1.55	0.92	1.23
Married	0.87	1.30	0.92	0.79	0.51	0.81	1.59
Living in stable accommodations	1.42	**2.09[c] 84%/71%**	0.61 58%/76%	1.48	**0.44[c]**	1.00	1.02
Working	1.28	1.33	0.73	**0.52[d] 22%/36%**	**0.32[c] 15%/36%**	0.88	1.15
Receiving social assistance	1.07	1.05	0.75	1.05	**2.32[c] 39%/22%**	1.44	0.68

[a] % mean of individuals in diagnostic category/% mean of individuals not in diagnostic category shown only when odds ratio is significant.
[b] No concurrent psychiatric disorder diagnosed.
[c] Likelihood χ^2 significant at $p < .01$.
[d] Likelihood χ^2 significant at $p < .05$.

TABLE 2.2. Odds-Ratios[a] for Lifetime Drug Use and Psychiatric Medication History by Type of Psychopathology

Substance	Mood (n = 228)	Anxiety (n = 165)	Adjustment (n = 43)	Organic (n = 63)	Psychotic (n = 48)	Axis II (n = 166)	No Dx[b] (n = 48)
Cannabis	0.88	0.72	1.51	1.40	1.03	1.32	1.09
Cocaine	1.05	0.64[c] 52%/63%	1.19	1.29	0.83	1.63[d] 68%/56%	1.00
Hallucinogens	0.95	0.74	0.69	1.49	1.13	1.48[c] 57%/47%	1.55
Heroin	1.13	0.60[c] 14%/21%	1.11	1.53	1.12	1.75[d] 26%/16%	1.00
Inhalant	0.67	0.77	0.56	1.56	1.71	1.83[d] 21%/13%	1.37
Nicotine	1.12	0.92	0.88	1.03	2.42	1.17	0.67
Stimulant	1.25	0.89	0.93	0.98	0.94	1.69[d] 39%/28%	1.18
Medication							
Anxiolytic	0.95	1.85[a] 79%/66%	0.92	1.06	1.21	1.70[d] 77%/67%	0.59
Prescribed opiate	0.94	1.33	0.99	1.14	0.47	2.40[d] 63%/41%	.24[d] 50%/19%
Antidepressant	2.78 72%/48%	1.21	0.62	0.29 30%/59%	2.84	1.33	0.53
Antipsychotic	0.54	0.97	0.51	0.73	13.61 67%/13%	0.89	0.52
Antabuse	1.25	0.83	1.14	0.55	0.76	1.65[c] 26%/18%	0.82

[a]% of individuals in diagnostic category/% of individuals not in diagnostic category shown only when odds ratio is significant.
[b]No concurrent psychiatric disorder diagnosed.
[c]Likelihood c^2 significant at $p < .05$.
[d]Likelihood c^2 significant at $p < .01$.

(adjustment disorder) to 11.6 years (organic disorder). Morning drinking was twice as likely in the organic sample in the 90 days of preassessment; these individuals were also four times as likely to rate their alcohol problem as major or very major than those without an organic disorder. (Conversely, the noncomorbid sample was half as likely to consume more than 10 alcoholic drinks at least once in the 90 days of preassessment).

There were no differences in the mean number of drinks per drinking day (ranging from 6.6 to 10 standard drinks across groups) or in the percent days abstinent in the 60 days prior to assessment (ranging from 44.0% to 57.6%).

Alcohol-Related Consequences

Patients with an organic psychiatric disorder were about twice as likely to report financial problems, physical violence, and relationship losses due to alcohol use in the 6 months prior to seeking treatment than those not diagnosed with this class of disorder (see Table 2.3). Financial problems were also two and a half times more likely to be reported from those who met criteria for a psychotic disorder diagnosis. Axis II patients were more likely to report physical aggression and legal convictions as a result of alcohol than those without a personality disorder diagnosis. Relationship losses were two and a half times more likely in patients assigned an adjustment disorder diagnosis than those without such a diagnosis.

Psychiatric and Addiction Treatment History

As Table 2.4 shows, patients diagnosed with an Axis II disorder were twice as likely to have attended Alcoholics Anonymous (AA) in the past year and one and a half times as likely to have ever had a psychiatric admission than patients not given this diagnosis. Consistent with this treatment history, Axis II patients were also less likely to be seeking treatment for their addiction for the first time. The noncomorbid subjects were about twice as likely to be seeking treatment for addictions for the first time, but less likely to have ever seen a mental health professional, been hospitalized on a psychiatric service, or been prescribed medications in the month prior to seeking treatment than subjects without a diagnosis. Anxiety-diagnosed patients were twice as likely to have been prescribed psychiatric medications in the month prior to seeking addiction treatment. Psychotic patients were seven times as likely to have had previous psychiatric admissions and three times as likely to have attended AA in the past year than those not assigned this diagnosis.

Family Psychiatric and Substance Use History

Table 2.4 shows that very few group differences were observed according to diagnosis except in those with an anxiety disorder, who were twice as likely to have a family member with a history of psychiatric disorder and treatment. Noncomorbid

TABLE 2.3. Odds Ratios[a] for Alcohol-Related Consequences
and Consumption by Type of Psychopathology

Consequences	Mood ($n = 228$)	Anxiety ($n = 165$)	Adjustment ($n = 43$)	Organic ($n = 63$)	Psychotic ($n = 48$)	Axis II ($n = 166$)	No Dx[b] ($n = 48$)
Physical aggression	**0.61**[c] 14%/21%	0.81	1.93	**1.97**[c] 29%/17%	0.73	**1.69**[c] 24%/16%	0.94
Health problem	0.70	1.42	0.74	0.79	0.94	1.62	0.63
Job lost	1.06	1.02	0.86	2.09	1.85	1.57	0.29
Legal conviction	0.70	0.71	1.61	1.49	0.85	**2.26**[c] 9%/4%	0.37
Financial problems	1.07	0.68	1.00	**2.17**[d] 42%/25%	**2.46**[d] 44%/25%	0.80	0.66
Relationship losses	0.87	0.76	**2.52**[d] 53%/31%	**2.15**[d] 49%/31%	0.61	0.91	1.16
Severity of Alcohol Problem							
M (SD) years heavy drinking	10.1 (9.6)	9.2 (7.2)	6.3 (7.5)	11.6 (9.7)	10.6 (9.4)	9.4 (8.9)	8.1 (8.3)
Any morning drinking— past year	0.88	1.11	0.81	**2.14**[c] 68%/50%	1.34	1.21	0.75
Ever drink 10+ drinks— past year	0.94	1.03	1.00	1.79	0.87	1.27	**0.47**[d] 51%/69%
Alcohol problem self-rated as (very) major	0.99	1.49	1.10	**3.73**[d] 83%/57%	0.73	0.76	0.53

[a]% of individuals in diagnostic category/% of individuals not in diagnostic category shown only when odds ratio is significant.
[b]No concurrent psychiatric disorder diagnosed.
[c]Likelihood χ^2 significant at $p < .05$.
[d]Likelihood χ^2 significant at $p < .01$.

TABLE 2.4. Odds Ratios[a] for Patient and Family Psychiatric and Alcohol Treatment History by Type of Psychopathology

Patient History	Mood (n = 228)	Anxiety (n = 165)	Adjustment (n = 43)	Organic (n = 63)	Psychotic (n = 48)	Axis II (n = 166)	No Dx[b] (n = 48)
First time seeking addiction treatment	**0.69**[c] 42%/51%	1.36	1.04	1.14	1.26	**0.64**[c] 40%/51%	**1.90**[c] 63%/47%
M (SD) times sought help	1.7 (1.7)	2.1 (1.9)	1.8 (1.9)	2.0 (2.3)	2.2 (1.7)	2.1 (2.0)/1.7 (1.6)[c]	1.6 (1.5)
Ever on psychiatric unit	1.27	1.13	0.54	0.92	**7.41**[d] 8%/37%	**1.58**[d] 49%/37%	**0.41**[d] 23%/42%
Ever attend AA—past year	0.78	1.24	0.86	0.99	**3.10**[d] 89.6/73.5	**2.08**[d] 83.7/71.2	1.50
Medication prescribed in month pretreatment	1.04	**1.83** 62%/47%	1.39	0.83	1.55	0.79	**0.56**[d] 40%/55%
Familial History of							
Excessive drinking	1.10	1.29	0.63	0.99	0.76	1.01	0.91
Alcohol treatment	1.28	1.45	0.66	0.99	0.96	1.20	**0.47**[c] 18%/32%
Psychiatric history	1.06	**1.76** 57%/43%	0.73	0.84	0.96	1.42	**0.52**[c] 33%/48%

[a]% of individuals in diagnostic category/% of individuals not in diagnostic category shown only when odds ratio is significant.
[b]No concurrent psychiatric disorder diagnosed.
[c]Likelihood χ^2 significant at $p < .05$.
[d]Likelihood χ^2 significant at $p < .01$.

patients were half as likely to have a family member who had received alcohol treatment or psychiatric treatment.

Psychological Distress at Assessment

Patients receiving an organic disorder diagnosis scored higher on most of the SCL-90 subscales than patients not given this diagnosis (see Table 2.5). As expected, anxiety-disordered patients scored higher on the SCL-90 subscales specific to anxiety (anxiety, phobic anxiety) and mood-disorder patients scored higher on subscales related to depression (depression, interpersonal sensitivity, and obsessive-compulsive subscale, the latter tapping into ruminative tendencies). The noncomorbid sample scored significantly lower than individuals with a concurrent psychiatric diagnosis on all subscales.

DISCUSSION

This chapter reports the characteristics of 586 treatment-seeking substance abusers who systematically underwent a comprehensive psychiatric diagnostic interview (*DSM-III-R* criteria) and completed a number of assessment instruments of current use in research-oriented addiction treatment centers. The sample was drawn from patients seeking treatment for substance abuse or dependence on an outpatient basis at an urban research and treatment facility. The generalizability of these findings to other samples of substance abusers must reflect the characteristics of this particular sample: urban, male, primarily nonpartnered, employed, and low to moderate socioeconomic status, with alcohol as the primary substance of abuse.

The complete clinical examination, the wealth of information gathered with those instruments, and the large number of subjects offered a rare opportunity for the drawing of descriptive profiles of the demographics as well as the addictive and psychosocial phenomenology of substance abusers with psychiatric comorbidity. Such information is nonetheless subject to possible inaccuracies, which this study is not in a position to rule out: the diagnostic data derive from a single psychiatric consultation and their reliability and validity were not tested;[15] the latter are of particular importance in the differential diagnosis between substance-induced and independent psychiatric disorders.[16] Nor were the subjects' responses to the questionnaires—including the self-reports on alcohol or drug use—independently confirmed. Those limitations notwithstanding, it was hoped that this exercise in clinical epidemiology would put in evidence disorder-specific vulnerabilities and clinical correlates of relevance to the identification of priorities in treatment planning and level-of-care allocation.

The setting of the study is a large clinical facility in a major urban center, and its wide variety of treatment programs cater to all sorts of substance misuse problems—from brief interventions with alcohol abuse cases to methadone maintenance for severe opiate addiction. A centralized intake service processes all cases

TABLE 2.5. Mean SCL-90-R Subscales[a] and Global Scores by Type of Psychopathology[b]

Subscale	Mood (n = 228)	Anxiety (n = 165)	Adjustment (n = 43)	Organic (n = 63)	Psychotic (n = 48)	Axis II (n = 166)	No Dx[b] (n = 48)
Somatization	1.3	1.2	1.1	**1.6/1.1**	1.0	1.3	**0.6/1.2**
Obsessive-compulsive	**1.8/1.5**	1.7	1.5	**2.2/1.6**	1.6	**1.9/1.6**	**1.1/1.7**
Interpersonal sensitivity	**1.8/1.5**	1.8	1.6	**2.1/1.6**	1.5	1.8	**1.0/1.7**
Depression	**2.4/2.0**	2.2	2.2	**2.5**	1.9	2.3	**1.5/2.2**
Anxiety	1.8	**1.9/1.6**	1.8	**2.1/1.6**	1.6	**1.9/1.6**	**1.0/1.7**
Anger-hostility	1.2	1.2	1.1	**1.6/1.0**	1.0	1.3	**0.6/1.2**
Phobic-anxiety	1.1	**1.4/0.9**	1.0	**1.4**	1.2	1.2	**0.5/1.1**
Paranoid ideation	1.6	1.4	1.7	**2.0/1.4**	1.6	1.6	**0.8/1.5**
Psychoticism	1.3	1.1	1.1	**1.8/1.2**	1.2	1.4	**0.7/1.3**
Global score	**1.6/1.4**	1.6	1.5	**2.0/1.5**	1.4	**1.7/1.5**	**0.9/1.6**

[a]Mean of individuals in diagnostic category/mean of individuals not in diagnostic category shown only when t test is significant.
[b]All t values significant at p < .01.
[c]No concurrent psychiatric disorder diagnosed.

arriving for treatment, and it can be confidently assumed that the sample of this study represents a cross section of the total patient population. The findings presented here, however, pertain only to individuals who gave positive answers to some psychiatric screening questions at the time of intake. After clinical evaluation, a small percentage of these (8.1%) were found to present no current psychiatric disorder; they are included in the data analysis as a separate group for comparison purposes. Much of the evidence gathered in the present study tends to support general assumptions about the effects of psychiatric comorbidity in individuals with addictive disorders, but some associations emerged that were not so obviously expected.

Personality disorders were found to be significantly associated with polydrug use and a greater utilization of both addiction and mental health services. These individuals may also face greater obstacles in complying with treatment, establishing therapeutic relationships, and completing treatment. Coordination of services and access to service policies are needed to decrease wasteful redundancy of interventions with this particular population. Given their rather chaotic drug use behavior and apparent inability to develop consistent service affiliation, some harm-reduction approaches might be the treatment of choice. Since these individuals are prone to antisocial behavior when intoxicated (e.g., physical aggression, legal problems), abstinence would be highly recommended.

Mood-disorder patients reported a greater tendency to seek addiction treatment repeatedly. This finding suggests the need for aggressive and continuing treatment of such disorders in order to improve long-term outcome.

Expectedly, the patients with diagnoses of psychotic disorder presented a profile of more severe psychosocial dysfunction and greater need for social assistance. Since they are generally poorer than those without such diagnoses, the financial impact of their substance abuse is relatively more severe and they are more likely to report it as a problem. The continuing case management model of care, with its ability to coordinate both medical and social assistance interventions, is obviously the most appropriate treatment approach for this category of patients. Their need for continuous support may explain in part why they reported a greater participation in the AA movement than other categories of patients.

Of note is the fact that the service's clinicians were more likely to diagnose the psychiatric symptoms as organic (i.e., substance induced) in patients who were male and who presented with alcohol dependence. This diagnosis was also more often made in individuals who reported higher levels of subjective distress. It is quite possible, of course, that such a tendency only reflects the clinical reality; but it is permissible to ask whether a diagnostic bias, a preconceived idea of the type of patient whose symptoms are likely to be of toxic origin, was at play among the examining clinicians. Several of the drugs abused by the subjects in this study—not just alcohol—are capable of inducing mood, anxiety, psychotic, or cognitive disorders (*DSM-IV*). Do clinicians tend to disregard this possibility? Are they less inclined to interpret as substance induced the psychiatric distress presented by female patients? Unfortunately, the present data do not answer these questions; the issue is mentioned here for future reference.

Female subjects were overrepresented in the anxiety disorder group, and it was not surprising to find that a diagnosis of anxiety is significantly associated with prescription drug abuse. Less obvious, however, is why clinicians tend to diagnose anxiety disorders less often in subjects who abuse illicit drugs. It is quite possible that they would feel that a diagnosis of personality disorder—the one most frequently made among illicit drug users—overrides that of anxiety disorder. Finally, adjustment-disorder patients appear to be in psychosocial crisis and may benefit from a crisis intervention combined with a brief pharmacotherapeutic intervention.

The across-diagnoses variance in clinical correlates elicited in the present study offers additional evidence in support of greater specificity in the clinical approach to the problem of comorbidity at addiction treatment centers. The issue of concurrent psychiatric disturbance is often defined in dimensional terms (e.g., overall levels of "severity") rather than on the basis of diagnostic specificity. The present findings point to the limitations inherent to such an approach.

REFERENCES

1. Anthenelli RM, Schuckit MA. Affective and anxiety disorders and alcohol and drug dependence: diagnosis and treatment. *J Addict Dis* 1993;12:73–87.
2. Lehman AF, Myers CP, Corty E. Assessment and classification of patients with psychiatric and substance abuse syndromes. *Hosp Community Psychiatry* 1989;40:1019–1025.
3. Mowbray CT, Ribisl KM, Solomon M, Luke DA, Kewson TP. Characteristics of dual diagnosis patients admitted to an urban, public psychiatric hospital: an examination of individual, social, and community domains. *Am J Drug Alcohol Abuse* 1997;23:309–326.
4. Penick EC, Powell BJ, Othmer E, Bingham S, Rice A. Subtyping alcoholics by coexisting psychiatric syndrome: course family history and outcome. In: Goodwin D, Van Dusen K, Mednick S, eds. *Longitudinal Research in Alcoholism*. Boston: Kluwer-Nijhoff Publishing; 1984.
5. Nace EP, Davis CW, Gaspari JP. Axis II comorbidity in substance abusers. *Am J Psychiatry* 1991;148:118–120.
6. Sloan KL, Rowe G. Substance abuse and psychiatric illness: psychosocial correlates. *Am J Addict* 1995;4:60–69.
7. Ojehagen A, Berglund M, Appel C-A, Nilsson B, Skjaerris A. Psychiatric symptoms in alcoholics attending outpatient treatment. *Alcohol Clin Exp Res* 1991;15:640–646.
8. Schuckit M. The clinical implications of primary diagnostic groups among alcoholics. *Arch Gen Psychiatry* 1985;42:1043–1049.
9. Hesselbrock MN, Meyer RE, Keener JJ. Psychopathology in hospitalized alcoholics. *Arch Gen Psychiatry* 1985;42:1050–1055.
10. Rounsaville BJ, Dolinsky ZS, Babor TF, Meyer R. Psychopathology as a predictor of treatment outcome in alcoholics. *Arch Gen Psychiatry* 1987;44:505–513.
11. Alterman AI, McLellan AT, Shifman RB. Do substance abuse patients with more

psychopathology receive more treatment? *J Nerv Ment Dis* 1993;181:576–582.

12. Sobell LC, Sobell MB. Timeline follow-back: a technique for assessing self-reported alcohol consumption. In: Litten R, Allen J, eds. *Measuring Alcohol Consumption: Psychosocial and Biological Methods.* Totowa, NJ: The Humana Press, Inc.; 1992:41–72.

13. Derogatis LR. *SCL-90: Administration, Scoring and Procedures Manual-I for the Revised Version and Other Instruments of the Psychopathology Rating Scale Series.* Baltimore, MD: Johns Hopkins University School of Medicine, Clinical Psychometrics Research Unit; 1983.

14. American Psychiatric Association. Committee on Nomenclature and Statistics. *Diagnostic and Statistical Manual of Mental Disorders, Revised Third Edition.* Washington, DC: American Psychiatric Association; 1987.

15. Weiss RD, Mirin SM, Griffin ML. Methodological considerations in the diagnosis of coexisting psychiatric disorders in the substance abuser. *Br J Addict* 1992;87:179–187.

16. Raskin VD, Miller NS. The epidemiology of the comorbidity of psychiatric and addictive disorders: a critical review. *J Addict Dis* 1993;12:45–57.

Chapter 3

Psychiatric Disorders Among Drug-Dependent Subjects

Are They Primary or Secondary?

Wilson M. Compton, III, M.D.
Linda B. Cottler, Ph.D.
Deborah L. Phelps, Ph.D.
Arbi Ben Abdallah, M.S.
Edward L. Spitznagel, Ph.D.

Psychiatric disorders are much more common than expected among patients with substance use disorders.[1-18] While this finding may be interesting in and of itself, it also has important treatment and prognostic implications. For example, psychiatric symptoms among patients with substance use disorders have been shown to be associated with higher rates of drug relapse following treatment.[13,14,19] In addition, comorbidity has been shown to complicate treatment of both drug and nondrug problems.[20]

Because of limited research, the causal link (if any) between drug dependence and other psychiatric disorders remains murky, especially where details on the progression from one illness to another are concerned. Lehman et al.[21] proposed several theoretical constructs: mental illness causes substance dependence; substance dependence causes mental illness; both diagnoses occur independently; and both could be caused by some common factor. These constructs are related to temporal association. For example, if mental illness results in substance dependence, then mental illness must, by definition, start first. If substance dependence

This study was supported by grants DA05619 (Dr. Cottler) and DA00209 (Dr. Compton) from the National Institute on Drug Abuse, Bethesda, MD.

results in mental illness, substance dependence would have to start first. If the two disorders occur independently or are caused by some common factor, no temporal association would necessarily be found. Robins et al. used the terms *primary* and *secondary* to identify a temporal sequence of syndromes, not necessarily implying a causal relationship.[22] In applying these definitions to dually diagnosed patients, a clearer understanding of the natural history of drug abuse may emerge.

We examined psychiatric disorders in a population of drug-dependent subjects newly admitted to treatment in order to clarify important issues about comorbidity: (1) Among persons diagnosed with both drug dependence and a comorbid psychiatric disorder (dual diagnosis respondents), does the onset of psychiatric illness precede the onset of drug dependence (primary psychiatric illness) or follow it (secondary psychiatric illness)? (2) Does the pattern of primary and secondary psychiatric illness vary according to the particular psychiatric diagnosis? and (3) Are there ethnic or other sociodemographic characteristics associated with psychiatric illness being primary to drug dependence?[23–26] Previous studies of comorbidity among intreatment substance abusers have included persons admitted to treatment without regard to presence or absence of a substance use disorder. In this study, the focus is on persons diagnosed with dependence so that only persons with a high level of substance abuse severity are included in the assessment of psychiatric comorbidity.

METHODS

Sample

Data for this study come from the Substance Abuse and Risk of AIDS (SARA) study, a NIDA-funded longitudinal study among St. Louis substance abusers who were recently admitted to drug treatment facilities in the City of St. Louis. Details about sampling, interviewing, and other study methods are provided in the companion paper by Compton et al.[27]

Instruments

All subjects were interviewed face-to-face using portions of the NIMH Diagnostic Interview Schedule Version III-R (DIS)[28,29] and other instruments focusing on human immunodeficiency virus (HIV) risk behaviors. For this report, all data are taken from the DIS, which has been used extensively in psychiatric epidemiologic studies[25] and can be administered by nonclinicians with adequate reliability.[30] Furthermore, in this version of the DIS, age of onset and recency of individual symptoms are elicited.[28] In a study of a closely related instrument, the reliability and validity of subjects' self-reported date of onset of symptoms were high.[31] In all cases, written informed consent was obtained prior to administration of any research instruments.

Diagnoses

Diagnostic algorithms written and checked by the authors of the DIS were used to compute lifetime prevalence rates of the *DSM-III-R* disorders listed in Tables 3.1 and 3.2. The definitions of primary and secondary psychiatric disorders were based on ages of onset of drug dependence and the psychiatric disorder as follows. Age of onset was defined as the age at which the full syndrome was first met. For example, the age of onset of drug dependence was defined as the age at which the third *DSM-III-R* criterion was first experienced (because the diagnosis requires at least three criteria); similarly, the age of onset of major depression was defined as the age at which the depressive syndrome was first experienced. A disorder was defined as primary to drug dependence if the threshold age of onset of the psychiatric syndrome preceded the threshold age of onset of drug dependence. A disorder was defined as secondary to drug dependence if the age of onset of drug dependence preceded the age of onset of the psychiatric syndrome. Same age of onset disorder was one in which the reported age of onset of drug dependence was the same as the age of onset of the psychiatric syndrome.

TABLE 3.1. Demographic and Drug Status of SARA
Study Drug-Dependent Subjects (*N* = 425)

Race	
African-American	61%
Caucasian	35%
Other	4%
Male	66%
High school graduate	57%
Mean age (*SD*)	32.5 yr. (6.5 yr.)
Currently unemployed	68%
Marital status	
Married	14%
Widowed	3%
Separated/divorced	33%
Never married	51%
Lifetime dependence on any illicit substance	100%
Cocaine dependence	68%
Opiate dependence	51%
Cannabis dependence	31%
Sedative dependence	17%
Amphetamine dependence	17%
Phencyclidine dependence	9%
Hallucinogen dependence	6%
Volatile inhalant dependence	2%
Mean number of dependence disorders (*SD*)[a]	2.2 (1.5)
Ever injected drugs	62%

[a]Excluding tobacco and alcohol dependence.

TABLE 3.2. *DSM-III-R* Lifetime Psychiatric Disorders among SARA Study Respondents with Drug Dependence (*N* = 425)

Psychiatric Disorder	%
Any disorder other than dependence on an illicit substance[a]	84
Any nonsubstance use disorder[b]	73
Alcohol dependence	64
Antisocial personality disorder	44
Phobic disorder	39
Major depressive disorder	24
Dysthymia	12
Generalized anxicty disorder	10

[a]Including alcohol dependence but not tobacco or illicit substance use disorders.
[b]Excluding tobacco, alcohol, or illicit substance use disorders.

Statistics

SAS statistical programs were used to analyze the data.[32] Descriptive statistics include the proportion of subjects affected with particular substance dependence disorders and psychiatric disorders. The age of onset for each disorder was also calculated as described above. These ages of onset were used to determine the proportion of the subjects with primary psychiatric disorders compared to those with secondary and those with identical ages of onset of both types of disorders.

Among those with a dual diagnosis, sociodemographic characteristics and history of injection drug use were tested for association with primary psychiatric disorders using the chi-square statistic for dichotomous variables and univariate logistic regression for continuous variables. Multivariate logistic regression models were used to determine the specificity of the associations. In these models, "primary psychiatric disorder" was the dependent variable compared to "all others," which included secondary and same age of onset disorders. Age, race, gender, and history of injection drug use were used as independent variables. The purpose of this model testing was to determine whether particular classes of drug-dependent persons were at particular risk for primary psychiatric illnesses. For all statistical tests, results were considered significant at $p < .05$.

RESULTS

The overall sample of 512 included 425 persons who had a history of dependence on one or more illicit substances. All results focus on the 425 persons with *DSM-III-R* drug dependence, and the demographic and drug dependence characteristics of these subjects are presented in Table 3.1. The sample of 425 drug-dependent persons was diverse (61% African-American and 66% male). The majority had graduated from high school (57%), were unemployed (68%), and were never married (51%). The mean age was 32.5 years. The most common lifetime dependence diagnosis was cocaine dependence (68%), followed by opiate (51%), cannabis (31%), sedative (17%), amphetamine (17%), phencyclidine (9%), hallucinogen (6%), and inhalant (2%) dependence. The subjects typically had more than one dependence diagnosis; the mean number of dependence disorders was 2.2. Sixty-two percent of the subjects had a history of injection drug use.

Rates of psychiatric disorders among the drug-dependent subjects (i.e., those with dual diagnoses) are displayed in Table 3.2. The prevalence of a nonsubstance use disorder was 72%; if alcohol dependence is included, the rate of comorbidity increased to 84%. The most common individual comorbid disorders were alcohol dependence (64%), antisocial personality (44%), phobias (39%), major depression (24%), dysthymia (12%), and generalized anxiety (10%).

Among drug-dependent subjects, ages of onset of drug dependence, alcohol dependence, and other comorbid psychiatric disorders (dual-diagnosis subjects) are shown in Table 3.3. On average, drug-dependent respondents had an onset of phobias at age 11.1 ($SD = 11.3$) and antisocial personality at age 13.1 ($SD = 2.5$)—that is, during childhood or early adolescence. Dysthymia and major depression started at ages 20.4 ($SD = 8.7$) and 20.7 ($SD = 8.1$), respectively. Generalized anxiety and alcohol dependence started at ages 23.0 ($SD = 8.5$) and 23.1 ($SD = 13.6$), respectively. Drug dependence had an average age of onset of 22.5 ($SD = 9.7$) years.

In Figure 3.1, primary and secondary distinctions are displayed. Drug dependence generally followed the onset of antisocial personality (91%) and phobias (90%); thus, these two conditions were usually primary to drug dependence. Alcohol dependence and drug dependence were evenly split in ranking their ages of onset, so primary (44%) and secondary (45%) alcohol dependence were nearly equal in prevalence. The remaining 11% of those with comorbid alcohol dependence reported identical ages of onset for alcohol and drug dependence. Similarly, 39% of the drug-dependent persons with major depression and 42% of those with dysthymia had primary psychiatric conditions, 55% and 44% of those with

TABLE 3.3. Age of Onset of Drug Dependence and Psychiatric Disorders among SARA Study Respondents with Drug Dependence

Psychiatric Disorder (N)	Age of Onset Years ± SD
Drug dependence[a] (425)	22.5 ± 9.7
Alcohol dependence (270)	23.1 ± 13.6
Antisocial personality (187)	13.1 ± 2.5
Phobic disorder (167)	11.1 ± 11.3
Major depressive disorder (101)	20.7 ± 8.1
Dysthymia (52)	20.4 ± 8.7
Generalized anxiety disorder (43)	23.0 ± 8.5

[a]Excluding tobacco and alcohol.

Antisocial Personality Disorder	
Cormobid diagnosis started before drug dependence	91%
Cormobid diagnosis started after drug dependence	5%
Same Age of Onset	4%
Phobic Disorder	
Cormobid diagnosis started before drug dependence	90%
Cormobid diagnosis started after drug dependence	8%
Same Age of Onset	2%
Major Depressive Disorder	
Cormobid diagnosis started before drug dependence	39%
Cormobid diagnosis started after drug dependence	55%
Same Age of Onset	6%
Alcohol Dependence	
Cormobid diagnosis started before drug dependence	44%
Cormobid diagnosis started after drug dependence	45%
Same Age of Onset	11%
Generalized Anxiety Disorder	
Cormobid diagnosis started before drug dependence	33%
Cormobid diagnosis started after drug dependence	65%
Same Age of Onset	2%
Dysthymia	
Cormobid diagnosis started before drug dependence	42%
Cormobid diagnosis started after drug dependence	44%
Same Age of Onset	14%

FIGURE 3.1. Primary and secondary psychiatric disorders among drug-dependent subjects from the SARA study ($N = 425$).

major depression and dysthymia had secondary disorders, and 6% and 14% had simultaneous ages of onset. Thus, there was no consistent pattern of comorbid depression or dysthymia starting before or after drug dependence, and these conditions could not be consistently categorized as either primary or secondary. For generalized anxiety, 65% began after the onset of drug dependence, indicating that most cases of generalized anxiety were secondary to drug dependence.

The association of primary disorders with demographic characteristics and history of injection drug use (IDU) was tested using both univariate and multivariate tests. In the univariate models, women were significantly more likely than men to have primary generalized anxiety disorders (53% vs. 19% primary in men, $p = .02$) but none of the other disorders. African-Americans were associated significantly with primary alcohol dependence (51% vs. 31% primary in Caucasians, $p = .008$), antisocial personality disorder (95% vs. 86% primary in Caucasians, $p = .04$), and phobias (96% vs. 80% primary in Caucasians, $p = .001$). Injection drug use was associated significantly with primary dysthymia (31% vs. 65% primary in noninjectors, $p = .02$). On the other hand, age was not a predictor of any primary disorders.

In order to test the specificity of these associations, multivariate logistic regression models were tested with primary (vs. nonprimary) disorders as the dependent variables. Independent variables were gender, race, age, and history of IDU. These models indicate that like the univariate models, the African-American race (compared to Caucasian/other race) was associated with primary phobias (odds ratio 9.2, $p < .001$) and primary alcohol dependence (odds ratio 1.7, $p = .04$), controlling for gender, age, and history of injection drug use. Similarly, female gender (compared to male) was associated with primary generalized anxiety disorder (odds ratio 1.8, $p = .02$). Also, like the univariate models, age was not associated with any primary disorders, and gender was not associated with primary alcohol dependence, antisocial personality, phobias, depression, or dysthymia. On the other hand, unlike the univariate models, racial group was not associated with primary antisocial personality in the multivariate model, nor was IDU status associated with primary dysthymia in the multivariate model.

DISCUSSION

Our study confirms the high rates of psychiatric disorders among drug-dependent subjects found by other research groups. It is clear that persons in treatment for drug dependence have very high rates of additional psychiatric disorders. In fact, comorbidity can be seen as the rule rather than the exception.

The definition of *primary* implies that the psychiatric disorder precedes and thus might cause drug dependence; conversely, a *secondary* psychiatric disorder follows and thus might be caused by the drug dependence. However, no conclusion concerning a definite causal link between the two syndromes is possible in the current study. We *can* say that when drug dependence follows a psychiatric disorder, the psychiatric disorder was *not* caused by drug dependence, and, similarly, that when a psychiatric disorder follows drug dependence, the drug dependence was *not* caused by the psychiatric disorder. The course of illness may be examined to see whether a relationship exists between two disorders.

Our findings confirm the primary nature of phobic and antisocial personality disorders. Because antisocial personality disorder requires a childhood onset, it is not surprising that it precedes drug dependence. To answer this potential confound, we analyzed the data by looking at the onset of drug dependence in comparison to the onset of conduct disorder *or* adult antisocial behaviors. Even with this broader definition that allowed for a full range of ages of onset (compared to a required childhood onset of *DSM-III-R* antisocial personality disorder), the vast majority still had primary antisocial behaviors—that is, they developed at least their first antisocial syndrome before drug dependence. Thus, children with conduct disorder symptoms may be a high-risk population in which drug abuse prevention measures may be focused. Furthermore, demographic characteristics (race gender, and age) and history of injection drug use were not associated with primary antisocial personality. This finding indicates that categories of primary and secondary antisocial personality apply equally well to the different racial, gender, and age groups, and to those who do and do not have a history of injection drug use. Perhaps most important, these results indicate that secondary antisocial syndromes are rare, and like Dinwiddie, we conclude that the concept of secondary antisocial syndromes is not supported.[33]

Phobias were also found to precede drug use in 90% of the drug-dependent subjects who were comorbid for phobic disorders. Given a typical onset of phobias during childhood, it may not be unexpected that phobias generally precede drug dependence, but, particularly for African-Americans, primary phobias are common. In fact, controlling for age, gender, and history of injection drug use, African-Americans were significantly associated with primary phobias. This association was particularly strong, with an odds ratio of 9.2. Not only were phobias very common but they were more likely to start before substance dependence among this race. An etiological relationship could be indicated, in that the rate of phobias was much higher than a general population sample.[24] Drug use may represent a form of self-medication for these subjects, and the interaction of phobias with drug use deserves further exploration. Children with phobic disorders, particularly African-American children, may be a useful target for drug-prevention efforts.

For the other common disorders, a more complex situation was seen. Alcohol dependence was nearly evenly divided into primary and secondary categories. The literature indicates that alcohol use (like tobacco use) may be a gateway substance,[34] but alcohol dependence does not always antedate drug dependence. Similarly, depression and dysthymia quite commonly preceded as well as followed drug dependence, making treatment and evaluation quite complicated. For generalized anxiety disorder, most cases (65%) started after drug dependence, possibly implicating drug dependence in the etiology of these conditions.

In a related paper, we showed that the rates of psychiatric disorders in this sample varied significantly according to gender and race, but the ages of onset of disorders did not differ much according to these same demographic characteristics.[27] Thus, race and gender may be important in determining the likelihood of having additional psychiatric disorders, but the pattern of these disorders, as reflected in their ages of onset, was generally not associated with demographic characteristics. The major exception to this rule was for primary phobic disorders, as described above, which were strongly associated with the African-American race. The other two statistically significant findings, for African-American race with primary alcohol dependence and for female gender with primary generalized anxiety, had odds ratios of less than 2.0. Thus, the relationship of these factors to primary psychiatric disorders was statistically significant but not very strong and probably not clinically meaningful. Furthermore, all other models did not find a significant association of race, gender, age, and IDU status with primary psychiatric disorders. We conclude that the rate of primary psychiatric disorders is generally independent of these factors and can be seen as consistently distributed across different race, gender, and age groups.

CONCLUSIONS

Despite the limitations of a treatment sample and some question concerning the validity of nonsubstance use DIS diagnoses ascertained by nonclinicians,[35,36] our results have implications for future research into comorbidity among substance users.[37] Because it is difficult to pinpoint the start of psychiatric disorders that are episodic or subacute, explicit definitions are particularly important. A precise nomenclature for *age of onset, primary,* and *secondary* is critical for understanding the interplay between drug dependence and other psychiatric disorders. Based on precise definitions for these concepts, we found that antisocial symptoms and phobias generally begin before drug dependence. Prospective research can confirm the importance of conduct symptoms and childhood phobias in predicting future drug dependence. Other psychiatric disorders were found to begin after drug dependence or to have a mixed onset in relationship to drug dependence. Research into comorbidity will need to take into account the onset of symptoms in relation to drug dependence if the relationship between dual diagnoses is to be understood.

REFERENCES

1. Regier DA, Farmer ME, et al. Comorbidity of mental disorders with alcohol and other drug abuse, results from the epidemiologic catchment area (ECA) study. *JAMA* 1990;262:2511–2518.
2. Ross HE, Glaser FB, et al. The prevalence of psychiatric disorders in patients with alcohol and other drug problems. *Arch Gen Psychiatry* 1988;45:1023–1031.
3. Weissman MM, Myers JK, Harding PS. Prevalence and psychiatric heterogeneity of alcoholism in a United States urban community. *J Stud Alcohol* 1980;41:672–681.
4. Mirin SM, Weiss RD, Michael J. Psychopathology in substance abusers: diagnosis and treatment. *Am J Drug Alcohol Abuse* 1988;14:139–157.
5. Mirin SM, Weiss RD. Affective illness in substance abusers. *Psychiatr Clin N Am* 1986;9:503–515.
6. Weiss RD, Mirin SM, et al. Psychopathology in chronic cocaine abusers. *Am J Drug Alcohol Abuse* 1986;12:17–29.
7. Rounsaville BJ, Weissman MM, et al. Heterogeneity of psychiatric diagnosis in treated opiate addicts. *Arch Gen Psychiatry* 1982;39:161–166.
8. Kosten TR, Rounsaville BJ. Psychopathology in opioid addicts. *Psychiatr Clin N Am* 1986;9:515–532.
9. Mirin SM, Weiss RD, et al. Psychopathology in substance abusers and their families. *Resident & Staff Physician* 1988;34:61–65.
10. Hesselbrock MN, Meyer RE, Keener JJ. Psychopathology in hospitalized alcoholics. *Arch Gen Psychiatry* 1985;42:1050–1055.
11. Khantzian EJ, Treece C. DSM-III psychiatric diagnosis of narcotic addicts, recent findings. *Arch Gen Psychiatry* 1985;42:1067–1071.
12. Powell BJ, Penick EC, et al. Prevalence of additional psychiatric syndromes among male alcoholics. *J Clin Psychiatry* 1982;43:404–407.
13. McLellan AT, Luborsky L, et al. Predicting response to alcohol and drug abuse treatment, role of psychiatric severity. *Arch Gen Psychiatry* 1983;40:620–625.
14. Croughan JL, Miller JP, et al. Psychiatric diagnosis and prediction of drug and alcohol dependence. *J Clin Psychiatry* 1982;43:353–356.

15. Jainchill N, De Leon G, et al. Psychiatric diagnoses among substance abusers in therapeutic community treatment. *J Psychoactive Drugs* 1986;18:209–213.
16. Hasin DS, Grant BF, Endicott J. Lifetime psychiatric comorbidity in hospitalized alcoholics: subject and familial correlates. *Int J Addict* 1988;23:827–850.
17. Rounsaville BJ, Anton SF, et al. Psychiatric diagnoses of treatment-seeking cocaine abusers. *Arch Gen Psychiatry* 1991;48:43–51.
18. Brooner R, King VL, Kidorf M, Schmidt CW, Bigelow GE. Psychiatric and substance use comorbidity among treatment-seeking opioid abusers. *Arch Gen Psychiatry* 1997;54:71–80.
19. LaPorte DJ, McLellan AT, et al. Treatment response in psychiatrically impaired drug abusers. *Compr Psychiatry* 1981;32:470–474.
20. Sullivan LW. *Drug Abuse and Drug Abuse Research.* Washington, DC: DHHS Pub. No. (ADM)91–1704;1991;61–83.
21. Lehman AF, Myers CP, Corty E. Assessment and classification of patients with psychiatric and substance abuse syndromes. *Hosp Community Psychiatry* 1989;400:1019–1025.
22. Robins E, Munoz RA, et al. Primary and secondary affective disorders. In: Zubin J, Freyhan FA, eds. *Disorders of Mood.* Baltimore: The Johns Hopkins University Press; 1972:33–45.
23. Compton WM, Helzer JE, Hwu HG, Yeh EK, McEvoy L, Tipp JE, Spitznagel EL. New methods in cross-cultural psychiatry: psychiatric illness in Taiwan and the United States. *Am J Psychiatry* 1991;148:1697–1704.
24. Helzer JE, Canino GJ, Yeh EK, Bland RC, Lee CK, Hwu HG, Newman S. Alcoholism: North America and Asia. *Arch Gen Psychiatry* 1990;47:313–319.
25. Robins LN, Regier DA. *Psychiatric Disorders in America: The Epidemiologic Catchment Area Study.* New York: The Free Press; 1991.
26. Hanson B. Drug treatment effectiveness: the case of racial and ethnic minorities in America—some research questions and proposals. *Int J Addict* 1985;20:99–137.
27. Compton WM, Cottler LB, Abdallah AB, Phelps DL, Spitznagel EL, Horton JC. Substance dependence and other psychiatric disorders among drug dependent subjects: race and gender correlates. *Am J Addict* 2000;9:113–125.
28. Robins LN, Helzer JE, et al. *National Institute of Mental Health Diagnostic Interview Schedule, Version III, Revised.* St. Louis, MO: Washington University; 1989.
29. Robins LN, Helzer JE, et al. National Institute of Mental Health Diagnostic Interview Schedule. *Arch Gen Psychiatry* 1981;38:381–389.
30. Robins LN, Helzer JE, Ratcliff KS, Seyfried W. Validity of the Diagnostic Interview Schedule, Version II: DSM-III diagnoses. *Psychol Med.* 1982;12:855–870.
31. Wittchen HU, Burke JD, Semler G, Pfister H, Von Cranach M, Zaudig M. Recall and dating of psychiatric symptoms. *Arch Gen Psychiatry* 1989;46:437–443.
32. SAS Institute, Inc. *SAS/STAT User's Guide, Version 6.* 4th Edition, Vol. 1. Cary, NC: SAS Institute, Inc.; 1989.
33. Dinwiddie SH, Reich T. Attribution of antisocial symptoms in coexistent antisocial personality disorder and substance abuse. *Compr Psychiatry* 1993;34:235–242.
34. Kandel D, Faust R. Sequence and stages in patterns of adolescent drug use. *Arch Gen Psychiatry* 1975;32:923–932.
35. Helzer JE, Robins LN, McEvoy LT, et al. A comparison of clinical and Diagnostic Interview Schedule diagnoses. *Arch Gen Psychiatry* 1985;42:657–666.
36. Anthony JC, Folstein M, Romanoski AJ, et al. Comparison of the lay Diagnostic Interview Schedule and a standardized psychiatric diagnosis. *Arch Gen Psychiatry* 1985;42:667–675.
37. Kessler RC, Crum RM, Warner LA, Nelson CB, Schulenberg J, Anthony JC. Life co-occurrence of DSM-III-R alcohol abuse and dependence with other psychiatric disorders in the National Comorbidity Survey. *Arch Gen Psychiatry* 1997;54:313–321.

Chapter 4

Reliability and Validity of Screening Instruments for Drug and Alcohol Abuse in Adults Seeking Evaluation for Attention-Deficit/ Hyperactivity Disorder

Barbara S. McCann, Ph.D.
Tracy L. Simpson, Ph.D.
Richard Ries, M.D.
Peter Roy-Byrne, M.D.

Substance abuse and dependence are common disorders among individuals in the United States, with 35% of males and 18% of females ages 15 to 54 meeting lifetime diagnostic criteria.[1] These disorders are not only socially and occupationally disabling but are associated with similarly disabling mental disorders in half of these individuals.[2] Thus, it is important to be able to quickly and accurately screen for substance use disorders in populations at high risk.

Adolescents and adults with attention-deficit hyperactivity disorder (ADHD) are at high risk for substance use disorders.[3,4] Roughly 50% of adults with ADHD have a history of psychoactive substance use disorders,[5] and a history of childhood ADHD has been found in 22% to 71% of substance-abusing adults.[3] Substance abuse is more common among individuals with a first-degree relative who has ADHD.[3,4] By default, ADHD, which requires childhood onset, always precedes substance abuse when the two co-occur. These findings have led many to speculate that ADHD is a risk factor for the development of substance abuse.[3]

In addition to high rates of substance use disorders among individuals with ADHD, various substance-related disorders share common characteristics with ADHD that may render differential diagnosis difficult. For example, cannabis intoxication is associated with impaired short-term memory, cognitive symptoms of substance-induced persisting dementia may include both memory impairment and disturbances in executive functioning, and intoxication from most illicit substances may include disturbances in social or occupational functioning.[6] Memory impairment (forgetfulness in daily activities) is a symptom of inattention, and the diagnosis of ADHD requires evidence of clinically significant impairment in social, academic, or occupational functioning.[6]

Between 8% and 10% of school-age children have been diagnosed with ADHD, and roughly half of these children continue to exhibit symptoms of the disorder as adults, resulting in a prevalence of ADHD in adults of between 4% and 5%.[7] Adults with ADHD report legal difficulties (including use of illicit substances), marital problems, frequent job changes, inconsistent work performance, and underemployment. These functional difficulties, coupled with recent widespread recognition that ADHD continues into adulthood, have led a growing number of adults to seek evaluation for this condition.

In light of the demonstrated high comorbidity between ADHD and substance use disorders in adults, as well as the ability of many substance-related disorders to mimic symptoms of ADHD, people seeking evaluation for ADHD should be screened for substance use disorders. However, there are no data on the reliability and validity of screening instruments for drug and alcohol abuse and dependence among adults seeking evaluation for ADHD. The present study attempts to fill this gap by describing the construct validity and internal consistency reliability of two widely used drug and alcohol screening instruments in adults seeking clinical evaluation for ADHD: the Drug Abuse Screening Test (DAST) and the Alcohol Use Disorders Identification Test (AUDIT).

METHOD

Participants

One hundred forty-three adults seeking evaluation at the Harborview Medical Center Adult ADHD Clinic during 1994 and 1995 have been described previously[8] and form the basis of this report. DAST and AUDIT were administered as part of a comprehensive test battery described in the earlier study.

Measures

DAST

DAST is a 28-item brief screening instrument that assesses drug-related consequences of use and abuse.[9] It assesses a wide range of problems associated with drug abuse and yields a single quantitative score.[9] Cutoff scores have been identified that are associated with *DSM-III* drug abuse and dependence diagnoses, with a cutoff score of 6 generally used.[10] In the original normative sample, the internal consistency was found to be high (.92), and a factor analysis revealed that the instrument measures a unidimensional construct. Sample items include "Have you engaged in illegal activities in order to obtain drugs?" and "Have you ever lost a job because of drug abuse?" The time frame for most of the DAST items can include past as well as current drug use (e.g., "Have you ever . . . ?"); eight items are written in the present tense (e.g., "Do you . . . ?"). Responses are in a yes/no format, and possible scores range from 0 to 28. Higher scores reflect greater drug use–related consequences. The original psychometric properties of DAST have been replicated in psychiatric patients, and its validity in discriminating patients with *DSM-III* substance abuse diagnoses from those with other *DSM-III* diagnoses has been established.[10]

AUDIT

AUDIT is a 10-item questionnaire developed in conjunction with a World Health Organization project on the detection of harmful alcohol consumption as a screening instrument for identifying harmful or hazardous drinkers in primary care settings.[11] AUDIT, like DAST, yields a single quantitative score based on quantity and sequelae of alcohol consumption, and cutoff scores have been established that distinguish hazardous from nonhazardous alcohol use.[11] Responses are scored from 0 (indicating minimal drinking or consequences) to 4 (indicating a high frequency of drinking or harmful consequences), with possible scores ranging from 0 to 40. A cutoff score of 8 or more has been recommended to distinguish hazardous from nonhazardous use, although other potential cutoff scores have been explored.[12,13] The first eight items of AUDIT cover drinking-related behavior in the present (e.g., "How often do you have a drink containing alcohol?") and during the past year (e.g., "How often during the last year have you failed to do what was normally expected of you because of drinking?"). The remaining two items can be construed as lifetime questions because of their wording (e.g., "Have you or someone else been injured as a result of your drinking?" and "Has a relative or friend, or a doctor or other health worker, been concerned about your drinking or suggested you cut down?" with possible responses including "No," "Yes, but not in the last year," and "Yes, during the last year"). Despite its relatively recent development, AUDIT has been studied extensively and has adequate internal reliability and validity.[14]

Procedure

Adults seeking evaluation in the Harborview Medical Center Adult ADHD Specialty Clinic received assessment in two phases. The first phase was 1 to 2 hours of psychological testing, which included administration of DAST and AUDIT.

The second phase was a clinical diagnostic interview conducted by one of four board-certified psychiatrists, all of whom are faculty in the Department of Psychiatry and Behavioral Sciences at the University of Washington. These psychiatrists made specific inquiry into the use of substances. A semistructured psychiatric interview previously validated against the Structured Clinical Interview for *DSM-III-R* was used to assess non-ADHD psychiatric diagnoses in this sample.[15] The ADHD diagnosis was made using *DSM-IV* criteria and a structured interview schedule provided by J. Biederman, M.D.

In the original report, patients were classified as "definite/probable" ADHD (*n* = 46), "possible" ADHD (*n* = 51), or non-ADHD (*n* = 46).[8] For the present report, written evaluations of the 51 patients classified as "possible" ADHD were reviewed independently by a board-certified psychiatrist (P.R.B.) and a senior psychologist (B.S.M.), both of whom have extensive experience in making the diagnosis of ADHD in adults. These 51 patients were reclassified as either ADHD or non-ADHD, resulting in 70 individuals with a diagnosis of ADHD and 73 individuals without the diagnosis of ADHD. Virtually every patient who did not receive a diagnosis of ADHD had some other form of psychiatric disorder, with mood disorders being the most common.[8]

Because diagnoses of conditions other than ADHD were made based on *DSM-III-R* criteria, the original written psychiatric evaluations were reevaluated for substance use disorders based on *DSM-IV* criteria. These evaluations were conducted by a clinical psychologist (B.S.M.) and a master's-level psychologist who completed her predoctoral internship at an APA-accredited program and had over 10 years of experience evaluating adults with substance use disorders (T.L.S.). Evaluators were blind to AUDIT and DAST scores, and had not conducted any of the diagnostic interviews. Each case was evaluated for alcohol abuse, alcohol dependence, drug abuse, and drug dependence, and was coded as current, past, or none. Abuse and dependence categories are mutually exclusive, and "use" refers to either abuse or dependence. The evaluators met to discuss the cases in which there was not 100% agreement and resolved these through consensus, consulting as necessary with a board-certified psychiatrist with extensive expertise in addictions research (R.R.). Four of the 143 cases did not contain sufficient information to reach a substance use diagnosis and were thus not included in the analyses, resulting in a final sample of 139 (68 with ADHD and 71 without ADHD).

RESULTS

Characteristics of the sample are shown in Table 4.1. Patients' ages ranged from 18 to 64 years (*M* = 36.4, *SD* = 10.5). The sample was predominantly male (69.1%) and Caucasian (95.7%). Current alcohol use diagnoses were made in 15.8% of patients, and current drug use diagnoses were made in 9.4%. Current combined alcohol and drug use disorders were assigned to 7 patients (5%). Based on the recommended AUDIT cutoff of 8 or above, 38 of 139 patients (27.3%) exceeded

TABLE 4.1. AUDIT and DAST Scores as a Function of Drug and Alcohol Abuse and Dependence Among Adults Seeking Evaluation for ADHD (N = 139)

			AUDIT		DAST	
Variable	Number of Patients	%	M	SD	M	SD
All patients	139	100.0 0.0	5.3	6.1	5.0	5.7
Alcohol use disorders						
Current	22	15.8	13.9$_a$	8.7	8.9$_a$	5.9
Past	24	17.3	6.0$_b$	4.2	8.4$_a$	7.1
None	93	66.9	3.2$_c$	3.3	3.3$_b$	4.3
Drug use disorders						
Current	13	9.4	7.5	9.6	10.1$_a$	4.6
Past	22	15.8	7.7	6.1	12.5$_a$	5.7
None	104	74.8	4.6	5.3	2.8$_b$	3.8
Any substance use disorder						
Current	27	19.4	12.0$_a$	8.8	8.9$_a$	5.8
Past	31	22.3	5.6$_b$	4.4	9.2$_a$	6.6
None	81	58.3	3.0$_b$	3.2	2.2$_b$	3.0

Note. Means with unshared subscripts differ in post hoc analyses (Scheffe's test), $p < .05$. AUDIT = Alcohol Use Disorders Identification Test; DAST = Drug Abuse Screening Test.

this score. Based on the recommended DAST cutoff score of 6 or above, 47 patients (33.8%) had a positive screen for drug abuse. AUDIT scores were highest for those with current alcohol use disorders, compared to those with past alcohol use disorders and those who never abused alcohol ($F[2, 136] = 46.9, p < .001$). In contrast, DAST scores were roughly comparable between those with current and past drug use disorders, and these individuals had higher scores than those who never abused drugs ($F[2,136] = 59.0, p < .001$). Individuals with current and past alcohol use disorders attained mean DAST scores that were significantly higher than individuals who never abused alcohol. Similarly, individuals with any current or past substance use disorder had higher DAST scores than individuals who never had a substance use disorder ($F[2,136] = 38.0, p < .001$).

Internal consistencies for AUDIT and DAST were determined by examining coefficient alpha and item-total correlations. Both scales exhibited adequate internal reliability consistent with prior results in a variety of patient populations. Cronbach's alpha was .92 for DAST and .87 for AUDIT. The two scores are moderately correlated ($r = .41$).

Item-total correlations on DAST were generally moderate to high (.40–.67). Items with lower item-total correlations included two items dealing with arrest ("Have you ever been arrested for possession of illegal drugs?" $r = .35$; "Have you ever been arrested for driving while under the influence of drugs?" $r = .38$), and two items reflecting ability to control use ("Do you try to limit your drug use to certain situations?" $r = .17$; "Can you get through the week without using drugs other than those required for medical reasons?" $r = .27$).

As with DAST, item-total correlations on AUDIT were generally moderate to high (.50–.74). The item-total correlation was low for one item that reflected failure to meet role expectations ("How often during the last year have you failed to do what was normally expected from you because of drinking?" $r = .19$).

Construct validity was assessed by performing cross-tabulations of various cutoff scores for both instruments, with the diagnostic categories of alcohol abuse or dependence (present/absent) and drug abuse or dependence (present/absent). This resulted in the identification of true positives, false positives, true negatives, and false negatives. Sensitivity, specificity, positive predictive power, negative predictive power, and diagnostic accuracy were computed for various cutoff scores. Table 4.2 shows the results of the validity analysis for various DAST cutoffs. Sensitivity, or the ability of DAST to detect individuals with active substance abuse, is greatest at the lowest cutoff points of 4 or 5, as expected. However, at these levels, positive predictive power is low due to the high number of false positives. The optimum cutoff point appears to be 6, as recommended when the test was originally developed.[9] At this cutoff, sensitivity is quite good, but below this point specificity declines considerably. Using the DAST cutoff of 6, 91% of people with past drug abuse or dependence were detected. Current drug abuse or dependence was detected in 85% of actual cases using this cutoff. Only 15% of nondrug abusers were incorrectly identified (false positives). The highest overall diagnostic accuracy is at the upper ranges of cutoff points, but the sensitivity becomes unacceptably low.

TABLE 4.2. Sensitivity, Specificity, Positive and Negative Predictive Power, and Diagnostic Accuracy of DAST at Various Cutoffs in Adults Seeking Evaluation for ADHD

DAST Cutoff ($\geq$)	Sensitivity	Specificity	Positive Predictive Power	Negative Predictive Power	Diagnostic Accuracy (%)
4	.92	.60	.19	.99	63.3
5	.92	.67	.22	.99	69.1
6	.85	.71	.23	.98	72.7
7	.69	.74	.21	.96	73.4
8	.69	.79	.25	.96	77.7
9	.69	.81	.27	.96	79.9
10	.54	.83	.25	.95	80.6
11	.54	.87	.29	.95	83.5
12	.54	.88	.32	.95	84.9
13	.31	.90	.24	.93	84.2
14	.15	.91	.14	.91	83.5
15	.15	.91	.15	.91	84.2

The validity analysis for AUDIT is shown in Table 4.3. Sensitivity is reasonably good at the recommended cutoff of 8 or above. However, sensitivity is better at a lower cutoff of 6 or above, with little reduction in specificity. Using the cutoff of 6, 82% of current abusers of alcohol were detected, compared to 77% using the cutoff of 8 or above. As expected, given the "current use" time frame for AUDIT questions, past alcohol abuse was not detected in 56% of prior abusers using the cutoff of 8 and was not detected in 50% using the cutoff of 6. As with DAST, 15% of nonalcohol abusers were incorrectly detected using the cutoff of 6 on AUDIT.

There was a notable number of false negatives using both screening instruments. The rate of false negatives using a DAST cutoff of 6 was fairly low. DAST did not detect 15% of current drug abusers and 9% of past drug abusers. Using the cutoff of 6, AUDIT failed to detect 18% of current alcohol abusers.

Current and past substance use disorders as a function of ADHD diagnosis are shown in Table 4.4. The prevalence of current and past substance use disorders was comparable in ADHD and non-ADHD patients: 44.1% of ADHD patients and 39.4% of non-ADHD patients had either a current or past substance use disorder. Table 4.4 also depicts DAST and AUDIT screening results for ADHD and non-ADHD patients, using cutoff scores of 6 for each instrument. As with the *DSM-IV* diagnoses, the ADHD and non-ADHD groups were comparable.

DISCUSSION

These results show that among adults seeking evaluation for ADHD, both DAST and AUDIT are acceptable screening measures for drug and alcohol abuse, re-

TABLE 4.3. Sensitivity, Specificity, Positive and Negative Predictive Power, and Diagnostic Accuracy of AUDIT at Various Cutoffs in Adults Seeking Evaluation for ADHD

AUDIT Cutoff (≥)	Sensitivity	Specificity	Positive Predictive Power	Negative Predictive Power	Diagnostic Accuracy (%)
5	.82	.69	.33	.95	71.2
6	.82	.78	.41	.96	78.4
7	.77	.81	.44	.95	80.6
8	.77	.82	.45	.95	81.3
9	.73	.86	.50	.94	84.2
10	.68	.90	.56	.94	86.3
11	.64	.92	.61	.93	87.8
12	.64	.95	.70	.93	89.9
13	.55	.97	.75	.92	89.9
14	.46	.98	.83	.91	89.9
15	.46	.99	.91	.91	90.6

TABLE 4.4. Substance Abuse and Dependence as a Function of ADHD Diagnosis

Variable	ADHD (n = 68)		non-ADHD (n = 71)	
	N	%	N	%
DSM-IV **Substance Use Disorders**				
Alcohol use disorders				
Current abuse	5	7.4	5	7.0
Current dependence	5	7.4	7	9.9
Past abuse	8	11.8	5	7.0
Past dependence	5	7.4	6	8.5
None	45	66.2	48	67.6
Drug use disorders				
Current abuse	3	4.4	1	1.4
Current dependence	6	8.8	3	4.2
Past abuse	8	11.8	9	12.7
Past dependence	3	4.4	2	2.8
None	48	70.6	56	78.9
Any substance use disorder				
Current abuse or dependence	14	20.6	13	18.3
Past abuse or dependence	16	23.5	15	21.1
None	38	55.9	43	60.6
AUDIT and DAST Screening				
AUDIT screening				
≥6	18	26.5	26	36.6
<6	50	73.5	45	63.4
DAST screening				
≥6	23	33.8	24	33.8
<6	45	66.2	47	66.2

spectively. AUDIT detected current but not past alcohol abuse, while DAST detected current and past drug abuse. Both instruments demonstrated adequate internal reliability consistent with findings in other clinical populations. However, the threshold level for AUDIT should be lower for this population.

It is important to note that both AUDIT and DAST are screening instruments and cannot be relied on as the sole basis for a diagnosis of a substance use disorder. Given that a small number of false positives will be identified using DAST or AUDIT, clinicians should approach the patient with a positive screen in a nonthreatening manner, as is recommended regarding the use of screening instruments in the primary care population.[16] Since a positive DAST screen also identifies patients with a prior (but not current) history of drug use disorder, the clinician needs to remain sensitive to patients who are in full remission rather than actively using substances. For these patients, follow-up questions should be directed toward encouraging behaviors that will deter relapse.

Likewise, a negative screen does not necessarily mean that a substance use problem does not exist. This is of particular concern in evaluating adults presenting to an ADHD specialty clinic. Stimulant therapy, in the form of methylphenidate, d-amphetamine, and pemoline, is the mainstay of pharmacological treatment for ADHD. Stimulant medications have abuse potential, and the possibility that an ADHD evaluation is sought in order to obtain stimulants should not be overlooked. In addition, due to the concerns regarding the abuse potential of stimulant therapy, many clinicians choose to avoid its use in individuals who have current, or even past, substance abuse histories,[17,18] although recent reports have suggested this approach can be adapted in selected individuals.[19]

There are other reasons to be on the alert for false negatives in using drug and alcohol screening measures in this population. Individuals with ADHD have a greater likelihood of having legal difficulties, ranging from minor traffic offenses to more severe forms of antisocial behavior.[7] Prior contact with the legal system may cause some patients to underreport their involvement with illicit substances. Finally, given the considerable attention that ADHD has received in the lay press,[20] the clinician should be wary of the individual who has a great deal invested in receiving an ADHD diagnosis and may therefore downplay the significance of other behaviors, including drug and alcohol use.

The prevalence of substance use disorders was similar among ADHD and non-ADHD patients in this sample of individuals who were referred to an adult ADHD specialty clinic. Current or past substance use disorders were present in 44% of patients with ADHD. These figures are comparable to the prevalence data reported in other studies of treatment-seeking adults with ADHD.[5,7,21,22] The equally high prevalence of current and past substance use disorders in non-ADHD patients (39%) is an important finding, since this population has other Axis I disorders and enough ADHD-like symptoms to find their way into the clinic. Overall, the relatively high rate of substance use disorders in this outpatient population highlights the need for accurate screening instruments as an aid in conducting a thorough assessment.

REFERENCES

1. Kessler RC, McGonagle KA, Zhao S, et al. Lifetime and 12-month prevalence of DSM-III-R psychiatric disorders in the United States: results from the National Comorbidity Survey. *Arch Gen Psychiatry* 1994;51:8–19.
2. Reiger DA, Farmer ME, Rae DS, et al. Comorbidity of mental disorders with alcohol and other drug abuse: results from the Epidemiological Catchment Area (ECA) study. *JAMA* 1990;264:2511–2518.
3. Wilens T, Biederman J, Spencer TJ. Attention-deficit hyperactivity disorder and the psychoactive substance use disorders. *Child Adolesc Psychiatr Clin N Am* 1996;5:73–91.
4. Wilens TE, Spencer TJ, Biederman J. Are attention-deficit hyperactivity disorder and the psychoactive substance use disorders really related? *Harv Rev Psychiatry* 1995;3:160–162.

5. Biederman J, Wilens T, Mick E, et al. Psychoactive substance use disorders in adults with attention deficit hyperactivity disorder (ADHD): effects of ADHD and psychiatric comorbidity. *Am J Psychiatry* 1995;152:1652–1658.

6. American Psychiatric Association. *Diagnostic and Statistical Manual of Mental Disorders, Fourth Edition.* Washington, DC: American Psychiatric Association; 1994.

7. Barkley RA. *Attention-Deficit Hyperactivity Disorder: A Handbook for Diagnosis and Treatment, Second Edition.* New York: Guilford; 1998.

8. Roy-Byrne P, Scheele L, Brinkley J, et al. Adult attention-deficit hyperactivity disorder: assessment guidelines based on clinical presentation to a specialty clinic. *Compr Psychiatry* 1997;38:1–9.

9. Skinner HA. The Drug Abuse Screening Test. *Addict Behav* 1982;7:363–371.

10. Staley D, El-Guebaly N. Psychometric properties of the Drug Abuse Screening Test in a psychiatric patient population. *Addict Behav* 1990;15:257–264.

11. Saunders JB, Aasland OG, Babor TF, et al. Development of the Alcohol Use Disorders Identification Test (AUDIT): WHO collaborative project on early detection of persons with harmful alcohol consumption—II. *Addiction* 1998;88:791–804.

12. Bohn MJ, Babor TF, Kranzler HR. The Alcohol Use Disorders Identification Test (AUDIT): validation of a screening instrument for use in medical settings. *J Stud Alcohol* 1995;56:423–432.

13. Conigrave KM, Hall WD, Saunders JB. The AUDIT questionnaire: choosing a cut-off score. *Addiction* 1995;90:1349–1356.

14. Allen JP, Litten RZ, Fertig JB, et al. A review of research on the Alcohol Use Disorders Identification Test (AUDIT). *Alcohol Clin Exp Res* 1997;21:613–619.

15. Tsuang D, Cowley D, Ries R, et al. The effects of substance use disorder on the clinical presentation of anxiety and depression in an outpatient psychiatric clinic. *J Clin Psychiatry* 1995;56:549–555.

16. Sullivan E, Fleming M. *A Guide to Substance Abuse Services for Primary Care Clinicians: Treatment Improvement Protocol (TIP) Series 24.* Department of Health and Human Services Publication No. (SMA) 97–3139;1997.

17. Wender PH. *Attention-Deficit Hyperactivity Disorder in Adults.* New York: Oxford University Press; 1995.

18. Riggs PD. Clinical approach to treatment of ADHD in adolescents with substance use disorders and conduct disorder. *J Am Acad Child Adolesc Psychiatry* 1998;37:331–332.

19. Levin FR, Evans SM, McDowell DM, et al. Methylphenidate treatment for cocaine abusers with adult attention-deficit/hyperactivity disorder. *J Clin Psychiatry* 1998;59:300–305.

20. Wallis C. Overdrive? *Time* 1994;43–50.

21. Shekim WO, Asarnow RF, Hess E, et al. A clinical and demographic profile of a sample of adults with attention deficit hyperactivity disorder, residual state. *Compr Psychiatry* 1990;31:416–425.

22. Wender PH, Reimherr FW, Wood DR. Attention deficit disorder ("minimal brain dysfunction") in adults: a replication study of diagnosis and drug treatment. *Arch Gen Psychiatry* 1981;38:449–456.

Chapter 5

Implementing Dual-Diagnosis Services for Clients with Severe Mental Illness

Robert E. Drake, M.D., Ph.D.
Susan M. Essock, Ph.D.
Andrew Shaner, M.D.
Kate B. Carey, Ph.D.
Kenneth Minkoff, M.D.
Lenore Kola, Ph.D.
David Lynde, M.S.W.
Fred C. Osher, M.D.
Robin E. Clark, Ph.D.
Lawrence Rickards, Ph.D.

Substance abuse is the most common and clinically significant comorbid disorder among adults with severe mental illness. In this chapter, the term *substance abuse* refers to substance use disorders, which include abuse and dependence. *Severe mental illness* refers to long-term psychiatric disorders such as schizophrenia that are associated with disability and that fall within the traditional purview of public mental health systems. *Dual diagnosis* denotes the co-occurrence of substance abuse and severe mental illness.

There are many populations with dual diagnoses, and there are other common terms for this particular group. Furthermore, dual diagnosis is a misleading

This review by a national panel was supported by grant 036805 from the Robert Wood Johnson Foundation and contract 280–00–8049 from the Center for Mental Health Services.

term because the individuals in this group are heterogeneous and tend to have multiple impairments rather than just two illnesses. Nevertheless, the term appears consistently in the literature and has acquired some coherence as a referent to particular clients, treatments, programs, and service system issues.

Since the problem of dual diagnosis became clinically apparent in the early 1980s,[1,2] researchers have established three basic and consistent findings. First, co-occurrence is common; about 50% of individuals with severe mental disorders are affected by substance abuse.[3] Second, dual diagnosis is associated with a variety of negative outcomes, including higher rates of relapse,[4] hospitalization,[5] violence,[6] incarceration,[7] homelessness,[8] and serious infections such as human immunodeficiency virus (HIV) and hepatitis.[9] Third, the parallel but separate mental health and substance abuse treatment systems so common in the United States deliver fragmented and ineffective care.[10] Most clients are unable to navigate the separate systems or make sense of disparate messages about treatment and recovery. Often they are excluded or extruded from services in one system because of the comorbid disorder and told to return when the other problem is under control. For those reasons, clinicians, administrators, researchers, family organizations, and clients themselves have been calling for the integration of mental health and substance abuse services for at least 15 years.[10,11]

Over that time, integrated dual-diagnosis services—that is, treatments and programs—have been steadily developed, refined, and evaluated.[11] This chapter, which is part of a series on specific evidence-based practices for persons with severe mental illness, provides an overview of the evolution of dual-diagnosis services, the evidence on outcomes and critical components, and the limitations of current research. We also address barriers to the implementation of dual-diagnosis services and current strategies for implementation in routine mental health settings.

DUAL-DIAGNOSIS SERVICES

Treatments, or interventions, are offered within programs that are a part of service systems. Dual-diagnosis treatments combine or integrate mental health and substance abuse interventions at the level of the clinical interaction. Hence, *integrated treatment* means that the same clinicians or teams of clinicians, working in one setting, provide appropriate mental health and substance abuse interventions in a coordinated fashion—that is, the caregivers take responsibility for combining the interventions into one coherent package. For the individual with a dual diagnosis, the services appear seamless, with a consistent approach, philosophy, and set of recommendations. The need to negotiate with separate clinical teams, programs, or systems disappears.

Integration involves not only combining appropriate treatments for both disorders but also modifying traditional interventions.[12–15] For example, social skills training emphasizes the importance of developing relationships but also the need to avoid social situations that could lead to substance use. Substance abuse counseling goes slowly, in accordance with the cognitive deficits, negative symptoms, vulnerability to confrontation, and greater need for support that are characteristic of many individuals with severe mental illness. Family interventions address understanding and learning to cope with two interacting illnesses.

The goal of dual-diagnosis interventions is recovery from two serious illnesses.[16] In this context, *recovery* means that the individual with a dual diagnosis learns to manage both illnesses so that he or she can pursue meaningful life goals.[17,18]

RESEARCH ON DUAL-DIAGNOSIS PRACTICES

In most states, the publicly financed mental health system bears responsibility for providing treatments and support services for clients with severe mental illness. Dual-diagnosis treatments for these clients have therefore generally been added to community support programs within the mental health system.

Studies of dual-diagnosis interventions during the 1980s examined the application of traditional substance abuse treatments, such as 12-step groups, to clients with mental disorders within mental health programs. These studies had disappointing results for at least two reasons.[19] The clinical programs did not take into account the complex needs of the population, and researchers had not yet solved basic methodologic problems. For example, early programs often failed to incorporate outreach and motivational interventions, and evaluations were limited by lack of reliable and valid assessment of substance abuse. Reviews based on these early studies were understandably pessimistic.[20]

At the same time, however, a series of demonstration projects using more comprehensive programs that incorporated assertive outreach and long-term rehabilitation began to show better outcomes. Moreover, the projects developed motivational interventions to help clients who did not perceive or acknowledge their substance abuse or mental illness problems.[21]

Building on these insights, projects in the early 1990s incorporated motivational approaches as well as outreach, comprehensiveness, and a long-term perspective, often within the structure of multidisciplinary treatment teams. These later studies, which were uncontrolled but incorporated more valid measures of substance abuse, generally showed positive outcomes, including substantial rates of stable remission of substance abuse.[22–25] Of course, uncontrolled studies of this type often produce findings that are not replicated in controlled studies; they should be considered pilot studies, which are often needed to refine the intervention and the methodologies of evaluation and which should be followed by controlled investigation to determine evidence-based practice.[26]

Controlled research studies of comprehensive dual-diagnosis programs began to appear in the mid-1990s. Eight recent studies with experimental or quasiexperimental designs support the effectiveness of integrated dual-diagnosis treatments for clients with severe mental illness and substance use disorders.[27-34] The type and array of dual-diagnosis interventions in these programs vary, but they include several common components that are reviewed below. The eight studies demonstrate a variety of positive outcomes in domains such as substance abuse, psychiatric symptoms, housing, hospitalization, arrests, functional status, and quality of life.[19] Although each has methodological limitations, together they indicate that current integrated treatment programs are more effective than nonintegrated programs. By contrast, the evidence continues to show that dual-diagnosis clients in mental health programs that fail to integrate substance abuse interventions have poor outcomes.[35]

CRITICAL COMPONENTS

Several components of integrated programs can be considered evidence-based practices because they are almost always present in programs that have demonstrated good outcomes in controlled studies and because their absence is associated with predictable failures.[21] For example, dual-diagnosis programs that include assertive outreach are able to engage and retain clients at a high rate, whereas those that fail to include outreach lose many clients.

Staged Interventions

Effective programs incorporate, implicitly or explicitly, the concept of stages of treatment.[14,36,37] In the simplest conceptualization, stages of treatment include forming a trusting relationship (engagement), helping the engaged client develop the motivation to become involved in recovery-oriented interventions (persuasion), helping the motivated client to acquire skills and supports for controlling illnesses and pursuing goals (active treatment), and helping the client in stable remission to develop and use strategies for maintaining recovery (relapse prevention).

Clients do not move linearly through stages. They sometimes enter services at advanced levels, skip over or pass rapidly through stages, or relapse to earlier stages. They may be in different stages with respect to mental illness and substance abuse. Nevertheless, the concept of stages has proved useful to program planners and clinicians because clients at different stages respond to stage-specific interventions.

Assertive Outreach

Many clients with a dual diagnosis have difficulty linking with services and participating in treatment.[38] Effective programs engage clients and members of their support systems by providing assertive outreach, usually through some combination of intensive case management and meetings in the client's residence.[21,32] For example, homeless persons with dual diagnoses often benefit from outreach, help with housing, and time to develop a trusting relationship before participating in any formal treatment. These approaches enable clients to gain access to services and maintain needed relationships with a consistent program over months and years. Without such efforts, noncompliance and dropout rates are high.[39]

Motivational Interventions

Most dual-diagnosis clients have little readiness for abstinence-oriented treatment.[40,41] Many also lack motivation to manage psychiatric illness and to pursue employment or other functional goals. Effective programs therefore incorporate motivational interventions that are designed to help clients become ready for more definitive interventions aimed at illness self-management.[12,14,21] For example, clients who are so demoralized, symptomatic, or confused that they mistakenly believe alcohol and cocaine are helping them to cope better than medications require education, support, and counseling to develop hope and a realistic understanding of illnesses, drugs, treatments, and goals.

Motivational interventions involve helping the individual to identify his or her own goals and, through a systematic examination of the individual's ambivalence, to recognize that not managing one's illnesses interferes with attaining those goals.[42] Recent research has demonstrated that clients who are not motivated can be reliably identified[43] and effectively helped with motivational interventions (Carey KB, Carey MP, Maisto SA, et al., unpublished data, 2000).

Counseling

Once clients are motivated to manage their own illnesses, they need to develop skills and supports to control symptoms and to pursue an abstinent lifestyle. Effective programs provide some form of counseling that promotes cognitive and behavioral skills at this stage. The counseling takes different forms and formats, such as group, individual, or family therapy or a combination.[15] Few studies have compared specific approaches to counseling, although one study did find preliminary evidence that a cognitive-behavioral approach was superior to a 12-step approach.[28] At least three research groups are actively working to refine cognitive-behavioral approaches to substance abuse counseling for dual-diagnosis clients.[12,13,44] These approaches often incorporate motivational sessions at the beginning of counseling and as needed in subsequent sessions rather than as separate interventions.

Social Support Interventions

In addition to helping clients build skills for managing their illness and pursuing goals, effective programs focus on strengthening the immediate social environment to help them modify their behavior. These activities, which recognize the role of social networks in recovery from dual disorders,[45] include social network or family interventions.

Long-Term Perspective

Effective programs recognize that recovery tends to occur over months or years in the community. People with severe mental illness and substance abuse do not usually develop stability and functional improvements quickly, even in intensive treatment programs, unless they enter treatment at an advanced stage.[19] Instead, they tend to improve over months and years in conjunction with a consistent dual-diagnosis program. Effective programs therefore take a long-term, community-based perspective that includes rehabilitation activities to prevent relapses and to enhance gains.

Comprehensiveness

Learning to lead a symptom-free, abstinent lifestyle that is satisfying and sustainable often requires transforming many aspects of one's life—for example, habits, stress management, friends, activities, and housing. Therefore, in effective programs attention to substance abuse as well as mental illness is integrated into all aspects of the existing mental health program and service system rather than isolated as a discrete substance abuse treatment intervention. Inpatient hospitalization, assessment, crisis intervention, medication management, money management, laboratory screening, housing, and vocational rehabilitation incorporate special features that are tailored specifically for dual-diagnosis patients. For example, hospitalization is considered a component of the system that supports movement toward recovery by providing diagnosis, stabilization, and linkage with outpatient dual-diagnosis interventions during acute episodes.[46] Similarly, housing and vocational programs can be used to support the individual with a dual diagnosis in acquiring skills and supports needed for recovery.[47]

Cultural Sensitivity and Competence

A fundamental finding of the demonstration programs of the late 1980s was that cultural sensitivity and competence were critical to engaging clients in dual-diagnosis services.[21] These demonstrations showed that African-Americans, Hispanics, and other underserved groups, such as farm workers, homeless persons, women with children, inner-city residents, and persons in rural areas, could be engaged in dual-diagnosis services if the services were tailored to their particular racial, cultural, and other group characteristics.

Many dual-diagnosis programs omit some of these critical components as evidence-based practices. However, one consistent finding in the research is that programs that show high fidelity to the model described here—those that incorporate more of the core elements—produce better outcomes than low-fidelity programs.[32,48,49] A common misconception about technology transfer is that model programs are not generalizable and that local solutions are superior. A more accurate reading of the research is that modifications for cultural and other local circumstances are important, but critical program components must be replicated to achieve good outcomes.

RESEARCH LIMITATIONS

The design and quality of research procedures and data across dual-diagnosis studies are inconsistent. In addition, researchers have thus far failed to address a number of issues.

Dual-diagnosis research has studied the clinical enterprise—that is, treatments and programs—with little attention to the policy or system perspective. Despite widespread endorsement of integrated dual-diagnosis services,[13,50–53] there continues to be a general failure at the federal and state levels to resolve problems related to organization and financing (see below). Thus, despite the emergence of many excellent programs around the country, few if any large mental health systems have been able to accomplish widespread implementation of dual-diagnosis services for persons with severe mental illness. We are aware of no specific studies of strategies to finance, contract for, reorganize, or train in relation to dual-diagnosis services.

Lack of data on the cost of integrated dual-diagnosis services and the cost savings of providing good care impedes policy development. Dual-diagnosis clients incur high treatment costs in usual services[54,55] and care is costly to their families,[56] but effective treatment may be even more costly. Some studies suggest cost savings related to providing good services,[57,58] but these are not definitive.

Another limitation of the research is the lack of specificity of dual-diagnosis treatments. Interventions differ across studies, manuals, and fidelity measures are rare, and no consensus exists on specific approaches to individual counseling, group treatment, family intervention, housing, medications, and other components. Current research will address some of these issues by refining specific components, although efficacy studies may identify complex and expensive interventions that will be impractical in routine mental health settings.

A majority of dual-diagnosis clients respond well to integrated outpatient services, but clients who do not respond continue to be at high risk of hospitalization, incarceration, homelessness, HIV infection, and other serious adverse outcomes. Other than one study of long-term residential treatment,[33] controlled research has not addressed clients who do not respond to outpatient services. Other potential interventions include outpatient commitment,[59] treatments aimed at trauma sequelae,[60] money management,[61] contingency management,[62] and pharmacological approaches using medications such as clozapine,[63] disulfiram,[64] or naltrexone.

Although a few studies ha   ...e specific treatment needs of dual-
diagnosis clients who are women·   ...iorities,[21,67] particular program modifications for these groups need further v. .dation. For example, many dual-diagnosis
programs have identified high rates of trauma histories and sequelae among
women,[46,68,69] and studies have suggested interventions to address trauma; however, no data on outcomes are yet available.

IMPLEMENTATION BARRIERS

Although integrated dual-diagnosis services and other evidence-based practices
are widely advocated, they are rarely offered in routine mental health treatment
settings.[70] The barriers are legion.

Policy Barriers

State, county, and city mental health authorities often encounter policies related
to organizational structure, financing, regulations, and licensing that militate against
the functional integration of mental health and substance abuse services.[71] The
U.S. public mental health and substance abuse treatment systems grew independently. In most states these services are provided under the auspices of separate
cabinet-level departments with separate funding streams, advocacy groups, and
lobbyists, enabling legislation, information systems, job classifications, and criteria for credentials. Huge fiscal incentives and strong political allies act to maintain the status quo.

Medicaid programs, which fund a significant and growing proportion of treatment for persons with severe mental illness, vary substantially from state to state
in the types of mental health and substance abuse services they fund. In most
states, mental health and substance abuse agencies have little control over how
Medicaid services are reimbursed or administered, which makes it difficult for
public systems to ensure that appropriate services are accessible. Medicare, the
federal insurance program for elderly and disabled persons, generally pays for a
more limited scope of mental health and substance abuse services. Together, Medicaid and Medicare pay for more than 30% of all behavioral health services, but
their impact on dual-diagnosis services has not been studied.[72]

Program Barriers

At the local level, administrators of clinics, centers, and programs have often
lacked the clear service models, administrative guidelines, contractual incentives,
quality assurance procedures, and outcome measures needed to implement dual-
diagnosis services. When clinical needs compel them to move ahead anyway, they
have difficulty hiring a skilled workforce with experience in providing dual-

diagnosis interventions and lack the resources to train current supervisors and clinicians.

Clinical Barriers

The beliefs of the mental health and substance abuse treatment traditions are inculcated in clinicians, which diminishes the opportunities for cross-fertilization.[73] Although an integrated clinical philosophy and a practical approach to dual-diagnosis treatment have been clearly delineated for more than a decade,[16] educational institutions rarely teach this approach. Consequently, mental health clinicians typically lack training in dual-diagnosis treatment and have to rely on informal self-initiated opportunities for learning current interventions.[74] They often avoid diagnosing substance abuse when they believe that it is irrelevant, that it will interfere with funding, or that they cannot treat it. Clinicians trained in substance abuse treatment, as well as recovering dual-diagnosis clients, could add expertise and training, but they are often excluded from jobs in the mental health system.

Consumer and Family Barriers

Clients and their families rarely have good information about dual diagnosis and appropriate services. Few programs offer psychoeducational services related to dual diagnosis, although practical help from families plays a critical role in recovery.[75] Family members are often unaware of substance abuse, blame all symptoms on drug abuse, or attribute symptoms and substance use to willful misbehavior. Supporting family involvement is an important but neglected role for clinicians.

Consumers often deny or minimize problems related to substance abuse[40] and, like other substance abusers, believe that alcohol or other drugs are helpful in alleviating distress. They may be legitimately confused about causality because they perceive the immediate effects of drugs rather than the intermediate or long-term consequences.[76] The net result is that the individual lacks motivation to pursue active substance abuse treatment, which can reinforce clinical inattention.

IMPLEMENTATION STRATEGIES

There are no proven strategies for overcoming the aforementioned barriers to implementing dual-diagnosis services, but some suggestions have come from systems and programs that have had moderate success.

Policy Strategies

Health care authorities in a majority of, and possibly all, states have current initiatives for creating dual-diagnosis services. Because health care policy is often administered at the county or city level, hundreds of individual experiments are occurring. One initial branch point involves the decision to focus broadly on the entire behavioral health system—that is, on all clients with mental health and substance abuse problems—or more narrowly on services for those with severe mental illness and co-occurring substance abuse. We examine here only strategies for dual-diagnosis clients with severe mental illness, for whom the implementation issues are relatively distinct.

Commonly used system-level strategies include building a consensus around the vision for integrated services and then conjointly planning; specifying a model; implementing structural, regulatory, and reimbursement changes; establishing contracting mechanisms; defining standards; and funding demonstration programs and training initiatives.[77] To our knowledge, few attempts have been made to study these efforts at the system level.

Anecdotal evidence indicates that blending mental health and substance abuse funds appears to have been a relatively unsuccessful strategy, especially early in the course of system change. Fear of losing money to cover nontraditional populations often leads to prolonged disagreements, inability to develop consensus, and abandonment of other plans. As a less controversial preliminary step, the mental health authority often assumes responsibility for comprehensive care including substance abuse treatment for persons with severe mental illness, while the substance abuse authority assists by pledging to help with training and planning.

This limited approach enables the mental health system to attract and train dual-diagnosis specialists who can subsequently train other clinicians. Without structural, regulatory, and funding changes to reinforce the training, however, the expertise may soon disappear—a common experience after demonstration projects. Thus many experts advise that policy issues should be addressed early in the process of implementation to avoid wasting efforts on training.[78–80]

New costs to the mental health system for dual-diagnosis training could be offset by greater effectiveness in ameliorating substance-abusing behaviors that are associated with hospitalizations. However, saving costs over time assumes that providers are at risk for all treatment costs—that is, that providers have incentives to invest more in outpatient services in order to spend less on inpatient services. Despite the growth of managed care, providers rarely bear complete financial responsibility for the treatment of clients with severe mental illness.

Program Strategies

At the level of the mental health clinic or program leadership, the fundamental task is to begin recognizing and treating substance abuse rather than ignoring it or using it as a criterion for exclusion.[81] After consensus-building activities to prepare for change, staff need training and supervision to learn new skills, and they must receive reinforcement for acquiring and using these skills effectively. One common strategy is to appoint a director of dual-diagnosis services whose job is to plan and oversee the training of staff, the integration of substance abuse awareness and treatment into all aspects of the mental health program, and the monitoring and reinforcement of these activities through medical records, quality assurance activities, and outcome data.

Experts identify the importance of having a single leader for program change.[82] Fidelity measures for integrated dual-diagnosis services can facilitate successful implementation at the program level.[50,83] Monitoring and reinforcing mechanisms also emphasize client-centered outcomes, such as abstinence and employment.

Clinical Strategies

Mental health clinicians need to acquire knowledge and a core set of skills related to substance abuse that includes assessing substance abuse, providing motivational interventions for clients who are not ready to participate in abstinence-oriented treatment, and providing counseling for those who are motivated to try to maintain abstinence. Clinicians adopt new skills as a result of motivation, instruction, practice, and reinforcement.[84] Because substance abuse affects the lives of the great majority of clients with severe mental illness—as a co-occurring disorder, family stressor, and/or environmental hazard—all clinicians should learn these basic skills. Otherwise, substance abuse problems will continue to be missed and untreated in this population.[85,86] For example, all case managers should recognize and address substance abuse in their daily interactions, as should housing staff, employment specialists, and other staff.

Until professional educational programs begin teaching current dual-diagnosis treatment techniques,[87] mental health system leaders will bear the burden of training staff. Some staff will become dual-diagnosis specialists and acquire more than the basic skills. These individuals will be counted on to lead dual-diagnosis groups, family interventions, residential programs, and other specialized services.

Consumer- and Family-Level Strategies

Clients and family members need access to accurate information. Otherwise, their opportunities to make informed choices, request effective services, and advocate for system changes are severely compromised. Consumer demand and family advocacy can move the health care system toward evidence-based practices, but concerted efforts at the national, state, and local levels are required. Researchers can facilitate their efforts by offering clear messages about the forms, processes, and expected outcomes of evidence-based practices. Similarly, local programs should provide information on available dual-diagnosis services to clients and their families.

As consumers move into roles as providers within the mental health system and in consumer-run services, they also need training in dual-diagnosis treatments. Local educational programs, such as community colleges, as well as staff training programs, should address these needs.

CONCLUSIONS

Substance abuse is a common and devastating comorbid disorder among persons with severe mental illness. Recent research offers evidence that integrated dual-diagnosis treatments are effective, but basic interventions are rarely incorporated into the mental health programs in which these clients receive care. Successful implementation of dual-diagnosis services within mental health systems will depend on changes at several levels: clear policy directives with consistent organizational and financing supports, program changes to incorporate the mission of addressing co-occurring substance abuse, supports for the acquisition of expertise at the clinical level, and availability of accurate information to consumers and family members.

REFERENCES

1. Pepper B, Krishner MC, Ryglewicz H. The young adult chronic patient: overview of a population. *Hospital and Community Psychiatry* 1981;32:463–469.
2. Caton CLM. The new chronic patient and the system of community care. *Hospital and Community Psychiatry* 1981;32:475–478.
3. Regier DA, Farmer ME, Rae DS, et al. Comorbidity of mental disorders with alcohol and other drug abuse. *JAMA* 1990;264:2511–2518.
4. Swofford C, Kasckow J, Scheller-Gilkey G, et al. Substance use: a powerful predictor of relapse in schizophrenia. *Schizophrenia Research* 1996;20:145–151.
5. Haywood TW, Kravitz HM, Grossman LS, et al. Predicting the "revolving door" phenomenon among patients with schizophrenic, schizoaffective, and affective disorders. *American Journal of Psychiatry* 1995;152:856–861.
6. Cuffel B, Shumway M, Chouljian T. A longitudinal study of substance use and community violence in schizophrenia. *Journal of Nervous and Mental Disease* 1994;182:704–708.
7. Abram KM, Teplin LA. Co-occurring disorders among mentally ill jail detainees: implications for public policy. *American Psychologist* 1991;46:1036–1045.
8. Caton CLM, Shrout PE, Eagle PF, et al. Risk factors for homelessness among schizophrenic men: a case-control study. *American Journal of Public Health* 1994;84:265–270.
9. Rosenberg SD, Goodman LA, Osher FC, et al. Prevalence of HIV, hepatitis B, and hepatitis C in people with severe mental illness. *American Journal of Public Health* 2001;91:31–37.
10. Ridgely MS, Osher FC, Goldman HH, et al. *Executive Summary: Chronic Mentally Ill Young Adults with Substance Abuse Problems: A Review of Research, Treatment, and Training Issues.* Baltimore: University of Maryland School of Medicine, Mental Health Services Research Center; 1987
11. Drake RE, Wallach MA. Dual diagnosis: 15 years of progress. *Psychiatric Services* 2000;51:1126–1129.
12. Barrowclough C, Haddock G, Tarrier N, et al. Cognitive-behavioral intervention for clients with severe mental illness who have a substance misuse problem. *Psychiatric Rehabilitation Skills* 2000;4:216–233.
13. Bellack AS, DiClemente CC. Treating substance abuse among patients with schizophrenia. *Psychiatric Services* 1999;50:75–80.

14. Carey KB. Substance use reduction in the context of outpatient psychiatric treatment: a collaborative, motivational, harm reduction approach. *Community Mental Health Journal* 1996;32:291–306

15. Mueser KT, Drake RE, Noordsy DL. Integrated mental health and substance abuse treatment for severe psychiatric disorders. *Journal of Practical Psychiatry and Behavioral Health* 1998;4:129–139.

16. Minkoff K. An integrated treatment model for dual diagnosis of psychosis and addiction. *Hospital and Community Psychiatry* 1989;40:1031–1036.

17. Mead S, Copeland ME. What recovery means to us: consumers' perspectives. *Community Mental Health Journal* 2000;36:315–328.

18. Torrey WC, Wyzik P. The recovery vision as a service improvement guide for community mental health center providers. *Community Mental Health Journal* 2000;36:209–216.

19. Drake RE, Mercer-McFadden C, Mueser KT, et al. Review of integrated mental health and substance abuse treatment for patients with dual disorders. *Schizophrenia Bulletin* 1998;24:589–608.

20. Ley A, Jeffery DP, McLaren S, et al. Treatment programmes for people with both severe mental illness and substance misuse. Cochrane Library, Feb 1999. Available at http://www.update-software.com/cochrane/cochrane-frame.html

21. Mercer-McFadden C, Drake RE, Brown NB, et al. The community support program demonstrations of services for young adults with severe mental illness and substance use disorders, 1987–1991. *Psychiatric Rehabilitation Journal* 1997;20(3):13–24.

22. Detrick A, Stiepock V. Treating persons with mental illness, substance abuse, and legal problems: the Rhode Island experience. *New Directions for Mental Health Services* 1992;56:65–77.

23. Drake RE, McHugo G, Noordsy DL. Treatment of alcoholism among schizophrenic outpatients: four-year outcomes. *American Journal of Psychiatry* 1993;150:328–329.

24. Durell J, Lechtenberg B, Corse S, et al. Intensive case management of persons with chronic mental illness who abuse substances. *Hospital and Community Psychiatry* 1993;44:415–416.

25. Meisler N, Blankertz L, Santos AB, et al. Impact of assertive community treatment on homeless persons with co-occurring severe psychiatric and substance use disorders. *Community Mental Health Journal* 1997;33:113–122.

26. Drake RE, Goldman HH, Leff HS, et al. Implementing evidence-based practices in routine mental health service settings. *Psychiatric Services* 2001;52:179–182.

27. Godley SH, Hoewing-Roberson R, Godley MD. *Final MISA Report.* Bloomington, IL: Lighthouse Institute; 1994.

28. Jerrell JM, Ridgely MS. Comparative effectiveness of three approaches to serving people with severe mental illness and substance abuse disorders. *Journal of Nervous and Mental Disease* 1995;183:566–576.

29. Drake RE, Yovetich NA, Bebout RR, et al. Integrated treatment for dually diagnosed homeless adults. *Journal of Nervous and Mental Disease* 1997;185:298–305.

30. Carmichael D, Tackett-Gibson M, Dell O, et al. *Texas Dual Diagnosis Project Evaluation Report, 1997–1998.* College Station, TX: Texas A&M University, Public Policy Research Institute; 1998.

31. Drake RE, McHugo GJ, Clark RE, et al. Assertive community treatment for patients with co-occurring severe mental illness and substance use disorder: a clinical trial. *American Journal of Orthopsychiatry* 1998;68:201–215.

32. Ho AP, Tsuang JW, Liberman RP, et al. Achieving effective treatment of patients with chronic psychotic illness and comorbid substance dependence. *American Journal of Psychiatry* 1999;156:1765–1770.

33. Brunette MF, Drake RE, Woods M, et al. A comparison of long-term and short-term

residential treatment programs for dual diagnosis patients. *Psychiatric Services* 2001;52:526–528.

34. Barrowclough C, Haddock G, Tarrier N, et al. Randomised controlled trial of motivational interviewing and cognitive behavioural intervention for schizophrenia patients with associated drug or alcohol misuse. *American Journal of Psychiatry*, in press.

35. Havassy BE, Shopshire MS, Quigley LA. Effects of substance dependence on outcomes of patients in a randomized trial of two case management models. *Psychiatric Services* 2000;51:639–644.

36. Osher FC, Kofoed LL. Treatment of patients with psychiatric and psychoactive substance use disorders. *Hospital and Community Psychiatry* 1989;40:1025–1030.

37. McHugo GJ, Drake RE, Burton HL, et al. A scale for assessing the stage of substance abuse treatment in persons with severe mental illness. *Journal of Nervous and Mental Disease* 1995;183:762–767.

38. Owen C, Rutherford V, Jones M, et al. Non-compliance in psychiatric aftercare. *Community Mental Health Journal* 1997;33:25–34.

39. Hellerstein DJ, Rosenthal RN, Miner CR. A prospective study of integrated outpatient treatment for substance-abusing schizophrenic patients. *American Journal on Addictions* 1995;42:33–42.

40. Test MA, Wallish LS, Allness DG, et al. Substance use in young adults with schizophrenic disorders. *Schizophrenia Bulletin* 1989;15:465–476.

41. Ziedonis D, Trudeau K. Motivation to quit using substances among individuals with schizophrenia: implications for a motivation-based treatment model. *Schizophrenia Bulletin* 1997;23:229–238.

42. Miller W, Rollnick S. *Motivational Interviewing: Preparing People to Change Addictive Behavior.* New York: Guilford; 1991.

43. Carey KB, Maisto SA, Carey MP, et al. Measuring readiness-to-change substance misuse among psychiatric outpatients: I. reliability and validity of self-report measures. *Journal of Studies on Alcohol;* in press.

44. Roberts LJ, Shaner A, Eckman T. *Overcoming Addictions: Skills Training for People with Schizophrenia.* New York: Norton; 1999.

45. Alverson H, Alverson M, Drake RE. An ethnographic study of the longitudinal course of substance abuse among people with severe mental illness. *Community Mental Health Journal* 2000;36:557–569.

46. Greenfield SF, Weiss RD, Tohen M. Substance abuse and the chronically mentally ill: a description of dual diagnosis treatment services in a psychiatric hospital. *Community Mental Health Journal* 1995;31:265–278.

47. Drake RE, Mueser KT. Psychosocial approaches to dual diagnosis. *Schizophrenia Bulletin* 2000;26:105–118.

48. Jerrell JM, Ridgely MS. Impact of robustness of program implementation on outcomes of clients in dual diagnosis programs. *Psychiatric Services* 1999;50:109–112.

49. McHugo GJ, Drake RE, Teague GB, et al. Fidelity to assertive community treatment and client outcomes in the New Hampshire dual disorders study. *Psychiatric Services* 1999;50:818–824.

50. Rach-Beisel J, Scott J, Dixon L. Co-occurring severe mental illness and substance use disorders: a review of recent research. *Psychiatric Services* 1999;50:1427–1434.

51. Mueser KT, Bellack A, Blanchard J. Comorbidity of schizophrenia and substance abuse. *Journal of Consulting and Clinical Psychology* 1992;60:845–856.

52. Osher FC, Drake RE. Reversing a history of unmet needs: approaches to care for persons with co-occurring addictive and mental disorders. *American Journal of Orthopsychiatry* 1996;66:4–11.

53. Woody G. The challenge of dual diagnosis. *Alcohol Health and Research World* 1996;20:76–80.

54. Bartels SJ, Teague GB, Drake RE, et al. Service utilization and costs associated with substance abuse among rural schizophrenic patients. *Journal of Nervous and Mental Disease* 1993;181:227–232.
55. Dickey B, Azeni H. Persons with dual diagnosis of substance abuse and major mental illness: their excess costs of psychiatric care. *American Journal of Public Health* 1996;86:973–977.
56. Clark RE. Family costs associated with severe mental illness and substance use. *Hospital and Community Psychiatry* 1994;45:808–813.
57. Clark RE, Teague GB, Ricketts SK, et al. Cost-effectiveness of assertive community treatment versus standard case management for persons with co-occurring severe mental illness and substance use disorders. *Health Services Research* 1998;33:1283–1306.
58. Jerrell JM. Cost-effective treatment for persons with dual disorders. *New Directions for Mental Health Services* 1996;70:79–91.
59. O'Keefe C, Potenza DP, Mueser KT. Treatment outcomes for severely mentally ill patients on conditional discharge to community-based treatment. *Journal of Nervous and Mental Disease* 1997;185:409–411.
60. Harris M. *Trauma Recovery and Empowerment Manual.* Anglin J, ed. New York: Free Press; 1998.
61. Ries RK, Dyck DG. Representative payee practices of community mental health centers in Washington State. *Psychiatric Services* 1997;48:811–814.
62. Shaner A, Roberts LJ, Eckman TA, et al. Monetary reinforcement of abstinence from cocaine among mentally ill patients with cocaine dependence. *Psychiatric Services* 1997;48:807–810.
63. Zimmet SV, Strous RD, Burgess ES, et al. Effects of clozapine on substance use in patients with schizophrenia and schizoaffective disorders: a retrospective survey. *Journal of Clinical Psychopharmacology* 2000;20:94–98.
64. Mueser KT, Noordsy DL, Essock S. Use of disulfiram in the treatment of patients with dual diagnosis. *American Journal of Addiction,* in press.
65. Brunette MF, Drake RE. Gender differences in patients with schizophrenia and substance abuse. *Comprehensive Psychiatry* 1997;38:109–116.
66. Alexander MJ. Women with co-occurring addictive and mental disorders: an emerging profile of vulnerability. *American Journal of Orthopsychiatry* 1996;66:61–70.
67. Quimby E. Homeless clients' perspectives on recovery in the Washington, DC, Dual Diagnosis Project. *Contemporary Drug Problems,* Summer 1995, pp 265–289.
68. Goodman LA, Rosenberg SD, Mueser KT, et al. Physical and sexual assault history in women with serious mental illness: prevalence, correlates, treatment, and future research directions. *Schizophrenia Bulletin* 1997;23:685–696.
69. Mueser KT, Goodman LB, Trumbetta SL, et al. Trauma and posttraumatic stress disorder in severe mental illness. *Journal of Consulting and Clinical Psychology* 1998;66:493–499.
70. Surgeon General's Report on Mental Health. Washington, DC: US Government Printing Office; 2000.
71. Ridgely M, Goldman H, Willenbring M. Barriers to the care of persons with dual diagnoses: organizational and financing issues. *Schizophrenia Bulletin* 1990;16:123–132.
72. Mark T, McKusick D, King E, et al. *National Expenditures for Mental Health, Alcohol, and Other Drug Abuse Treatment.* Rockville, MD: Substance Abuse and Mental Health Services Administration; 1998.
73. Drainoni M, Bachman S. Overcoming treatment barriers to providing services for adults with dual diagnosis: three approaches. *Journal of Disability Policy Studies* 1995;6:43–55.
74. Carey KB, Purnine DM, Maisto SM, et al. Treating substance abuse in the context of

severe and persistent mental illness: clinicians' perspectives. *Journal of Substance Abuse Treatment* 2000;19:189–198.

75. Clark RE. Family support and substance use outcomes for persons with mental illness and substance use disorders. *Schizophrenia Bulletin*, 2001.

76. Mueser KT, Drake R, Wallach M. Dual diagnosis: a review of etiological theories. *Addictive Behaviors* 1998;23:717–734.

77. *Co-occurring Psychiatric and Substance Disorders in Managed Care Systems.* Rockville, MD: Mental Health Services; 1998.

78. Hesketh B. Dilemmas in training for transfer and retention. *Applied Psychology* 1997:46:317–386.

79. Milne D, Gorenski O, Westerman C, et al. What does it take to transfer training? *Psychiatric Rehabilitation Skills* 2000;4:259–281.

80. Rapp CA, Poertner J. *Social Administration: A Client-Centered Approach.* White Plains, NY: Longman; 1992.

81. Mercer-McFadden C, Drake RE, Clark RE, et al. *Substance Abuse Treatment for People with Severe Mental Disorders.* Concord, NH: New Hampshire–Dartmouth Psychiatric Research Center; 1998.

82. Corrigan PW. Wanted: champions of rehabilitation for psychiatric hospitals. *American Psychologist* 1995;40:514–521.

83. Mueser KT, Fox L. *Stagewise Family Treatment for Dual Disorders: Treatment Manual.* Concord, NH: New Hampshire–Dartmouth Psychiatric Research Center; 1998.

84. Torrey WC, Drake RE, Dixon L, et al. Implementing evidence-based practices for persons with severe mental illnesses. *Psychiatric Services* 2001;52:45–50.

85. Shaner A, Khaka E, Roberts L, et al. Unrecognized cocaine use among schizophrenic patients. *American Journal of Psychiatry* 1993;150:777–783.

86. Ananth J, Vandewater S, Kamal M, et al. Missed diagnosis of substance abuse in psychiatric patients. *Hospital and Community Psychiatry* 1989;40:297–299.

87. Carey KB, Bradizza CM, Stasiewicz PR, et al. The case for enhanced addictions training in graduate programs. *Behavior Therapist* 1999;22:27–31.

Chapter 6

Motivational Interviewing With Psychiatrically Ill Substance-Abusing Patients

Steve Martino, Ph.D.
Kathleen M. Carroll, Ph.D.
Stephanie S. O'Malley, Ph.D.
Bruce J. Rounsaville, M.D.

Motivational interviewing, developed by Miller and his associates,[1] is an effective strategy for engaging and treating patients with substance-related disorders.[2-4] However, investigation of the efficacy of motivational interviewing with *psychiatrically ill* substance-abusing patients has not been evaluated. We adapted motivational interviewing for use with substance-abusing patients with *DSM-IV* mood and psychotic disorders and conducted a pilot study to assess how effective it is for preparing them to participate in a partial hospital program. We hypothesized that motivational interviewing would increase dual-diagnosis patients' participation in the program and improve treatment outcome.

METHODS

Subjects

Subjects were 23 adults who had *DSM-IV* substance-related disorders and concurrent mood or psychotic disorders. Inclusion criteria were (1) use of drugs or

This work was supported as part of a National Institute of Drug Abuse psychotherapy research center grant NIDA1-P50-DA-09241 (Dr. Rounsaville).

The authors thank Stacey Bernasconi for her assistance with data collection and analysis.

alcohol within 2 months of study entry and (2) current psychiatric pharmaco-therapy. Subjects were excluded if they (1) required inpatient hospitalization, (2) were incapable of giving informed consent, (3) had insufficient English fluency, or (4) were prohibited from participating in a 12-week partial hospital program. The subjects' demographic and diagnostic characteristics were age (M = 35.35, SD = 6.4), sex (male = 65%, female = 35%), race (white = 61%, black = 26%, Hispanic = 13%), marital status (single = 83%, separated/divorced = 17%), years of education (M = 10.74, SD = 2.2), unemployment (100%), number of prior hospitalizations (M = 8.18, SD = 8.9), admission Global Assessment of Functioning (M = 44.83, SD = 6.2), distribution of mood disorders (dysthymia = 22%, major depression = 13%, depressive disorder NOS = 13%), psychotic disorders (schizoaffective disorder = 22%, paranoid schizophrenia = 17%, undifferentiated schizophrenia = 4%, schizophreniform disorder = 4%, psychotic disorder NOS = 4%), and substance abuse or dependence disorders (alcohol = 82%, cocaine = 56%, opioid = 39%, cannabis = 35%, anxiolytic = 26%, amphetamine = 8%). Through a medical record review, we also established a demographically and di-agnostically similar (p > .05) historical control group (n = 71) of patients who had participated in the same program during the year preceding the study and who met the study's eligibility criteria.

Procedure

After subjects gave informed consent, we determined *DSM-IV* diagnoses using a clinical consensus method. All subjects completed preadmission questionnaires that included the Behavior and Symptom Identification Scale (BASIS),[5] Beck Depression Inventory (BDI),[6] Change Assessment Scale (CAS),[7] Thoughts About Abstinence Scale (TAAS),[8] Addiction Severity Index—Drug and Alcohol subsections only (ASI-D/A),[9] and Timeline Follow-Back Assessment (TLFB).[10] We modified TAAS and TLFB to assess goal commitment to medication compliance and days of medication compliance, respectively.

Subsequently, we randomly assigned subjects per psychiatric group (mood or psychotic disorder) to receive a 45- to 60-minute motivational interview (MI; n = 13) or standard preadmission interview (SI; n = 10), both delivered by this study's first author. MI consisted of querying subjects to elicit self-motivational statements, providing feedback from preadmission questionnaires, and completing a decisional balance activity. SI involved a standard psychiatric interview and program description. After the interview, subjects completed the CAS, TAAS, and Client Satsifaction Scale.[11] Finally, we tallied subjects' unexcused (i.e., without staff approval) tardiness, early departures, and absences, daily attendance, frequency and days of drug and alcohol use, and days of medication compliance during their program participation.

For the historical control group, two raters independently collected basic treatment outcome data from the charts. Reliability ratings using Pearson prod-uct-moment correlations between the two raters on a random sample of 20 charts were (1) unexcused absences = .85, (2) attendance = .99, and (3) frequency of drug/alcohol use = .99.

RESULTS

No significant baseline differences existed between MI and SI groups on demographic variables and for indicators of level of functioning, substance abuse severity, motivation for change, or goal commitment. In contrast, SI subjects reported more psychiatric symptomatology on the BASIS ($t[1,21] = -2.24, p < .05$) and the BDI ($t[1,21] = -2.04, p < .05$). We found no significant differences from pre- to postinterview in motivational level, goal commitment for abstinence or medication compliance, and session satisfaction. Most subjects entered the study with high baseline levels of motivation for change (83%) and endorsed goals consistent with a commitment to absolute abstinence (87%) and medication compliance (65%). Retention rates for the subjects at 4, 8, and 12 weeks were 57%, 35%, and 26%, respectively.

To examine treatment outcome, we created indices from the dependent measures. We divided these measures by the subjects' program length of stay (LOS) to adjust for different tenures (e.g., 5 days of substance use over a 50-day LOS yielded an indexed score of 5/50 or .10). Treatment outcome results for interview and diagnostic conditions are reported in Table 6.1.

To determine the direction of outcome data within conditions, we applied the sign test because of its usefulness for testing whether one random variable in

TABLE 6.1. Mean Treatment Outcomes Indices

Dependent Variable	Type of Interview		Diagnostic Group	
	Motivational Interview (*n* = 13)	Standard Interview (*n* = 10)	Psychotic Disorder (*n* = 12)	Mood Disorder (*n* = 11)
Treatment Participation				
Tardiness	0.00	.18	.04	.12
Early departures	0.00	.17	.01	.15
Unexcused absences	.13	.21	.11	.21
Attendance	.72	.59	.75	.58
Total PHP days attended[a]	31.00	22.00	33.00	21.00
Substance Use				
Frequency drug/alcohol use	.06	.12	.05	.11
Days used alcohol or drugs	.08	.15	.07	.16
Days medication compliant	.89	.86	.80	.96

[a]Total PHP days attended is not expressed as an index because it represents treatment outcome in which all subjects shared the same common denominator of a 12-week program.

a pair tends to be larger than another random variable in a pair.[12] With $T = 8$ (frequency MI > SI), $n = 0$ (frequency MI = SI), and a p value of .0352, we found MI subjects had better overall treatment outcomes than SI subjects. Two-tailed pairwise t tests indicated that MI subjects had significantly less tardiness ($t[1,21] = -2.17, p < .05$) and early departures ($t[1,21] = -2.23, p < .05$) than SI subjects. We also found psychotically disordered (PD) subjects had better overall treatment outcomes than mood-disordered (MD) subjects ($T = 8$ [frequency PD > MD], $n = 1$ [frequency PD = MD], $p = .0352$). Two-tailed pairwise t-tests on the specific treatment outcomes, however, were not significant. Comparison of the interview conditions with the historical control group on treatment outcomes using one-way ANOVAs revealed one significant difference among the groups for number of program days attended ($F[2,20] = 3.54, p < .05$). Using post hoc t tests (Tukey-B; $p < .05$), MI subjects attended the partial hospital program for significantly more days than subjects in the historical control group, with SI subjects falling in between these two groups.

DISCUSSION

Our pilot study suggests that a one-session preadmission motivational interview with dual-diagnosis patients as a prelude to entering a partial hospital program yielded some overall treatment outcome benefit, most readily apparent in the patients' attendance patterns (less tardiness and early departures and greater number of days attended). We believe that because the outcome data were consistently in the predicted direction, and that in a few instances statistically significant effects were found with a relatively small sample size, motivational interviewing shows promise for further study, albeit with several methodological improvements (e.g., increasing sample size, recruiting subjects with wider motivational range and greater diagnostic homogeneity, balancing psychiatric severity across conditions, and using structured diagnostic interviewing).

REFERENCES

1. Miller WR. Motivational interviewing: research, practice, and puzzles. *Addict Behav* 1996;21:835–842.
2. Bein TH, Miller WR, Boroughs JM. Motivational interviewing with alcoholic outpatients. *Behav Cognitive Psychother* 1993;21:347–356.
3. Brown JM, Miller WR. Impact of motivational interviewing on participation and outcome in residential alcoholism treatment. *Psychol Addict Behav* 1993;7:211–218.
4. Project MATCH Research Group. Matching alcoholism treatment to client heterogeneity: Project MATCH posttreatment drinking outcomes. *J Stud Alcohol* 1997;58:7–29.
5. Eisen SV, Dill DL, Grob MC. Reliability and validity of a brief patient-report instrument for psychiatric outcome evaluation. *Hosp Community Psychiatry* 1994;45:242–247.

6. Beck AT, Ward CH, Mendelson M. An inventory for measuring depression. *Arch Gen Psychiatry* 1961;4:461–471.
7. DiClemente CC, Hughes SO. Stages of change profiles in alcoholism treatment. *J Subst Abuse* 1990;2:217–235.
8. Hall SM, Havassy BE, Wasserman DA. Commitment to abstinence and acute stress in relapse to alcohol, opiates, and nicotine. *J Consult Clin Psychol* 1990;58:175–181.
9. McLellan AT, Luborsky L, Woody GE, et al. An improved diagnostic evaluation instrument for substance abuse patients: the Addiction Severity Index. *J Nerv Ment Dis* 1980;168:26–33.
10. Sobell MB, Maisto SA, Sobell LC, et al. Developing a prototype for evaluating alcohol treatment effectiveness. In: Sobell LC, Sobell MB, Ward E, eds. *Evaluating Alcohol and Drug Abuse Treatment Effectiveness: Recent Advances*. New York: Pergamon Press; 1980.
11. Larsen DL, Attkisson CC, Hargreaves WA, et al. Assessment of client/patient satisfaction: development of a general scale. *Evaluation and Program Planning* 1979;2:197–207.
12. Conover WJ. *Practical Nonparametric Statistics, Second Edition*. New York: John Wiley & Sons; 1980.

Chapter 7

Current Concepts in the Treatment of Depression in Alcohol-Dependent Patients

Patrick J. McGrath, M.D.
Edward V. Nunes, M.D.
Frederic M. Quitkin, M.D.

MEDICAL SIGNIFICANCE OF ALCOHOLISM

Because most psychiatric residencies limit training in the diagnosis and treatment of substance use disorders, psychiatrists may be insufficiently aware of the high rate and significant clinical impact of comorbidity of alcoholism and various psychiatric disorders, including depression. (In this chapter, *alcoholism* is used synonymously with *alcohol dependence*, as defined by *DSM-IV*.[1]) Alcoholism is a leading cause of morbidity and mortality in developed and developing countries. Some statistics concerning alcoholism help to illustrate its enormous medical importance. If contributions to physical illness, suicide, homicide, and accidental death are considered,[26] alcoholism is the fourth leading cause of death in the United States. In multiple studies, alcoholism has been found to be associated with approximately 25% of the deaths by suicide[39] and more than 50% of fatal motor vehicle accidents.[33] Because many alcoholics die at younger ages than do nonalcoholics, more years of potential life are lost to alcoholism than to heart disease or cancer.[18] According to the World Health Organization,[40] alcohol use

This work was supported by grant AA 08030 and AA 09539 from the National Institute of Alcohol Abuse and Alcoholism and the Office of Mental Health of the State of New York.

disorders are the fourth leading cause of disability and premature mortality worldwide.

RELATIONSHIP BETWEEN ALCOHOLISM AND DEPRESSION

Because alcoholic individuals commonly experience depressive symptoms, clinicians and researchers postulate a relationship between the two disorders. People might drink because they are depressed, using alcohol to medicate underlying depression. This is called the *self-medication hypothesis.*[30,52,64] Alternatively, because depressive symptoms often resolve with abstinence, the causal relationship may be reversed; that is, depression may occur mainly as a toxic effect of alcohol dependence.[7] Which viewpoint is correct? The answer has important consequences for how clinicians think about and treat individuals with both disorders.

Multiple epidemiologic studies, including the Epidemiologic Catchment Area study, the National Comorbidity Study, and the National Longitudinal Alcohol Epidemiologic Survey, show that the syndrome of major depression is commonly comorbid with alcoholism at rates that clearly exceed chance.[22,29,54] The elevated odds ratios for comorbidity in epidemiologic samples essentially eliminate the possibility that the co-occurrence of these disorders is as likely as a chance co-occurrence of any two common disorders or an illusion[6] created by individuals with two disorders being more likely to seek treatment. For example, the Epidemiologic Catchment Area data show that, among persons with any alcohol use disorder, the lifetime prevalence of any affective disorder is an estimated 13.4%,[54] which is approximately 2-fold the rate in the general population. Examined from the converse perspective, among those with any affective disorder, the lifetime risk for alcohol use disorders is 21.8%, which is 1.9-fold the rate among those without affective disorders.

Another large study estimated current alcohol comorbidity with other disorders.[22] Among patients with a current or past-year alcohol use disorder, 9.6% also had major depression, which was significantly more than the 3.3% rate in patients without current alcohol abuse. Conversely, 21.4% of patients with current major depression had a current alcohol use disorder, which was significantly greater than the 7.4% rate for those without major depression. Regardless of time frame, the risk for alcohol use disorder was increased approximately 4-fold among patients with major depression. As expected, even higher rates of comorbid major depression, ranging from 8% to 53%, occur in treatment-seeking samples and in primary care settings.[36] Prospective follow-up data from the Collaborative Study on the Psychobiology of Depression show that 28% of alcoholics without affective disorder at intake developed major depression within 6 years, compared with 12% of healthy subjects.[13] These episodes of depression were characterized by more symptoms, longer duration, and more suicide attempts than were episodes in patients without an antecedent nonaffective disorder.

The comorbidity of alcoholism and depression also seems to have prognostic importance.[24,38] For example, in a 10-year follow-up study[38] of depressed probands, patients who were never alcoholic or who were alcoholic but in remission had twice the likelihood of recovery from major depression compared with actively alcoholic probands. Another careful 5-year follow-up study[24] of patients with major depression and alcoholism showed that improvement in depression was strongly associated with reduced alcoholic relapse. Strikingly, other studies have shown that 58% of alcoholic patients who committed suicide had major depression.[39] Although convincingly demonstrating an association of depression and alcohol abuse treatment outcomes, such studies cannot necessarily show the nature of this association.

Clearly, the co-occurrence of depressive disorders and alcoholism is common and of clinical importance. With the availability of effective antidepressant medications, treatment of comorbid depression could improve the outcome for patients with both disorders. Because antidepressant medication is neither generally euphoriant nor self-administered, the understandable concern about cross-addiction to another substance is generally agreed not to apply here. The high prevalence of alcoholism among depressed people in general indicates that improvement in treatment outcome for even a small subset of alcoholics who have treatable depression clearly could have a significant public health impact.

POSSIBLE EXPLANATIONS FOR COMORBIDITY

Competing theories explain the comorbidity of alcoholism and depression. Data support the self-medication and toxicity hypotheses. The self-medication hypothesis proposes that depressed patients drink to alleviate the dysphoric affect of depression or anxiety,[30,52,64] which suggests that a subset of depressed patients becomes secondarily alcoholic and that treatment of the antecedent depression might improve outcome.

In a series of careful studies, Schuckit et al.[7,8] found that patients with primary alcoholism admitted for detoxification have marked resolution of comorbid major depression with abstinence, showing that most depression present at admission in patients with primary alcoholism improves without antidepressant treatment.[7,57,60] However, because the study focused on people with primary alcoholism admitted for detoxification, the results may not apply to unselected clinical samples in other treatment settings or in primary care settings. From a broader sample of 2,945 alcoholics selected for high familial loading for alcoholism among first-degree relatives, Schuckit et al.[59] estimated that episodes of depression independent of alcohol abuse occurred in 15.2% of alcoholics and alcohol-induced depression in 26.4%. These estimates mean that approximately one-third of depressions in alcoholics represent primary depressive illness, a probable underestimate because the sample was selected for high alcoholism familial loading.

Lines of evidence to address the relationship of depression and alcoholism include family studies to assess the genetics of each disorder; formal studies of comorbidity, including assessment of which disorder preceded the other; and treatment studies that assess the response of the disorders to therapies specific to each. Although a critical review of this evidence is beyond the scope of this chapter, a summary may be useful in thinking about the clinical realities and decisions regarding treatment. Many of the studies in this area have used clinical samples that are unreliable in the assessment of comorbidity because comorbid patients are more likely to seek treatment and therefore are overrepresented (i.e., Berkson's bias).[6] This bias may cause an overestimate of the incidence of comorbid cases in the population and distort the comorbid associations as they relate to treatment outcome and other variables. Only epidemiologic samples fully address this issue and provide reliable data on the prevalence of comorbidity and its correlates.

Genetics

Reviews of family studies suggest that alcoholism and depression are not manifestations of the same underlying disorder and are mainly independently transmitted in families.[10,36] Data indicate a possible common genetic predisposition for alcoholism and depression in women, although this predisposition accounts for only a small portion of the variance.[28] Also, bipolar depression may be more commonly antecedent to alcoholism, and unipolar depression may be more commonly a consequence of alcoholism.[37,54] One family study suggests that although most variance in the transmission of alcoholism in families is unique to alcoholism, alcoholism is associated significantly with depression and anxiety; depression and anxiety, in turn, are strongly associated with each other.[37] Because of these comorbid associations, the genetic independence of the disorders may not be as complete as was previously believed, but additional research is necessary to establish this theory.

Course

Researchers think about the relationship between comorbid disorders based on which disorder is chronologically primary—that is, had the earlier onset. They presume that chronologically primary depression is more likely an independent entity that might persist in abstinence and require antidepressant therapy.[56,59] Conversely, chronologically secondary depression is thought more likely to be the result of toxicity and therefore to remit with abstinence. Studies show that depression that occurs in subjects with primary alcoholism remits with abstinence from alcohol and that depression that occurs in the course of alcoholism affects ultimate treatment outcome.[7,56–58] How commonly depression might be the primary disorder is unclear; researchers determine which disorder had the first onset by asking subjects. This technique may be unreliable, especially when subjects have had chronic disorders and may bias their answers to appear more favorable to the researchers. In an unpublished review (2000) of 10 studies that determined which disorder was primary, the authors found a median rate for primary depression among alcoholics of 13%, which is 1.4 times the Epidemiologic Catchment Area study community rate for adults. The National Longitudinal Alcohol Epidemiologic Survey epidemiologic data set has assessed carefully the primary or secondary distinction among 9,985 alcoholic subjects with depression.[23] The rates of primary, concurrent, and secondary depression were 41.0%, 16.5%, and 42.5%, respectively. Even among a sample highly loaded for familial alcoholism, approximately one-third of cases of major depression seem to be primary.[59] These data strongly suggest that previous reports of relatively low incidences of primary depression among alcoholics are underestimates because of sampling alcoholics in treatment rather than using an epidemiologic sample.

Another approach to the methodologic problem of unreliability of dating age of onset is to study adolescents, whose age is closer to the usual age of onset of alcohol abuse, limiting artifacts of memory and retrospective distortion. The only such published community study found that 22.8% of subjects with alcohol abuse disorder had major depression, compared with 6.9% for nonabusers.[16] Also, in most cases, the onset of major depression was before that of alcohol abuse. Taken together, these data suggest that a significant minority of alcoholics have primary depression that may contribute to the development of alcoholism or exacerbate its course after it has developed.

Which disorder is primary differs by gender[25] and gender determines the effect of comorbid depression on prognosis. The prognosis for comorbidly depressed men is worse than that for nondepressed men; the prognosis for comorbidly depressed women is better.[55] The reason for this difference has not been explained. It may mean that the type of depression differs between women and men. Perhaps in women the increased prevalence of primary depressive illness results in more comorbidly depressed cases involving primary depression, which has a spontaneously remitting course. In men, primary depression may be less common, and the major depressions are phenocopies that do not have a large genetic component and are more likely the result of toxic physiologic effects of alcohol or its psychosocial consequences. This idea is consistent with data showing remission of comorbid depression with abstinence in male alcoholic patients seen in Veterans Affairs settings.[7,8] Although other explanations are possible, these data, at the least, suggest that heterogeneity exists among comorbid patients—heterogeneity that may determine how physicians treat these patients.

TREATMENT

Several important treatment studies using contemporary diagnostic instruments, dosage regimens, and definitions of outcome have been published. These studies generally have distinguished between primary depression, which was antecedent to alcoholism or occurred during long periods of sobriety, and secondary depression, which occurred only after alcoholism was established.

The authors have reported on two studies of antidepressant therapy for primary depression among alcoholic outpatients in whom the primacy of depression was determined by clinical history.[45] In a pilot study,[15] the authors showed that 58% of patients with primary depression had significant improvement in alcoholism and depression when treated with an open-labeled regimen of imipramine therapy plus counseling. *Primary depression* was defined as having antedated the onset of alcoholism or occurred during 6 months of sobriety. Also, in a 6-month randomized discontinuation portion of the study, 7 of 10 patients randomized to placebo relapsed (70%), whereas only 4 of 13 maintained on imipramine therapy (31%) did so (Fisher's exact test, $p = 0.09$).[45] Following this trial, the authors conducted a randomized, placebo-controlled study of imipramine therapy in alcoholic subjects with a history of primary depression.[35] The study included 69 actively alcoholic outpatients who received weekly individual relapse-prevention counseling in addition to pharmacotherapy. The study demonstrated a clear antidepressant effect, but no independent effect of imipramine on drinking occurred. Patients whose depression improved with imipramine therapy, however, showed statistically and clinically significant improvements in their heavy drinking. These studies support the idea that subjects with primary depression, as determined by history rather than by observing protracted depression during abstinence, respond to antidepressant medication.

Only one controlled trial has addressed the treatment of clearly defined secondary depression among alcoholics.[34] In a placebo-controlled trial of desipramine therapy, subjects who remained depressed after at least 1 week of abstinence showed significantly less depression when given desipramine therapy, compared with placebo, and had significantly longer abstinence. Although the rate of relapse to drinking was higher on placebo (40.0%) than on active medication (8.3%), this difference was not statistically significant with the small sample size of depressed patients ($N = 22$) in the study. Of interest, desipramine did not reduce relapse to drinking in nondepressed alcoholic subjects, which is consistent with earlier studies showing no benefit from tricyclic antidepressant therapy in alcoholic subjects not selected for comorbid depression.[9]

Interest in the possible role of selective serotonin reuptake inhibitors (SSRIs) in treating depression has been engendered by laboratory studies that show serotonin reuptake inhibitors, including fluoxetine, fluvoxamine, zimelidine, citalopram, and viqualine, reduce the consumption of alcohol among animal species.[21] Naranjo et al.[41–44] have conducted double-blind, placebo-controlled studies showing modest but significant reductions (10–26%) in alcohol consumption in nonaffectively ill alcohol abusers. This benefit seemed to require higher dosage levels than those usually required in treating depression.[41] Encouraged by these data to hypothesize that SSRIs may be effective therapy for alcoholism, Kranzler et al.[31] conducted a placebo-controlled trial of fluoxetine therapy in alcoholic subjects not selected for comorbid affective disorder. This study showed no benefit of active fluoxetine therapy in reducing relapse. Unfortunately, the number of alcoholic subjects with significant depression was too small to assess the effect of fluoxetine therapy.

Cornelius et al.[11,12] have conducted a pilot study and a controlled study of patients admitted to a psychiatric unit with severe major depression and comorbid major depression. Although the chronology of depression was not described, depression was clearly a major and severe clinical problem warranting hospital admission. In the pilot study and preliminary results from the controlled study, patients on active medication experienced significant improvements in depression and alcohol consumption; improvement in alcohol consumption seemed to be independent of improvement in depression. This study suggests that fluoxetine therapy does have some selective benefits in reducing alcohol consumption in depressed alcoholic patients and may be a treatment of choice in this group if its safety can be established. A study conducted by the authors (unpublished observations, 2000) compared fluoxetine therapy with placebo in 77 actively alcoholic outpatients, all of whom received concurrent individual weekly relapse-prevention counseling. Subjects were selected for primary depression, defined as depression that antedated the onset of alcohol use disorder or continued during 6 months of abstinence. Preliminary analyses of the data have shown no advantage of fluoxetine therapy over placebo in treating depression. Trends toward less alcohol consumption were seen on some drinking measures, although this finding did not seem to be clinically significant. The inconsistency between these two trials may be the result of marked sampling differences. The subjects in the Pittsburgh study were all hospitalized for depression, mainly because of suicidality. A serotonergic antidepressant may be effective for this subgroup, whereas tricyclic antidepressants (TCAs) or other noradrenergic treatments are more useful in nonsuicidal patients.

The controlled studies indicate that antidepressant medications, including SSRIs, have no utility in nondepressed alcoholic patients. Comorbid depression, whether chronologically primary or secondary to alcoholism, seems to respond to antidepressant medication. Although the improvements in depression are clinically meaningful, improvements in alcohol abuse are much less robust. TCAs seem to have no effect on drinking behavior apart from improving depression; SSRIs may reduce alcohol consumption more than TCAs and may show some benefits even in the absence of improved depression. Given that SSRIs do not reduce drinking significantly in nondepressed alcoholic patients, this finding is surprising and bears examination in additional studies. SSRIs were strikingly effective in one study and ineffective in another, which suggests that their spectrum of action may be more limited to severely depressed subjects, perhaps those with considerable suicidality.

Although the mechanism of the relationship between alcoholism and depression is undetermined, an interesting hypothesis relates both disorders to the regulation of the endogenous opiate system. Strong evidence shows that alcohol increases the release of endogenous opiate peptides in alcohol-preferring animals[15] and that opiate receptor antagonists diminish relapse among detoxified alcoholics.[48,63] If endogenous opiates are related to depressive disorders, as has been hypothesized, both disorders may share pathophysiologic features in their interaction with this system. This possible relationship, although intriguing, is highly speculative and requires considerably more research.

MANAGEMENT

Diagnosis

How to diagnose major depression in the face of active alcohol dependence or abuse is controversial. The goal is to distinguish a substance-induced mood disorder or secondary depression, which is likely to remit with abstinence, from an independent or primary mood disorder, which is best treated with specific pharmacotherapy. Work by Schuckit et al.[7,8] and others has shown that a minimum of 3 weeks of abstinence is required for resolution of depressive symptoms caused by alcohol intoxication and withdrawal,[8] which has led to the recommendation in *DSM-IV* of at least 1 month of abstinence before making a diagnosis of a mood disorder in alcoholics with depression.[1] Mood disorder that occurs before achieving this duration of abstinence is considered substance related. This situation is clearly ideal, and efforts to achieve a period of abstinence should be made to make the most accurate diagnosis. Unfortunately, this period of abstinence is often difficult to attain in clinical settings. The distinction of primary from secondary depression is fraught with the vagaries of memory because the onset of both disorders is usually many years before presentation for treatment. Also, social acceptability can be problematic; having a "reason" to drink may be seen as exculpatory in the minds of patients, so a history suggesting primary depression may be proffered. Because substantial evidence indicates that depression combined with alcohol use worsens prognosis, depressed alcohol abusers often have the most difficulty attaining abstinence.[55]

In the situation in which prolonged abstinence cannot be attained, studies of primary and secondary depression cited earlier show that depression can be treated successfully with antidepressant medications and that improvement often is associated with diminished alcohol abuse. This treatment can be done after briefer periods of abstinence or even in the face of ongoing alcohol abuse. Clinical features of depression in such patients may be helpful in deciding whether antidepressant therapy is warranted (Table 7.1). The diagnosis of depression in alcohol-abusing or alcohol-dependent patients cannot be made accurately using self-rated depression scales. An accurate syndromal diagnosis of the depressive disorder is necessary to determine whether a trial of antidepressant medication is warranted, whether a mood stabilizer is indicated, and whether a trial of abstinence first is preferable. These determinations are made best by a careful diagnostic interview, establishing the ages of onset of depression and alcohol abuse, their chronology, and any persistence of one during periods of remission from the other.

Clinicians should establish whether any depressive disorder is unipolar or bipolar and characterize it as major depression, dysthymia, or other depressive disorder. The assessment of other comorbid disorders, such as panic disorder, posttraumatic stress disorder, or abuse of other drugs in addition to alcohol, is also important because these comorbidities have treatment implications of their own. Patients with panic disorder may need gradual institution of antidepressants because some medications may initially exacerbate panic, particularly SSRIs. Insomnia and nightmares caused by posttraumatic stress disorder may not respond as fully to antidepressant treatment as would be expected in uncomplicated cases, and may require alternative treatment. Clinicians should assess the abuse of other drugs because this abuse commonly accompanies alcohol abuse and is often less clinically obvious. Routine urine screening for drugs of abuse is often helpful in identifying occult use of other drugs and in monitoring the treatment response of such patients. Seventy-five percent to 90% of alcoholics are smokers,[62] which is 3-fold higher than among the general population. Such high comorbidity of nicotine dependence and the severe health consequences of smoking indicate that attention should be paid to smoking in patients who abuse alcohol or other drugs.

Triage

Clinicians face a critical decision in whether to detoxify alcohol-dependent patients. Although rating scales exist to help clinicians decide, in most clinical settings the history of recent consumption, periods of abstinence, and any withdrawal symptoms are usually sufficient for this decision.[46] Patients who frequently abstain for 1 or 2 days during their usual drinking without significant withdrawal do not need detoxification and can begin with outpatient treatment. Patients with unstable medical problems, suicidal ideation, and alcoholism that is acutely endangering them or others usually require at least brief hospitalization for detoxification. Patients who cannot abstain or have histories of withdrawal symptoms should be detoxified as inpatients or in an intensive outpatient program, if available. Detoxification in outpatient settings is an increasingly attractive alternative because of its cost advantages;[20] however, it should be reserved for patients who are free of histories of severe withdrawal and severe medical complications of alcoholism, and who have a reliable and cooperative significant other.

TABLE 7.1. Clinical Features Indicating Antidepressant Therapy

Clinical Indications	Depressive Characteristic
Clear	Persists in prolonged abstinence (e.g., ≤ months)
Probable	Primary by history; persisted in past periods of abstinence; chronic; emerges during stable use
Possible	Positive family history of mood or anxiety disorder

Treatment Algorithm

Psychosocial Therapy

A comprehensive discussion of the psychosocial and pharmacologic treatment of alcoholism is beyond the scope of this chapter and is available elsewhere.[53] Although investigators generally agree that all patients with alcoholism require significant psychosocial support, the kind of treatment that is effective is undefined. Three highly structured psychotherapies have undergone evaluation in a large treatment assessment program in the United States called Project Match, which is examining ways of matching patients to a psychosocial treatment best suited for their needs.[50,51] Although the hoped-for ability to match patients to specific psychotherapies best suited for them was not achieved, the outcomes of all three treatments were quite good, which suggests that well-defined and relatively time-limited psychosocial therapies seem useful in managing alcoholic patients. These treatments are illustrative of state-of-the-art standardized treatment approaches in use (Table 7.2).

Family approaches are often desirable in conjunction with other treatment to provide education about the disease concepts of alcoholism and depression and to assist family members' support of treatment.[20,46] Generally, psychosocial treatment efforts should first address the substance abuse and only later deal with depression.

Pharmacologic Therapy

Although treatment studies using modern diagnostic criteria and vigorous antidepressant medication trials are scarce, some recommendations can be made based on these studies and on clinical experience (Table 7.3). Because these studies have generally excluded patients with severe hepatic disease, unstable cardiovascular diseases, seizure disorders, and severe dependence on other drugs, the following recommendations also exclude these patients. Patients with mild liver disease evidenced by minor elevations of transaminases without jaundice or cirrhosis need not be excluded from treatment with antidepressants. Patients with

TABLE 7.2. Psychotherapeutic Therapies for Alcoholism

Treatment Type	Description	Duration (wk)
12-step facilitation	Alcoholics Anonymous meetings and weekly individual 12-step reinforcement sessions	12
Cognitive-behavioral	Coping skills training for relapse prevention	12
Motivational enhancement	Feedback of risks for impairment and elicitation of motivation for change	4

TABLE 7.3. Antidepressant Medication Selection

Desirability	Class	Reasons and Comments
First choice	SSRI	Effective for depression, possibly especially for severe or suicidal patients; well tolerated with minimal sedation; may reduce alcohol consumption by direct action
	Tricyclic	Effective for depression; less well tolerated than SSRIs; alcohol abuse reduced only in mood responders
Relatively contraindicated	Bupropion	Proconvulsive
Contraindicated	Nonselective MAOIs	Potential severe toxicity with alcohol
Other options	Venlafaxine, mirtazapine, others	Unstudied, but may be useful for resistant depression
	Lithium	Indicated for bipolar depression; useful for antidepressant augmentation; no direct benefit for alcoholism[17]

Note. SSRI = selective serotonin reuptake inhibitor; MAOI = monoamine oxidase inhibitor.

significant hepatic compromise may metabolize antidepressant medications slowly and therefore be more prone to medication toxicity.

As in other depressive states, adequate doses and duration of a therapeutic trial are necessary. Careful monitoring of possible interactions between alcohol consumption and the medication are essential. Any antidepressant can potentiate the sedating effects and impairment of coordination resulting from alcohol, making driving and the operation of dangerous machinery more hazardous. Although this effect is uncommon, occasional instances occur and patients should be warned in advance. In studies published to date, patients have received full therapeutic doses without evidence of severe toxicity, even during slips back to drinking. Because these studies have included relatively few carefully selected subjects, more studies are necessary to establish the degree of safety, and clinical caution is warranted.

Monitoring Treatment

In addition to self-report, the report of a significant other is useful to help ensure the patient's probity in reporting alcohol consumption. A nonjudgmental attitude on the part of the treating clinician is important to avoid driving out of treatment patients who are unable to abstain. Useful laboratory testing includes monitoring gamma-glutamyltransferase, aspartate aminotransferase, alanine aminotransferase, and mean corpuscular volume, all of which are responsive to alcohol abuse and normalize with reduced drinking.[4,5] These measurements are useful only if they were abnormal at baseline. Newer experimental techniques, such as the measurement of carbohydrate-deficient transferrin, a transferrin isoform produced in the context of heavy alcohol consumption, may provide better objective evidence of improved drinking in the future.[2,61] Breathalyzer or saliva dipstick screening for alcohol is occasionally useful but is insensitive to alcohol consumed more than approximately 12 hours before testing.[27]

Treatment Resistance

Patients with clear primary depression whose depression does not respond to an adequate clinical trial of antidepressant therapy should be treated with a second antidepressant trial or a potentiation strategy. Patients whose depression responds but whose drinking does not should be given maximal outpatient psychosocial treatment aimed at treating alcohol dependence. The authors' clinical experience suggests that combining naltrexone therapy with antidepressant therapy is occasionally helpful and does not result in significant adverse effects. Naltrexone therapy has been shown to be effective in the treatment of alcoholism in nondepressed alcoholics.[48,63] An epidemiologic study of naltrexone therapy in approximately 800 patients, many of whom were receiving antidepressants, showed no evidence of toxic interaction.[14] Naltrexone is given in daily doses of 50 mg or thrice weekly in supervised doses of 100 mg each. Although disulfiram has been shown not to be generally effective in the treatment of alcoholism,[19] disulfiram administered by a reliable significant other, typically a spouse, is sometimes strikingly helpful.[47]

Finally, an intensive daily outpatient program or hospitalization for detoxification may be recommended. Intensive treatment sometimes is more acceptable to patients as an alternative if vigorous outpatient treatment has failed. Intensive treatment has a further advantage of conserving treatment resources in the increasingly cost-conscious treatment environment in most countries.

FUTURE ISSUES

Etiology

The causes of primary mood disorders and alcoholism have been shown to be largely genetic,[28,36] although the exact nature of this component is unknown. Genetic markers for both of these disorders probably will be found and will clarify their relationship enormously. In the meantime, more clinical studies may help to clarify the gender differences observed with respect to the differential prognosis of alcoholism when accompanied by depressive disorders in men and women. Unitary explanations are unlikely to be fully satisfactory, and whether "self-medication" or depression caused by the toxicity of alcohol are etiologically relevant probably varies among individual cases.

Medication

Future studies must verify whether SSRIs are especially effective in treating depressed alcoholic patients as indicated by one study.[11] The advent of opiate receptor antagonists, such as naltrexone, has been a major breakthrough in the search for an effective pharmacotherapy for alcoholism.[3,48,63] Other new treatments, such as the excitatory amino acid receptor inhibitor (e.g., acamprosate), are also in development.[32,49] One of these medications, naltrexone, in combination with an antidepressant, ultimately may prove to be a treatment of choice for depressed alcoholic patients. Clinical studies are needed of the safety and efficacy of these combinations and of clinical and possibly biochemical typologies that may guide treatment selection. Ultimately, other types of medication may be developed to block craving for alcohol or inhibit reinforcement from drinking to help to restore neurochemical imbalances created by alcohol abuse.

Perspectives

Depression is commonly comorbid with alcoholism or alcohol abuse. Careful clinical evaluation often can differentiate patients with primary mood disorders from those with secondary alcoholism. Comorbid patients often can be treated with antidepressant therapy on an outpatient basis combined with counseling to address alcohol abuse, with good remission of depression and improvement in alcohol abuse, especially for those whose mood improves. More severely depressed patients with alcoholism have been studied and may show a selective improvement of their symptoms on SSRI antidepressant therapy. Finally, even patients with secondary depression who are recently abstinent can be treated effectively with antidepressant medication. Although more studies are necessary, clinicians can apply these research findings today to the management of depressed patients with alcoholism. More definitive answers will be found to the many questions presented by the combination of these disorders.

REFERENCES

1. American Psychiatric Association. *Diagnostic and Statistical Manual of Mental Disorders, Fourth Edition.* Washington, DC: American Psychiatric Association; 1994.
2. Anton R, Moak D, Latham P. Carbohydrate-deficient transferrin as an indicator of drinking status during a treatment outcome study. *Alcohol Clin Exp Res* 1996;20:841–846.
3. Anton R, Moak D, Waid L, et al. Naltrexone and cognitive behavioral therapy for the treatment of outpatient alcoholics: results of a placebo-controlled trial. *Am J Psychiatry* 1999;156:1758–1764.

4. Beresford T, Blow F, Hill E, et al. Comparison of CAGE questionnaire and computer-assisted laboratory profiles in screening for covert alcoholism. *Lancet* 1990;336:482–485.
5. Beresford T, Low D, Hall R, et al. A computerized biochemical profile for detection of alcoholism. *Psychosomatics* 1982;23:713–720.
6. Berkson J. Limitations of the application of the 4-fold table analyses to hospital data. *Biometrics* 1946;2:47–53.
7. Brown S, Schuckit MA. Changes in depression among abstinent alcoholics. *J Stud Alcohol* 1988;49:412–417.
8. Brown S, Inaba R, Gillin J, et al. Alcoholism and affective disorder: clinical course of depressive symptoms. *Am J Psychiatry* 1995;152:45–52.
9. Ciraulo D, Salloum I, Cornelius M. Tricyclic antidepresants in the treatment of depression associated with alcoholism. *J Clin Psychopharmacol* 1981;1:146–150.
10. Cloninger C, Reich T. Alcholism and affective disorders: Familial association and genetic models. In: Goodwin D, Erickson C, eds. *Alcholism and Affective Disorders: Clinical, Genetic, and Biochemical Studies.* New York: SP Medical and Scientific Books; 1979.
11. Cornelius JR, Salloum IM, Ehler JG, et al. Fluoxetine in depressed alcoholics. *Arch Gen Psychiatry* 1997;54:700–705.
12. Cornelius J, Salloum I, et al. Preliminary report: double-blind placebo-controlled study of fluoxetine in depressed alcoholics. *Psychopharmacol Bull* 1995;31:297–303.
13. Coryell W, Endicott J, Keller M. Major depression in a nonclinical sample. *Arch Gen Psychiatry* 1992;49:117–125.
14. Croop RS, Faulkner EB, Labriola DF. The safety profile of naltrexone in the treatment of alcoholism: results from a multicenter usage study. *Arch Gen Psychiatry* 1997;54:1130–1135.
15. de Waele J, Kiianmaa K, Gianoulakis C. Spontaneous and ethanol-stimulated in vitro release of beta endorphin by the hypothalamus of AA and ANA rats. *Alcohol Clin Exp Res* 1994;18:1468–1473.
16. Deykin E, Levy J, Wells V. Adolescent depression, alcohol, and drug abuse. *Am J Public Health* 1987;77:178–182.
17. Dorus W, Ostrow D, Anton R, et al. Lithium treatment of depressed and nondepressed alcoholics. *JAMA* 1989;262:1646–1652.
18. Dufour M. Death certificates as a data base for health research? Only with your help. *Bull Pathol Educ* 1984;9:57–59.
19. Fuller R, Branchley L, Brightwell D, et al. Disulfiram treatment of alcoholism: a Veterans Administration cooperative study. *JAMA* 1986;256:1449–1455.
20. Galanter M: Network therapy for addiction: a model for office practice. *Am J Psychiatry* 1993;150:28–36.
21. Gorelick D. Serotonin uptake blockers and the treatment of alcoholism. *Recent Dev Alcohol* 1989;7:267–281.
22. Grant BF, Harford TC. Comorbidity between DSM-IV alcohol use disorders and major depression: results of a national survey. *Drug Alcohol Depend* 1995;39:197–206.
23. Grant BF, Hasan DS, Dawson DA. The relationship between DSM-IV alcohol use disorders and DSM-IV major depression: examination of the primary-secondary distinction in a general population sample. *J Affect Disord* 1996;38:113–128.
24. Hasin D, Tsai W, Endicott J, et al. The effects of major depression on alcoholism. *Am J Addict* 1996;5:144–155.
25. Helzer J, Pryzbeck T. The co-occurrence of alcoholism with other psychiatric disorders in the general population and its impact on treatment. *J Stud Alcohol* 1988;49:219–224.

26. Institute of Medicine. *Causes and Consequences of Alcohol Problems.* Washington, DC: National Academy Press, 1987.

27. Kapur B, Israel Y. Alcohol dipstick: A rapid method for analysis of ethanol in body fluids. In: Chang N, Chao H, eds. *Early Identification of Alcohol Abuse.* DHHS Publications, Research Monograph 17. Rockville, MD; 1985, pp 1–30.

28. Kendler K, Heath A, Neale MC, et al. Alcoholism and major depression in women: a twin study of the causes of comorbidity. *Arch Gen Psychiatry* 1993;50:690–698.

29. Kessler R, McGonagle K, Camelley K, et al. The epidemiology of psychiatric comorbidity. In: Tsuang M, Cohen M, Zahner G, eds. *Textbook of Psychiatric Epidemiology.* New York: John Wiley & Sons; 1996, pp 179–197.

30. Khantzian E. The self-medication hypothesis of addictive disorders: Focus on heroin and cocaine dependence. *Am J Psychiatry* 1985;142:1259–1264.

31. Kranzler H, Burleson J, Korner P, et al. Placebo-controlled trial of fluoxetine as an adjunct to relapse prevention in alcoholics. *Am J Psychiatry* 1995;152:391–397.

32. Littleton J. Acamprosate in alcohol dependence: How does it work? *Addiction* 1995;90:1179–1188.

33. Lowenfels A, Wynn P. One less for the road: International trends in alcohol consumption and vehicular fatalities. *Ann Epidemiol* 1992;2:249–256.

34. Mason BJ, Kocsis JH, Ritvo EC, et al. A double-blind, placebo-controlled trial of desipramine for primary alcohol dependence stratified on the presence or absence of major depression. *JAMA* 1996;275:761–767.

35. McGrath PJ, Nunes EV, Stewart JW, et al. Imipramine treatment of alcoholics with primary depression: a placebo-controlled clinical trial. *Arch Gen Psychiatry* 1996;53:232–240.

36. Merikangas K, Gelernter C. Cormorbidity for alcoholism and depression. *Psychiatr Clin North Am* 1990;13:613–632.

37. Merikangas K, Risch N, Weissman M. Comorbidity and co-transmission of alcoholism, anxiety, and depression. *Psychol Med* 1994;24:69–80.

38. Mueller T, Lavori P, Keller MB, et al. Prognostic effect of the variable course of alcoholism on the 10-year course of depression. *Am J Psychiatry* 1994;151:701–706.

39. Murphy G, Wetzel R, Robins E, et al. Multiple risk factors predict suicide in alcoholism. *Arch Gen Psychiatry* 1992;49:459–463.

40. Murray C, Lopez A (eds). *The Global Burden of Disease: A Comprehensive Assessment of Mortality and Disability from Diseases, Injuries, and Risk Factors in 1990 and Projected to 2020.* Boston: Harvard School of Public Health; 1996.

41. Naranjo C, Kadlec K, Sanhueza P, et al. Fluoxetine differentially alters alcohol intake and other consummatory behaviors in problem drinkers. *Clin Pharmacol Ther* 1990;47:490–498.

42. Naranjo C, Sellers E, Roach C, et al. Zimelidine-induced variations in alcohol intake by nondepressed heavy drinkers. *Clin Pharmacol Ther* 1984;35:374–381.

43. Naranjo C, Sellers E, Sullivan J, et al. The serotonin uptake inhibitor citalopram attenuates ethanol intake. *Clin Pharmacol Ther* 1987;41:266–274.

44. Naranjo C, Sullivan J, Kadlec K, et al. Differential effects of viqualine on alcohol intake and other consummatory behaviors. *Clin Pharmacol Ther* 1989;46:301–309.

45. Nunes E, McGrath P, Quitkin F, et al. Imipramine treatment of alcoholism with comorbid depression. *Am J Psychiatry* 1993;150:963–965.

46. O'Farrell T. Marital and family therapy. In: Reid H, Miller W, eds. *The Handbook of Alcoholism Treatment Approaches: Effective Alternatives.* New York: Allyn & Bacon; 1995.

47. O'Farrell T, Bayog R. Antabuse contract for married alcoholics and their spouses: a method to maintain Antabuse ingestion and decrease conflict about drinking. *J Subst Abuse Treat* 1986;3:1–8.

48. O'Malley S, Jaffe A, Schottenfeld R. Naltrexone and coping skills therapy for alcohol dependence: a controlled study. *Arch Gen Psychiatry* 1993;49:881–887.
49. Paille F, Guelfi J, Perkins A, et al. Double-blind randomized multicenter trial of acamprosate in maintaining abstinence from alcohol. *Alcohol* 1995;30:239–247.
50. Project MATCH Research Group. Matching alcoholism treatments to client heterogeneity: Project MATCH three-year drinking outcomes. *Alcohol Clin Exp Res* 1998;22:1300–1311.
51. Project MATCH Research Group. Matching alcoholism treatments to client heterogeneity: treatment main effects and matching effects on drinking during treatment. *J Stud Alcohol* 1988;59:631–639.
52. Quitkin F, Rifkin A, Kaplan J, et al. Phobic anxiety syndrome complicated by drug dependence and addiction: a treatable form of drug abuse. *Arch Gen Psychiatry* 1972;27:159–162.
53. Reid H, Miller W. (eds). *The Handbook of Alcoholism Treatment Approaches: Effective Alternatives.* New York: Allyn & Bacon, 1995
54. Regier D, Farmer M, Rae D, et al. Comorbidity of mental disorders with alcohol and other drug abuse: results from the epidemiologic catchment area study. *JAMA* 1990;264:2511–2519.
55. Rounsaville B, Dolinsky Z, Babor T, et al. Psychopathology as a predictor of treatment outcome in alcoholics. *Arch Gen Psychiatry* 1987;44:505–513.
56. Schuckit M. Alcoholism and affective disorder: diagnostic confusion. In: Goodwin D, Erickson C, eds. *Alcoholism and Affective Disorders.* New York: Spectrum; 1979, pp 9–19.
57. Schuckit M. The clinical implications of primary diagnostic groups among alcoholics. *Arch Gen Psychiatry* 1985;42:1043–1049.
58. Schuckit M, Winokur G. A short-term follow-up of women alcoholics. *Diseases of the Nervous System* 1972;33:672–678.
59. Schuckit M, Tipp J, Bergman M, et al. Comparison of induced and independent major depressive disorders in 2,945 alcoholics. *Am J Psychiatry* 1997;154:948–957.
60. Schuckit M, Tipp J, Bucholz K, et al. The life-time rates of three major mood disorders and four major anxiety disorders in alcoholics and controls. *Addiction* 1997;92:1289–1304.
61. Stibler H. Carbohydrate-deficient transferrin in serum: a new marker of potentially harmful alcohol consumption reviewed. 1991;37:2029–2037.
62. Toneatto A, Sobell L, Sobell M, et al. The effect of cigarette smoking on alcohol treatment outcome. *J Subst Abuse* 1995;7:245–252.
63. Volpicelli J, Alterman A, Hayashida M, et al. Naltrexone in the treatment of alcohol dependence. *Arch Gen Psychiatry* 1992;49:876–880.
64. Weiss R, Griffin M, Mirin S. Drug abuse as self-medication for depression: an empirical study. *Am J Drug Alcohol Abuse* 1992;18:121–129.

Chapter 8

Utilization of Psychosocial Treatments by Patients Diagnosed with Bipolar Disorder and Substance Dependence

Roger D. Weiss, M.D.
Monika E. Kolodziej, Ph.D.
Lisa M. Najavits, Ph.D.
Shelly F. Greenfield, M.D., M.P.H.
Lisa M. Fucito, B.A.

Bipolar and substance use disorders frequently coexist. In a literature review on the subject, Brady and Lydiard[1] estimated that alcohol or drug problems occur in 21% to 58% of patients with bipolar disorder. More recently, Keck and colleagues[2] found that of 106 bipolar patients who were followed for 12 months after hospitalization for either a manic or a mixed-mood episode, 55% met criteria for a substance use disorder. Comorbidity between these two disorders is associated with a worse prognosis than with either diagnosis alone, including slower recovery time[3] and more psychiatric hospitalizations.[4]

Despite the high prevalence rate and negative clinical consequences associated with the comorbidity of bipolar and substance use disorders, to our knowledge only one study[5] to date has examined psychosocial interventions among

This study was supported by grants DA09400 (Dr. Weiss), DA00326 (Dr. Weiss), DA00407 (Dr. Greenfield), DA08631 (Dr. Najavits), and DA00400 (Dr. Najavits) from the National Institute on Drug Abuse, Bethesda, MD; grant AA12181 (Dr. Najavits) from the National Institute on Alcoholism and Alcohol Abuse, Bethesda, MD; and a grant from the Dr. Ralph and Marian C. Falk Medical Research Trust, Chicago, IL (Dr. Weiss).

persons diagnosed with these disorders. O'Sullivan et al.[5] found that abstinent patients reported more frequent attendance at Alcoholics Anonymous (AA) meetings than did nonabstinent patients. In addition to attendance at self-help groups, psychotherapy interventions are considered to be an important component of effective treatment for both bipolar[6,7] and substance use disorders.[8] Although several authors[2,9,10] have advocated increased utilization of a broad range of psychosocial interventions for persons with bipolar and substance use disorders, it is unknown to what extent patients make use of these treatments.

The main goal of this study was to examine the naturally occurring course of psychosocial treatment utilization in a sample of this dually diagnosed population; since all patients had to be receiving pharmacotherapy with a mood stabilizer to enter the study, we focused on psychosocial treatment in this report. Data were collected monthly over a 6-month posthospitalization period from patients who served as a comparison group in a study aiming to develop and pilot test a new manualized group psychotherapy for patients with coexisting bipolar and substance use disorders.[11] The patients in the current study received "treatment as usual"—that is, the treatment that they would ordinarily receive as recommended to them by their treating clinicians. They were evaluated monthly to assess their mood, substance use, overall functioning, and treatment utilization (see below for details of the assessment battery). Indeed, one of the goals of the larger study and the purpose of this report was to help define what "treatment as usual" is for this population. In this context, we also examined their mood symptoms and their alcohol and drug use monthly during the 6-month assessment period. By highlighting naturally occurring psychosocial treatment patterns and their concurrent symptomatology, we aim to better understand the course of this combination of disorders.

METHOD

Subjects

Subjects were recruited from an inpatient setting at McLean Hospital by reviewing admission notes and approaching all patients with admitting diagnoses of current bipolar disorder and substance use disorder. Patients were told that we were interested in better understanding the course of bipolar and substance use disorders and therefore wished to see them monthly for the next 6 months to follow their progress. All patients signed a written informed consent form after having the study explained to them, and they were paid $20 or $50 for each assessment, depending on its length. Patients who agreed to participate were administered the Structured Clinical Interview (SCID) for *DSM-IV*[12] after detoxification to confirm the diagnoses of current bipolar disorder and substance dependence. Other inclusion criteria included (1) substance use within 30 days before admission, (2) ongoing pharmacotherapy with a mood stabilizer, (3) consent for us to communicate with their pharmacotherapist, and (4) ability and willingness to give written informed consent.

Assessment and Procedure

Substance use and mood symptoms were rated by a trained research assistant using the Addiction Severity Index (ASI), fifth edition,[13] the 17-item Hamilton Depression Rating Scale,[14] and the Young Mania Rating Scale.[15] The research assistant also administered the following structured interviews to inquire about utilization of treatment: the Treatment Services Review,[16] which provides information about treatment sought for medical, psychosocial, and substance use problems, and the Treatment Summary, created and used by our group to inquire about the types of past and current treatment interventions sought, as well as the main focus of these interventions (e.g., bipolar disorder, substance use, both, or other). All measures were completed during the initial intake while the person was hospitalized, and then monthly for 6 months following hospital discharge.

RESULTS

Sociodemographic and Diagnostic Characteristics

Twenty-four patients (13 men, 11 women) who served as the comparison group for the experimental group therapy were included in this study. The mean age of the sample was 33.0 years ($SD = 6.4$). Patients were primarily white ($n = 20$; 83.3%), single or divorced ($n = 19$; 79.2%), and unemployed ($n = 16$; 66.6%). A majority of the patients ($n = 17$; 70.8%) were diagnosed with both drug and alcohol dependence; 4 patients (16.7%) were diagnosed solely with drug dependence; and 3 patients (12.5%) were only alcohol dependent. Most patients ($n = 18$; 75.0%) were diagnosed with bipolar I disorder; 3 patients (12.5%) had bipolar II disorder; and 3 patients (12.5%) had bipolar disorder not otherwise specified.

Treatment Utilization

Treatment utilization patterns during the 6-month posthospitalization period are shown in Figure 8.1. The most common behavioral treatment received was individual psychotherapy and the number of patients who participated in individual psychotherapy ranged from 17 (70.8%) in Month 1 to 9 (52.9%) in month 6 (McNemar test, *ns*). For those attending individual psychotherapy, frequency of attendance decreased from a mean of 5.3 ± 2.6 days in Month 1 to 3.9 ± 2.1 days in Month 6 ($t = -2.66$, 20 df, $p = .02$). Table 8.1 shows the main focus of psychotherapy as reported by the patients. Whereas in Month 1 nearly half of the patients reported that treatment focused on both bipolar and substance use disorders, this was significantly less common by Month 6. At that time, nearly half of the patients

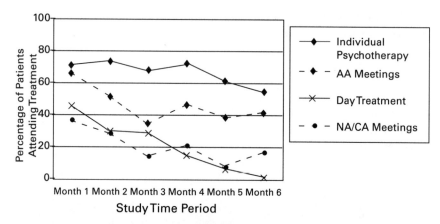

FIGURE 8.1. Treatment use over 6-month period.

reported that treatment focused mainly on other topics (exact McNemar test, p = .03).

Only 1 patient (4.2%) ever participated in group therapy and 3 patients (12.5%) participated in either family or couples' therapy during the 6-month period. Twelve patients (50.0%) attended a day treatment program during Month 1, though no patients were attending day treatment during Month 6 (McNemar test, p = .01). Six patients (25.0%) visited an alcohol or drug counselor or participated in some form of residential treatment during the study period. Sixteen patients (66.7%) attended AA meetings during the first month; attendance decreased to 41.2% (n = 7) in Month 6 (McNemar test, p = .03). For those attending AA, frequency of attendance decreased from a mean of 11.2 ± 11.5 days in Month 1 to 5.3 ± 8.2 days in Month 6 (t = −2.49, 16 df, p = .02). Attendance at Cocaine Anonymous (CA) or Narcotics Anonymous (NA) dropped from 9 patients (38.0%) in Month 1

TABLE 8.1. Primary Focus of Individual Psychotherapy in Month 1 and Month 6

	Frequency			
	Month 1 (n = 17)[a]		Month 6 (n = 9)[a]	
Primary Psychotherapy Focus	n	%	n	%
Bipolar disorder only	3	17.6	3	33.3
Substance use disorder only	0	0.0	1	11.1
Both bipolar and substance use disorders	8	47.1[b]	1	11.1[b]
Other[c]	6	35.3	4	44.4

[a]n specifies number of people engaged in individual psychotherapy.
[b]Exact McNemar test, p = .03.
[c]The "other" category includes treatment focusing on family, school, work, and personality disorders.

to 3 patients (17.6%) in Month 6, but this change was not statistically significant (McNemar test, ns).

Mood Symptoms and Substance Use

Mood symptoms, ASI alcohol and drug composite scores ranging from 0 (no substance use problem) to 1 (most severe substance use problem), and number of days of alcohol and drug use were compared between Month 1 and Month 6. Differences in degrees of freedom reflect missing data. Patients' mean substance use composite scores on the ASI at Month 1 (mean alcohol composite = 0.15 ± 0.16; mean drug composite = 0.08 ± 0.09) were not significantly different from scores obtained at Month 6 (mean alcohol composite = 0.16 ± 0.23; mean drug composite = 0.10 + 0.23). Similarly, no differences were noted between mean Hamilton Depression Rating Scale scores at Month 1 (16.7 ± 9.9) and at Month 6 (15.7 ± 9.0) or between mean Young Mania Rating Scale scores at Month 1 (8.0 ± 9.5) and at Month 6 (5.4 ± 4.6). Figure 8.2 shows the mean number of days of alcohol and drug use over the 6-month period. Although the mean number of days of substance use increased over time, differences between Months 1 and 6 were not statistically significant for alcohol use ($t = 0.68$, 16 df, ns). There was a trend, however, showing an increase in drug use from Month 1 to Month 6 ($t = 2.03$, 17 df, $p = .06$).

DISCUSSION

The goal of our study was to prospectively examine patterns of psychosocial treatment utilization by patients who have recently been hospitalized with comorbid bipolar disorder and substance dependence. The results indicate that the most commonly used treatments were individual psychotherapy and AA. Other treat-

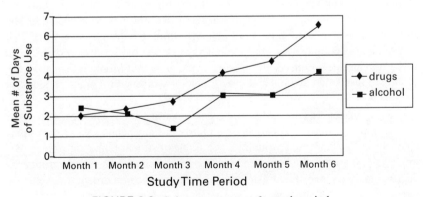

FIGURE 8.2. Substance use over 6-month period.

ments, such as family or group therapy, substance abuse counseling, and attendance at CA/NA, were much less frequently used.

These findings may be considered in light of suggestions that psychosocial interventions are thought to enhance bipolar patients' overall functioning.[9] Although rigorous clinical trials of the effectiveness of these interventions are lacking,[17] preliminary studies conducted with bipolar patients (with the substance use status unstated) suggest that interventions such as group and family therapy and psychoeducation regarding bipolar disorder may effectively reduce functional morbidity.[7,18] Moreover, some authors[10,19] have recommended that informing bipolar patients of risks associated with substance use ought to be an important component of treatment. Although we cannot ascertain the degree to which psychoeducation concerning bipolar and substance use disorders was part of the treatment received by our sample, patients in our study reported that individual psychotherapy focusing on both bipolar disorder and substance use occurred less often over time. We also found that most patients never made use of other psychosocial treatment modalities, such as family or group psychotherapy. Hence, it appears that these patients underutilized currently recommended treatments.

In addition to reductions in formal professional treatment, we found that AA attendance decreased over time. The association between AA attendance and substance use among bipolar patients was investigated by O'Sullivan and colleagues,[5] who interviewed bipolar patients with alcohol dependence at 3, 12, and 20 months following discharge from a psychiatric hospital. The percentage of bipolar patients reporting abstinence from alcohol decreased steadily from 75% at 3 months to 50% at 12 months and 42% at 20 months. Abstinent patients reported more frequent attendance at AA meetings and more frequent contact with their general practitioners than did the group that had relapsed. As with other populations of patients with substance use disorders,[20] it is thus possible that AA attendance may facilitate decreased substance use among patients diagnosed with bipolar and substance use disorders.

There were no statistically significant differences in mood symptoms or substance use between Month 1 and Month 6. However, it is noteworthy that number of days of alcohol and drug use increased over time, suggesting a clinically relevant concern. It is possible that this difference would have reached statistical significance with a larger number of patients. Similarly, even though the ASI alcohol and drug compositem were at relatively low severity levels at Months 1 and 6, the standard deviations of these scores were greater at Month 6 than at Month 1. This suggests that alcohol and drug problems worsened for some patients but became less severe for others.

Study limitations may affect the generalizability of our findings. This was a small sample composed of patients with fairly homogeneous sociodemographic characteristics who were hospitalized at a single treatment center and who agreed to participate in monthly assessments. The small sample prevents us from conducting analyses investigating any causal links between treatment use, self-help attendance, mood symptoms, and substance use. Moreover, it is unclear if these findings can be generalized to a larger population. Our results are also based solely on patients' retrospective self-reports. Without research data from the treating psychotherapists, we are uncertain to what degree the reported changes in psychotherapy and self-help group attendance were reflective of patients' formal treatment plans. Moreover, self-reports may be associated with biased reporting of substance use.[21] However, it is important to note that in other research conducted by our group with this population,[22] self-reports concerning substance use were highly valid when compared to data obtained from urine screens.

The advocacy by some authors[1,23] for specialized treatments for patients with bipolar disorder and substance use disorder does not appear to be matched by patients' perceptions of their treatment experiences over time. Given the generally poor prognosis associated with this combination of disorders,[2-4] the development of dually focused psychosocial treatments for this population may help improve their outcomes. Our group is currently in the process of testing the efficacy of a specialized group therapy for patients with comorbid bipolar and substance use disorders.[11] Future studies may focus on the effectiveness of such interventions and on other factors (e.g., characteristics of patients, clinicians, and systemic issues, such as access to adequate health insurance) that affect treatment utilization by patients diagnosed with these disorders.

REFERENCES

1. Brady KT, Lydiard RB. Bipolar affective disorder and substance abuse. *J Clin Pharmacol* 1992;12:17S–22S.
2. Keck PE Jr., McElroy SL, Strakowski SM, et al. 12-month outcome of patients with bipolar disorder following hospitalization for a manic or mixed episode. *Am J Psychiatry* 1998;155:646–652.
3. Keller MB, Lavori PW, Coryell W, et al. Differential outcome of pure manic, mixed/cycling, and pure depressive episodes in patients with bipolar illness. *JAMA* 1986;255:3138–3142.
4. Haywood TW, Kravitz HM, Grossman LS, et al. Predicting the "revolving door" phenomenon among patients with schizophrenic, schizoaffective, and affective disorders. *Am J Psychiatry* 1995;152:856–861.
5. O'Sullivan K, Rynne C, Miller J, et al. A follow-up study on alcoholics with and without coexisting affective disorder. *Br J Psychiatry* 1988;152:813–819.
6. Miklowitz DJ. Psychotherapy in combination with drug treatment for bipolar disorder. *J Clin Psychopharmacol* 1996;16(Suppl 1):56S–66S.
7. Parikh SV, Kusumakar V, Haslam DRS, et al. Psychosocial interventions as an adjunct to pharmacotherapy in bipolar disorder. *Can J Psychiatry* 1997;42(Suppl 2):74S–78S.
8. Najavits LM, Weiss RD. The role of psychotherapy in the treatment for substance use disorders. *Harv Rev Psychiatry* 1994;2:84–96.
9. Brady KT, Sonne SC, Anton R, et al. Valporate in the treatment of acute bipolar affective episodes complicated by substance abuse: a pilot study. *J Clin Psychiatry* 1995;56:118–121.
10. Goodwin FK, Jamison KR. *Manic-Depressive Illness*. New York: Oxford University Press; 1990.

11. Weiss RD, Najavits LM, Greenfield SF. A relapse prevention group for patients with bipolar and substance use disorders. *J Subst Abuse Treat* 1999;16:47–54.
12. First MB, Spitzer RL, Gibbon, M, et al. *Structured Clinical Interview for Axis I DSM-IV Disorders, Patient Edition (SCID-I/P, Version 2.0).* New York: Biometric Research, New York State Psychiatric Institute; 1994.
13. McLellan AT, Kushner H, Metzger D, et al. The fifth edition of the Addiction Severity Index. *J Subst Abuse Treat* 1992;9:199–213.
14. Hamilton M. A rating scale for depression. *J Neurol Neurosurg Psychiatry* 1960;23:56–62.
15. Young R, Biggs J, Ziegler V, et al. A rating scale for mania: reliability, validity, and sensitivity. *Br J Psychiatry* 1978;133:429–435.
16. McLellan AT, Alterman AI, Cacciola J, et al. A new measure of substance abuse treatment: initial studies of the Treatment Services Review. *J Nerv Ment Dis* 1992;180:101–110.
17. Prien RF, Potter WZ. NIMH workship on treatment of bipolar disorder. *Psychopharmacol Bull* 1990;26:409–427.
18. Solomon DA, Keitner GI, Miller IW, et al. Course of illness and maintenance treatments for patients with bipolar disorder. *J Clin Psychiatry* 1995;56:5–13.
19. Brady KT, Sonne SC. The relationship between substance abuse and bipolar disorder. *J Clin Psychiatry* 1995;56:19S–24S.
20. Miller NS, Ninonuevo FG, Klamen DL, et al. Integration of treatment and post-treatment variables in predicting results of abstinence-based outpatient treatment after one year. *J Psychoactive Drugs* 1997;29:239–248.
21. Babor TF, Stephens RS, Marlatt GA. Verbal report methods in clinical research on alcoholism: response bias and its minimization. *J Stud Alcohol* 1987;48:410–424.
22. Weiss RD, Greenfield SF, Najavits LM, et al. Medication compliance among patients with bipolar disorder and substance use disorder. *J Clin Psychiatry* 1998;59:172–174.
23. Strakowski SM, DelBello MP. The co-occurrence of bipolar and substance use disorders. *Clin Psychol Rev*, in press.

Chapter 9

Screening and Diagnosis of Anxiety and Mood Disorders in Substance Abuse Patients

Ingmar H. A. Franken, M.Sc.
Vincent M. Hendriks, Ph.D.

In the past two decades, the prevalence of comorbid psychopathological disorders in the population of substance abuse patients has received ample attention.[1,2] Studies indicate that the prevalence of co-occurring Axis I and Axis II disorders in substance abuse patients is high.[2,3] Moreover, these studies show that anxiety and mood disorders are the most prevalent comorbid Axis I disorders in this population. Patients with this psychiatric comorbidity have worse response rates in substance abuse treatment compared to patients with a substance abuse disorder only.[1,4,5] In addition, studies show that patients with poorer psychiatric functioning have increased risk for dropout during substance abuse treatment.[6] To adequately treat these co-occurring psychiatric disorders and consequently reduce substance abuse treatment dropout rates and improve outcome, it is of major importance to screen for these disorders early in treatment.

There are several methods for diagnosing psychiatric morbidity. The most common methods are psychiatric interviewing and (semi)structured interviewing. Psychiatric interviewing by a psychiatrist and the administration of structured interviews, such as the Composite International Diagnostic Interview (CIDI)[7] and the Structured Clinical Interview for *DSM-III-R* (SCID),[8] are time-consuming and therefore are often not applicable as standard assessments for all admissions in substance abuse services. In addition, the availability of trained psychiatric staff is often limited in substance abuse treatment services.[9] The result is that only small proportions of patients in substance abuse treatment services are being referred for additional psychiatric consultation.[10] An easy-to-use questionnaire as a screening instrument for comorbid psychiatric disorders is needed in order to improve clinical decisions on the referral process. Because psychiatric symptoms are often confounded by symptoms that are the result of entering a detoxification period (e.g., withdrawal, intoxication, need for help), it is unknown when these screening instruments have to be administered. Although this need for psychopathology screening instruments in substance abuse populations is stressed by several researchers,[11–13] studies addressing this early screening are scarce.

In the current study, the Symptom Checklist-90 Revised (SCL-90)[14] is used as a screening instrument for psychiatric comorbidity. SCL-90 is a frequently used and widely accepted screening instrument for psychiatric comorbidity. In the general population, SCL-90 is a reliable and valid instrument for screening on comorbidity.[15] In clinical samples, SCL-90 is found to be suitable for measuring neurotic symptoms.[16] Furthermore, in a selective sample of detoxified female alcoholics, Haver[17] found that SCL-90 holds high specificity and sensitivity in detecting psychiatric comorbidity.

Given the addressed problems, three research questions are investigated in the present study. First, is pre- and postdetoxification change in SCL-90 score in this population different for subjects with psychopathology compared to subjects without psychopathology? Second, what is the value of SCL-90 as a clinical diagnostic screening instrument for psychopathology, and does it provide additional diagnostic value for the frequently used Addiction Severity Index–Psychiatric Problems Scale (ASI-PSY)?[13] Third, what is the prevalence of anxiety and mood disorders in a clinical substance abuse population? Because mood and anxiety disorders are the most common nonsubstance abuse–related psychiatric disorder in this population,[3] the current study is limited to these disorders.

SUBJECTS

The study sample consisted of 116 subjects who where consecutively admitted to the inpatient substance abuse treatment program of Parnassia Psychiatric Centre, The Hague, Netherlands. All patients were clinically detoxified at time of admission to the program. Ages ranged from 15 to 47 years ($M = 29.8$; $SD = 7.5$). The percentage of male subjects was 84% (97 male, 19 female). The majority of subjects were white (87%); 3% were North African; 5%, Asian; and 5%, Surinamese. The majority (96%) were polydrug users. The mean age of first regular (i.e., at least 3 days a week) heroin use was 20.7 years ($n = 72$; range: 13–39; $SD = 4.6$), and the mean years of regular heroin use was 5.7 ($SD = 6.2$). The mean age of first regular cocaine use was 21.5 years ($n = 92$; range: 13–41; $SD = 5.5$), and the mean years of regular cocaine use was 5.8 ($SD = 5.1$). Of the cohort, 51% indicated that heroin was their drug of choice, followed by cocaine (23%), amphetamine (8%), methadone (3%), and other (15%). The main routes of administration were smoking (67%), injecting (11%), and intranasal use (12%). The mean ASI Drug Use Severity composite score (range: 0–1) was 0.51 (SD = 0.27). Although no single subject mentioned alcohol as drug of choice, 3 subjects (3%) met the *DSM-III-R* criteria for alcohol dependence as measured by CIDI.

INSTRUMENTS

The Addiction Severity Index (ASI) is a semistructured interview[18,19] that collects data on several areas of addiction-related problems. For the present study, only the ASI Drug Use Severity Composite Score (ASI-DRUG) and ASI Psychiatric Severity Composite Score (ASI-PSY) were used.

The revised SCL-90[14] is a multidimensional self-report instrument consisting of 90 items representing 8 psychopathological areas: depression, anxiety, agoraphobia, somatization, interpersonal sensitivity and paranoid ideation, hostility, cognitive-performance difficulties, and sleep disturbance. SCL-90 is a valid and reliable indicator of psychopathology[20] in the general population. In a recent study on SCL-90 factor structure in a comorbid substance abuse population, the authors concluded that SCL-90 subscales in this population may be distorted for the evaluation of psychiatric comorbidity, and the use of the total SCL-90 score is advised.[21] Therefore, in the present study the total score of SCL-90 was used as a general indicator of psychopathology.

The CIDI[7] was used to assess anxiety and mood disorders according to *DSM-III-R* criteria.[22] Both lifetime and current prevalence were assessed. The diagnosis was current when criteria were met in the 30 days before the interview. A positive anxiety disorder diagnosis consisted of at least one of the *DSM-III-R* anxiety disorders. A positive diagnosis of mood disorders consisted of at least one of the *DSM-III-R* mood disorders, including bipolar disorders and dysthymia. CIDI results in a dichotomous score, indicating presence or absence of the psychiatric diagnosis. The CIDI diagnosis—in particular, anxiety, mood disorders, and substance abuse—provides good concordance with assessment by clinicians.[23,24]

PROCEDURES

Before entering detoxification treatment, the SCL-90 questionnaire, ASI, and background variables were administered by trained members of the intake staff. After detoxification and when the withdrawal symptoms had waned, a trained psychologist administered the CIDI. In addition, the SCL-90 was completed for a second time during this postdetoxification period. The mean time in detoxification was 19.8 days (SD = 17.8). This time in detoxification was not different for persons with or without a current co-occurring psychiatric disorder, $t(114) = .91, p = .366$.

ANALYSIS

Change in SCL-90 scores is analyzed with 2 × 2 mixed design analysis of variance (ANOVA) with psychiatric comorbidity (presence vs. absence of an anxiety or mood disorder) as between subjects variable and time (pre- vs. postdetoxification) as within subjects variable. In addition, change in SCL-90 scores is analyzed for anxiety, mood, and both disorders separately by two one-way ANOVAs with the pre- and postdetoxification SCL-90 scores as a dependent variable. In order to analyze the diagnostic value of SCL-90 as a screening instrument for psychiatric comorbidity, receiver-operating characteristic (ROC) curve analysis is employed. ROC curves provide a pure index of accuracy of clinically employed instruments by combining sensitivity and specificity scores of the instrument.[25] Furthermore, clinical performance of the SCL-90 postdetoxification score as a screening instrument for psychiatric comorbidity is compared with predetoxification SCL-90 and ASI-PSY by employment of analysis of areas under ROC curve.[26] For all the screening instrument scores, sensitivity and specificity of clinical relevant cutoff points are computed. Determination of clinical relevant cutoff scores for screening instruments is done by keeping sensitivity high[25] in order to avoid false negative cases as much as possible. In this study, the cutoff score and specificity of the instruments are computed with the use of a sensitivity of at least 90%. All statistical testing was two-tailed with a significance level of p < .05.

RESULTS

Prevalence of Psychiatric Comorbidity

The prevalence of anxiety and mood disorders is summarized in Table 9.1. As shown in this table, the majority of subjects (69.8%) had a lifetime anxiety or mood disorder. Current prevalence of any nonsubstance-related diagnosis was 46.6%. Both lifetime prevalence (53.4%) and current prevalence (38.8%) of anxiety disorders were more common than mood disorders, 49.1% and 21.6%, respectively. Current co-occurring anxiety and mood disorders were observed in 46.6%.

Psychiatric Disorder and Change in SCL-90 Score

In the 2 × 2 mixed-design ANOVA, a significant main effect of psychiatric comorbidity on SCL-90 score was observed, $F(1,114) = 13.57$, $p < .001$. The SCL-90 total score of subjects without psychiatric comorbidity ($M = 154.1$) was significantly lower than subjects with an anxiety or mood disorder ($M = 185.0$). In addition, a significant main effect of time on the SCL-90 total score has been observed. After detoxification, a general decline was observed in the SCL-90 score compared to predetoxification ($M_{pre} = 181.8$ vs. $M_{post} = 155.7$).

TABLE 9.1. *DSM-III-R* Anxiety and Mood Disorders (CIDI)[a]

Disorder	Lifetime Prevalence (%)	Current Prevalence (%)
Anxiety disorders		
Panic disorder without agoraphobia	3.4	2.6
Generalized anxiety disorder	10.3	6.1
Panic disorder with agoraphobia	5.2	4.3
Agoraphobia without panic disorder	15.5	5.1
Social phobia	31.0	18.1
Simple phobia	32.8	21.5
Obsessive compulsive disorder	4.3	2.6
Any anxiety disorder	53.4	38.8
Mood disorders		
Dysthymia	17.2	13.8
Major depression	35.3	9.5
Bipolar disorder	7.8	5.2
Any mood disorder	49.1	21.6
Any anxiety or mood disorder	69.8	46.6

[a]$n = 116$.

A significant interaction effect for time × psychiatric comorbidity was observed, $F(1,114) = 4.75, p < .001$. As shown in Figure 9.1, the decline in the SCL-90 score is more pronounced for subjects without psychiatric comorbidity compared to persons with psychiatric comorbidity.

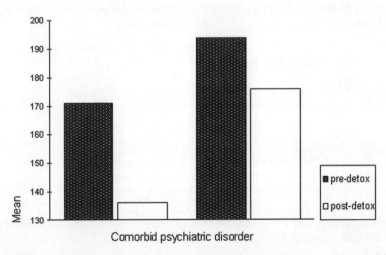

FIGURE 9.1. SCL-90 scores before and after detoxification of subjects with and without psychiatric comorbidity.

TABLE 9.2.　Pre- and Postdetoxification SCL-90 Scores of Substance Abuse Patients by Psychiatric Disorder

	N	Mean	*SD*
Predetoxification SCL-90 Score			
No anxiety or mood disorders	62	172.4	52.0
Mood disorder	9	171.0	44.8
Anxiety disorder	29	185.4	54.5
Anxiety and mood disorder	16	217.9	48.4
Total	116	181.8	53.4
Postdetoxification SCL-90 Score			
No anxiety or mood disorders	62	137.7	36.6
Mood disorder	9	160.3	33.2
Anxiety disorder	29	165.4	44.9
Anxiety and mood disorder	16	205.2	60.4
Total	116	155.7	47.9

Mood vs. Anxiety Disorder

Table 9.2 shows mean SCL-90 scores by psychopathology and detoxification status. Subanalysis showed a main effect of group on the SCL-90 score both predetoxification, $F(3) = 3.46$; $p < .019$, and postdetoxification, $F(3) = 11.49$; $p < .001$. Post hoc Scheffé tests demonstrate that subjects with both an anxiety and a mood disorder have significantly higher SCL-90 predetoxification scores ($p < .024$) than subjects without a disorder. No other group differences were found. Furthermore, Scheffé tests showed higher postdetoxification SCL-90 scores for subjects with both disorders than subjects without disorders ($p < .001$) and anxiety disorders ($p < .033$). Subjects without disorders had lower postdetoxification SCL-90 scores than subjects with an anxiety disorder ($p = .044$).

SCL-90 Clinical Performance

Specificity and sensitivity of both the pre- and postdetoxification SCL-90 scores for a mood or anxiety disorder are summarized in Table 9.3. Analysis of areas

TABLE 9.3.　Cutoff Score and Related Sensitivity and Specificity of Three Screening Instruments

	Cutoff Score	Sensitivity (95% CI)	Specificity (95% CI)
Predetox SCL-90	>123	92.7 (82.4–97.9)	19.7 (10.6–31.8)
Postdetox SCL-90	>24	90.9 (80.0–96.9)	49.2 (36.1–62.3)
ASI-PSY	>0	91.3 (79.2–97.5)	24.1 (13.5–37.6)

under ROC curve shows that the SCL-90 postdetoxification score, area = 0.751, is a significantly better indicator of mood or anxiety disorder than the predetoxification SCL-90 score, area = 0.638 (difference = 0.114, 95% CI = 0.018–0.209, $z = 2,54$, $p = 0.006$). In addition, the SCL-90 predetoxification score is a significantly better indicator of psychiatric comorbidity than the ASI-PSY score (difference = 0.120, 95% CI = –0.006–0.064, $z = 2.10$, $p = 0.018$). ROC curves of the screening instruments are displayed in Figure 9.2. A larger area under the curve indicates better diagnostic characteristics in terms of sensitivity and specificity.

DISCUSSION

The present study underscores the finding of previous studies that the prevalence of anxiety and mood disorders in a substance abuse population in treatment is high.[27] In our study sample, almost half (47%) of the subjects had a current anxiety or mood disorder, and more than half (70%) of the subjects had a lifetime disorder. Furthermore, the present results indicate that the ASI-PSY score is a limited indicator of psychiatric comorbidity. When a predetoxification screening for psychopathology is warranted, the present results show that the use of SCL-90 is preferable

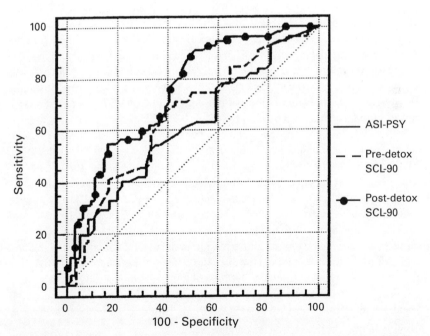

FIGURE 9.2. ROC curve indicating sensitivity and specificity of 3 screening scores of comorbid psychiatric disorder.

to ASI-PSY. Of the three screening scores under study, the postdetoxification SCL-90 score is found to be the most valid screening instrument for diagnosis of anxiety and mood disorders in a clinical substance abuse population.

One of the limitations of the present study is that the time in detoxification was variable. The mean time in detoxification was of relatively long duration—that is, 20 days. Treatment effects during this detoxification period possibly confounded current findings. However, time in detoxification was not found to be different for persons with or without comorbid disorders. In addition, in a previous study we found no differences on psychopathology (SCL-90 and ASI-PSY) between detoxification completers and noncompleters.[28]

The detoxification regimen for opiate-dependent patients consisted of a rapid reduction schedule during the first week. Benzodiazepines were used very occasionally when necessary. It is possible that the use of these medications affects self-reported psychiatric symptoms. However, in the present study we used the postdetoxification SCL-90 score as the second measurement. At this point, all medications were stopped.

ASI is a frequently used instrument in substance abuse treatment settings. Although the ASI-PSY scale is a valid and reliable indicator of psychological distress,[19] the present results show this scale has considerable limitations when used as a screening instrument for comorbid anxiety and mood disorders in clinical practice. When sensitivity of ASI-PSY is set on 90%, the cutoff score is zero, and specificity is low (24%). These findings correspond with Eland-Goossensen et al.,[29] who found moderate sensitivity and low specificity of the ASI-PSY score. In contrast to SCL-90 scores, no postdetoxification ASI-PSY scale was administered. According to the goals of ASI and clinical practice, the instrument has to be administered before detoxification in order to obtain valid scores.[18] Nonetheless, it may be that the ASI-PSY scale can validly be assessed in an inpatient sample. Further study on the value of the postdetoxification ASI-PSY score in screening on comorbid psychopathology is needed.

Detoxification of substance abuse patients without a co-occurring psychiatric disorder results in a considerable decline of SCL-90 scores.[30] This decline in SCL score is in line with findings of other studies that address the use of self-report questionnaires in drug abuse patients. For example, Husband et al.[31] found a significant decline in self-reported dysphoria, as measured by BDI, after treatment entry in an inner-city cocaine addict population. Strain et al.[32] found a comparable decline in depressive symptoms in opiate addicts during the first 7 days of admission. It has to be noted that regression to the mean effects[33] may be responsible for the observed decline. However, the difference between the sharp decline in the SCL-90 score in patients without psychiatric comorbidity and the more slight decline in patients with comorbid diagnosis may indicate that psychopathological symptoms as measured by SCL-90 are caused by factors other than psychiatric comorbidity.

As with ASI-PSY, the use of SCL-90 as a predetoxification indicator of psychiatric comorbidity is limited. When sensitivity of this measure is kept high, specificity is low (20%), resulting in a high number of false positive scores. An earlier study already demonstrated that the use of the predetoxification SCL-90 is limited in predicting detoxification outcome.[28] In the present study, ROC analysis shows that the postdetoxification SCL-90 score is a more accurate screening score than both the predetoxification SCL-90 score and the ASI-PSY score. Postdetoxification SCL-90 scores differentiate between patients with comorbid anxiety and mood disorder. Patients with an anxiety disorder had significantly higher SCL-90 scores than patients without a comorbid disorder and significantly lower scores than patients with both anxiety and mood disorder. For patients with a mood disorder only, no significant effect could be found. It is likely that the relatively small number of mood-disorder patients in the population under study resulted in too low a statistical power to detect significant results in this subgroup.

The choice of a certain cutoff score should take into consideration the nature of the sample and the purpose for which the instrument is being used. For screening purposes in clinical populations, for example, to determine the necessity of additional clinical evaluation, sensitivity is of primary interest. Although elevation of cutoff scores in SCL-90 results in fewer false positive diagnoses, it also reduces sensitivity and consequently usefulness as a screening instrument. Although it is the most accurate screening instrument in this study, the postdetoxification SCL-90 holds merely moderate specificity (50%); applying this instrument in clinical practice results in a substantial reduction (50%) of patients unnecessarily referred for further psychiatric diagnostic evaluation.

Additional study on the usefulness of screening instruments for psychiatric comorbidity in this specific population is needed. As stated at the beginning of this chapter, the number of referrals to specialized clinicians for psychiatric diagnosing is relatively low. An adequate screening instrument that combines high sensitivity with improved specificity will result in higher efficiency and, consequently, may result in a higher number of referrals of patients with comorbidity to clinical professionals. The results of the present study indicate that the postdetoxification SCL-90 score may be an important starting point. Future studies may address improvement in specificity of this score by modifying test instructions, for example, excluding symptoms that are drug related or an adapted time frame.

Many clinical treatment settings use information regarding comorbidity in the decision making of adequate treatment referrals. This decision is often made before the patient is detoxified. However, screening instruments that are used in this preclinical stage are possibly confounded by such factors as withdrawal symptoms, need for help, and substance intoxication.

REFERENCES

1. Rounsaville BJ, Kosten TR, Weissman MM, et al. Prognostic significance of psychopathology in treated opiate addicts: a 2.5-year follow-up study. *Arch Gen Psychiatry* 1986;43:739–745.

2. Brooner RK, King VL, Kidorf M, et al. Psychiatric and substance use comorbidity among treatment-seeking opioid abusers. *Arch Gen Psychiatry* 1997;54:71–80.
3. Hendriks VM. Psychiatric disorders in a Dutch addict population: rates and correlates of DSM-III diagnosis. *J Consult Clin Psychol* 1990;58:158–165.
4. Rounsaville BJ, et al. Diagnosis and symptoms of depression in opiate addicts: course and relationship to treatment outcome. *Arch Gen Psychiatry* 1982;39:151–156.
5. McLellan AT, Luborsky L, Woody GE, et al. Predicting response to alcohol and drug abuse treatment: role of psychiatric severity. *Arch Gen Psychiatry* 1983;40:620–625.
6. Carroll KM, Power M-ED, Bryant KJ, et al. One-year follow-up status of treatment-seeking cocaine abusers: psychopathology and dependence severity as predictors of outcome. *J Nerv Ment Dis* 1993;181:71–79.
7. Robins LN, Wing J, Wittchen HU, et al. The Composite International Diagnostic Interview: an epidemiologic instrument suitable for use in conjunction with different diagnostic systems and in different cultures. *Arch Gen Psychiatry* 1988;45:1069–1077.
8. Spitzer RL, Williams JB, Gibbon M, et al. The Structured Clinical Interview for DSM-III-R (SCID). I: History, rationale, and description. *Arch Gen Psychiatry* 1992;49:624–629.
9. Keaney F, Crimlisk H, Bearn J. Comorbidity of mental disorders with substance misuse. *Br J Psychiatry* 1997;171:484–485.
10. Craig TJ, Dibuono M. Recognition of comorbid psychopathology by staff of a drug detoxification unit. *Am J Addict* 1996;5:76–80.
11. Hall W, Farrell M. Comorbidity of mental disorders with substance misuse. *Br J Psychiatry* 1997;171:4–5.
12. Scott J, Gilvarry E, Farrell M. Managing anxiety and depression in alcohol and drug dependence. *Addict Behav* 1998;23:919–931.
13. Dixon L, Myers P, Johnson J, et al. Screening for mental illness with the Addiction Severity Index. *Am J Addict* 1996;5:301–307.
14. Derogatis LR. *The Symptom Checklist 90-R: Administration, Scoring, and Procedures Manual, Third Edition.* Minneapolis, MN: National Computer Systems; 1994.
15. Koeter MW. Validity of the GHQ and SCL Anxiety and Depression scales: a comparative study. *J Affect Disord* 1992;24:271–279.
16. Peveler RC, Fairburn CG. Measurement of neurotic symptoms by self-report questionnaire: validity of the SCL-90R. *Psychol Med* 1990;20:873–879.
17. Haver B. Screening for psychiatric comorbidity among female alcoholics: the use of a questionnaire (SCL-90) among women early in their treatment programme. *Alcohol Alcohol* 1997;32:725–730.
18. McLellan AT, Luborski L, Woody GE, et al. An improved diagnostic evaluation instrument for substance abuse patients: the Addiction Severity Index. *J Nerv Ment Dis* 1980;168:26–33.
19. Hendriks VM, Kaplan CD, Van Limbeek J, et al. The Addiction Severity Index: reliability and validity in a Dutch addict population. *J Subst Abuse Treat* 1989;6:133–141.
20. Arrindell WA, Ettema H. Dimensionele structuur, betrouwbaarheid en validiteit van de Nederlandse bewerking van de Symptom Checklist-SCL90 (Dimensional structure, reliability, and validity of the Dutch Symptom Checklist-SCL90). *Ned Tijdsch Psychol* 1981;36:77–108.
21. Zack M, Toneatto T, Streiner DL. The SCL-90 factor structure in comorbid substance abusers. *J Subst Abuse* 1998;10:85–101.
22. American Psychiatric Association. *Diagnostic and Statistical Manual of Mental Disorders: DSM-III-R, Third Edition Revised.* Washington, DC: American Psychiatric Association; 1987.
23. Janca A, Robins LN, Cottler LB, et al. Clinical observation of assessment using the

Composite International Diagnostic Interview (CIDI): an analysis of the CIDI field trials–wave II at the St. Louis site. *Br J Psychiatry* 1992;160:815–818.
24. Janca A, Robins LN, Bucholz KK, et al. Comparison of Composite International Diagnostic Interview and clinical DSM-III-R criteria checklist diagnoses. *Acta Psychiatr Scand* 1992;85:440–443.
25. Zweig MH, Campbell G. Reciever-operator characteristics (ROC) plots: a fundamental evaluation tool in clinical medicine. *Clin Chem* 1993;39:561–577.
26. Hanley JA, McNeil BJ. A method of comparing the areas under receiver operating characteristic curves derived from the same cases. *Radiology* 1983;148:839–843.
27. Regier DA, Farmer ME, Rae DS, et al. Comorbidity of mental disorders with alcohol and other drug abuse. *JAMA* 1990;264:2511–2518.
28. Franken IHA, Hendriks VM. Predicting outcome of inpatient detoxification of substance abusers. *Psychiatr Serv* 1999;50:813–817.
29. Eland-Goossensen A, Vandegoor I, Garretsen H, et al. Screening for psychopathology in the clinical practice. *J Subst Abuse Treat* 1997;14:585–591.
30. Franken IHA, Hendriks VM. Comorbidity of mental disorders with substance misuse. *Br J Psychiatry* 1997;171:485.
31. Husband SD, Marlowe DB, Lamb RJ, et al. Decline in self-reported dysphoria after treatment entry in inner-city cocaine addicts. *J Consult Clin Psychol* 1996;64:221–224.
32. Strain EC, Stitzer ML, Bigelow GE. Early treatment time course of depressive symptoms in opiate addicts. *J Nerv Ment Dis* 1991;179:215–221.
33. Yudkin PL, Stratton IM. How to deal with regression to the mean in intervention studies. *Lancet* 1996;347:241–243.

Substance Use Disorders in Patients with Posttraumatic Stress Disorder

A Review of the Literature

Leslie K. Jacobsen, M.D.
Steven M. Southwick, M.D.
Thomas R. Kosten, M.D.

Substance use disorders, particularly abuse of and dependence on central nervous system (CNS) depressants, are common in patients with posttraumatic stress disorder (PTSD). This chapter reviews clinical, epidemiologic, and neurobiologic studies relevant to the problem of comorbid PTSD and substance use disorders and discusses the clinical implications of these findings.

CLINICAL PHENOMENOLOGY AND EPIDEMIOLOGY

PTSD develops in some people after exposure to a severe traumatic event. The *DSM-IV* diagnosis of PTSD consists of symptoms in three clusters: (1) reexperiencing symptoms, including intrusive recollections of the trauma that are triggered

Received May 11, 2000; revision received Aug. 22, 2000; accepted Nov. 17, 2000. From the Department of Psychiatry, Yale University School of Medicine, New Haven, CT, and the VA Connecticut Healthcare System. Address correspondence to Dr. Jacobsen, Department of Psychiatry (116A), VA Connecticut Healthcare System, Yale University–West Haven Campus, 950 Campbell Ave., West Haven, CT 06516; leslie.jacobsen@yale.edu (e-mail).

Supported in part by grants DA-00167, DA-04060, and DA-09250 from the National Institute on Drug Abuse.

by exposure to cues symbolizing the trauma; (2) avoidance symptoms, which involve diminished participation in activities and avoidance of thoughts, people, places, and memories associated with the trauma; and (3) arousal symptoms, which include difficulty sleeping, irritability, difficulty concentrating, hypervigilance, and exaggerated startle response.

Although intoxication and withdrawal symptoms vary across abused substances, all substance use disorders share key features. They include a maladaptive pattern of substance use leading to failure to fulfill work, school, or home obligations; legal problems; and substance-related interpersonal problems. Substance dependence further includes tolerance, withdrawal symptoms upon cessation of use, unsuccessful efforts to control use, and continued use despite persistent substance-related physical or psychological problems.

Persons with PTSD have elevated rates of comorbid psychiatric disorders. Studies of both combat veterans and civilians with PTSD have demonstrated that alcohol abuse or dependence is the most common co-occurring disorder among men with PTSD, followed by depression, other anxiety disorders, conduct disorder, and nonalcohol substance abuse or dependence.[1,2] Among women with PTSD, rates of comorbid depression and other anxiety disorders are highest, followed by alcohol abuse and dependence.[1,2] High rates of comorbidity of PTSD and substance use disorders were first reported in war-related studies, in which as many as 75% of combat veterans with lifetime PTSD also met criteria for alcohol abuse or dependence.[2] Among civilian populations, estimates of the prevalence of lifetime substance use disorders have ranged from 21.6% to 43.0% in persons with PTSD, compared with 8.1% to 24.7% in persons without PTSD.[1,3,4] Similarly, among substance abusers in the general population, the reported rate of PTSD is 8.3%.[5] Rates of PTSD appear to be higher among patients in inpatient substance abuse treatment (up to 42.5%)[6] and among pregnant women in residential treatment for substance abuse (62%).[7] Surveys of substance-dependent adolescents have also found rates of PTSD ranging up to 19.2%.[8]

Patients with both PTSD and a substance use disorder have significantly higher rates of comorbid Axis I and II disorders, psychosocial and medical problems, substance- or alcohol-related inpatient admissions, and relapse to substance use, compared with patients whose substance use is not complicated by PTSD.[4,9] Furthermore, patients with PTSD and substance use disorders tend to suffer from more severe PTSD symptoms, particularly those in the avoidance and arousal symptom clusters, than do patients with PTSD alone.[10] Conversely, one longitudinal study of patients with PTSD and a comorbid substance use disorder found at 6-month posttreatment follow-up that patients whose PTSD symptoms had remitted reported significantly less substance use than did patients with unremitted PTSD.[11]

RELATIONSHIP OF SUBSTANCE USE TO PTSD SYMPTOMS

Elevated rates of comorbid depressive and anxiety disorders in patients with PTSD greatly complicate any effort to develop a model of the relationship between PTSD and substance use. High rates of comorbidity suggest that PTSD and substance use disorders are functionally related to one another. Two primary pathways have been described to explain these high rates of comorbidity. In the first, substance abuse precedes PTSD. To sustain their habit, some substance abusers repetitively place themselves in dangerous situations and, as a result, experience high levels of physical and psychological trauma.[5] For example, in a study of patients with PTSD and comorbid cocaine abuse, PTSD developed as a result of trauma sustained in the context of procurement and use of cocaine.[12] Given that chronic substance use can lead to higher levels of arousal and anxiety as well as to sensitization of neurobiologic stress systems,[13] substance abuse may result in a higher level of vulnerability to development of PTSD after exposure to trauma.

In the second pathway, PTSD precedes development of substance use disorders. In this model, the use of substances is a form of self-medication. Patients report that CNS depressants, such as alcohol, cannabis, opioids, and benzodiazepines, acutely improve PTSD symptoms.[14] Consistent with this, patients with PTSD report that onset and severity of substance abuse parallel the onset and escalation of PTSD symptoms.[14] In addition, clinical evidence suggests that the choice of substances of abuse (CNS depressants vs. CNS stimulants) may stem from the particular constellation of PTSD symptoms that patients experience. For example, PTSD patients with alcohol dependence exhibit significantly more arousal symptoms than do PTSD patients with cocaine dependence.[10]

In the second model, withdrawal from substances, particularly CNS depressants, may initiate a cycle that perpetuates relapse and continued substance use. The withdrawal syndromes associated with many CNS depressants overlap extensively with the arousal symptoms of PTSD[15] (Table 10.1). Substances may be taken initially to ameliorate PTSD symptoms. As noted earlier, patients with PTSD have reported that CNS depressants acutely provide symptom relief.[14] Furthermore, objectively measured startle responses are reduced by alcohol.[16] However, the physiologic arousal resulting from substance withdrawal may have an additive

TABLE 10.1. Symptoms of Increased Arousal in PTSD and Symptoms Associated With Withdrawal From CNS Depressants[a]

PSD Symptoms of Increased Arousal	Symptoms of CNS Depressant Withdrawal
Difficulty falling/staying asleep	Insomnia
Irritability or outbursts of anger	Phychomotor agitation
Difficulty concentrating	Anxiety
Hypervigilance	Autonomic hyperactivity
Exaggerated startle response	Increased hand tremor
	Transient hallucinations
	Nausea or vomiting
	Seizures

[a]From the *DSM-IV* criteria for PTSD, alcohol withdrawal, and sedative, hypnotic, or anxiolytic withdrawal.

effect with arousal symptoms stemming from PTSD. The resulting hyperaroused state may serve as a conditioned reminder of traumatic events and thus precipitate an increase in reexperiencing symptoms. Exacerbation of PTSD symptoms may then prompt relapse to substance use in an attempt to self-medicate. Thus, for the PTSD patient who already has symptoms of arousal, the additional arousal that accompanies withdrawal from substances may be intolerable. Alternatively, substances may be used to cope with the traumatic event itself.[17] This pattern may particularly apply when trauma that leads to PTSD occurs during adulthood. The initial calming effects from substance use may cue patients to resume substance use when PTSD symptoms reemerge.

Most published data support the second model, in which substance use follows or parallels traumatic exposure and the development of PTSD.[18] In a longitudinal study conducted by Chilcoat and Breslau,[19] 1,007 adults were reevaluated 3 and 5 years after an initial assessment. The researchers found that preexisting substance abuse did not increase subjects' risk of subsequent exposure to trauma or their risk of developing PTSD after exposure to trauma. The relationship between exposure to trauma and increased risk for development of a substance use disorder was found to be specific to PTSD, as exposure to trauma without subsequent development of PTSD did not increase risk for development of a substance use disorder.[19] Of note is one study of patients with cocaine dependence and PTSD that found patients in whom PTSD preceded the onset of cocaine use were significantly more likely to suffer from comorbid major depression and to use benzodiazepines and opiates than were patients in whom PTSD developed after the onset of cocaine use.[12]

PATHOPHYSIOLOGY

Our review of the literature on the pathophysiologic basis of comorbid PTSD and addiction selectively focuses on studies of the hypothalamic-pituitary-adrenal (HPA) axis and the noradrenergic system, as these have been most extensively studied in PTSD. It must be emphasized that many other neurobiological systems are involved in both the acute and chronic adaptation to stress and to substance use. These systems include the dopaminergic, gamma-aminobutyric acid, benzodiazepine, and serotonergic systems, as well as the thyroid axis. Interactions among these systems in patients with comorbid PTSD and substance dependence are enormously complex. Thus, the potential relationships we discuss between the HPA axis, the noradrenergic system, and symptoms in patients with comorbid PTSD and substance use disorders should be viewed as one part of a far more complex whole.

HPA Axis in PTSD and Addiction

In humans and animals, acute stress elicits a cascade of neurohormonal events, including increased turnover of norepinephrine in terminal projection regions of the locus ceruleus and liberation of hypothalamic corticotropin-releasing hormone (CRH) into the pituitary portal system, which stimulates release of ACTH from the pituitary, in turn triggering release of cortisol (human) or corticosterone (rat) from the adrenals.[20] Animal and human research has implicated this cascade in the pathophysiology of both substance use disorders and PTSD.

Humans with substance dependence most frequently identify stress and negative mood states as reasons for relapse and ongoing substance abuse.[21] Recently, a personalized stress imagery task was shown to reliably increase cocaine craving and salivary cortisol in cocaine-dependent patients.[22] Animal studies have shown that stress induces relapse to heroin and to cocaine self-administration in rats trained to self-administer these substances and then subjected to a prolonged drug-free period.[23,24] Similarly, in animals naive to illicit substances, a large range of stressors increases the proclivity toward drug self-administration.[25] Initial work on the pathophysiology of this phenomenon indicated that stress-induced or stress-enhanced drug self-administration is mediated by corticosterone.[26]

Evidence has accumulated to support a role for CRH in mediating the effects of stress on drug self-administration. Central, but not peripheral, administration of CRH has been shown to induce a long-lasting enhancement (sensitization) of the locomotor response to d-amphetamine,[27] and pretreatment with a CRH antagonist has been shown to block the development of stress-induced sensitization to d-amphetamine.[28] Indeed, central administration of anti-CRH antibody or the CRH receptor antagonist alpha-helical CRH has been found to block the locomotor hyperactivity induced by cocaine.[29]

Withdrawal from chronic cocaine or alcohol administration in rats produces anxiety-like behavior and decreased exploration associated with selective increases in CRH in the hypothalamus, amygdala, and basal forebrain.[30,31] Pretreatment with anti-CRH immunoserum or alpha-helical CRH, blocking the effects of CRH, completely prevents the development of these withdrawal-associated behaviors.[30] Consistent with these observations, CSF CRH is elevated in humans in acute alcohol withdrawal and then normalizes or decreases below normal levels with extended abstinence and resolution of withdrawal symptoms.[32] Shaham and colleagues[33] found that intracerebroventricular injection of CRH reinstated heroin seeking after extinction in rats trained to self-administer the drug. In addition, alpha-helical CRH attentuated the reinstatement effect of foot-shock stress.[33] Neither adrenalectomy nor chronic or acute exposure to the corticosterone synthesis inhibitor metyrapone interfered with the reinstatement effects of priming injections of heroin or of foot-shock stress. A potent, selective CRF1 receptor antagonist, CP-154,526, has been found to attenuate reinstatement of drug seeking induced by foot-shock stress after up to 14 days of extinction in rats trained to self-administer heroin or cocaine.[34]

Findings from both animal and human studies of the effects of chronic stress or PTSD on HPA axis function vary depending on the experimental paradigm used or the population studied. In patients with PTSD, elevated,[35] reduced,[36] and normal[37] levels of cortisol secretion have been reported. A series of studies performed by Yehuda and colleagues demonstrated that patients with PTSD have an elevated number of lymphocyte glucocorticoid receptors,[38] enhanced suppression of cortisol after administration of dexamethasone,[39] a greater than normal decrease in the number of lymphocyte glucocorticoid receptors after administration of dexamethasone,[39] and higher than normal increases in ACTH after metyrapone blockade of cortisol synthesis.[40] All of these findings suggest that glucocorticoid negative feedback is enhanced in PTSD.

Animal studies examining the effects of uncontrollable stress on HPA axis function have reported initial increases of corticosterone secretion, followed by normalization of corticosterone secretion with ongoing chronic stress.[41] However, some investigators have failed to demonstrate normalization of corticosterone secretion with chronic uncontrollable stress,[42] particularly in animals that have been reared under stressful conditions[43] or when levels of chronic stress are high.[44] In a pattern similar to that found in humans with PTSD, animals subjected to a single episode of prolonged stress and then briefly restressed after a stress-free period showed enhancement of glucocorticoid negative feedback.[45]

Although both animal and human studies have suggested that glucocorticoid negative feedback may be enhanced in PTSD, the implications of these observations for CRH secretion in this disorder are unclear. As noted earlier, CRH-producing cells and CRH receptors exist both in the hypothalamus and in extrahypothalamic sites. Findings from some studies have suggested that hypothalamic and extrahypothalamic CRH-producing cells may respond differently to corticosterone. Specifically, corticosterone appears to restrain hypothalamic CRH-producing cells while stimulating extrahypothalamic CRH-producing cells, particularly those in the amygdala.[46] Replacement of corticosterone in adrenalectomized rats decreases CRH production in the parvocellular nucleus of the hypothalamus while increasing CRH production in the central nucleus of the amygdala.[47] This region-specific pattern of regulation is also seen in adrenally intact rats treated with high-stress levels of corticosterone for extended periods of time.[48] Thus, while glucocorticoid feedback may decrease CRH production and release in the hypothalamus, it may stimulate CRH production and release in other brain regions, including the amygdala. This possibility has been addressed in two studies of patients with PTSD: one that examined CSF concentrations of CRH at a single time point[49] and one that examined CSF concentrations of CRH at serial time points over a 6-hour period.[37] Both found significantly higher levels of CSF CRH in patients with PTSD than in normal comparison subjects. However, although elevated CSF CRH suggests that brain CRH may be elevated, the specific brain tissues producing CRH elevations cannot be determined from CSF data alone.

The possibility that brain CRH levels are elevated in PTSD is of great interest because of a rich preclinical literature indicating that elevated levels of CRH in the brain, particularly in the amygdala, potentiate fear-related behavioral responses, including the startle response.[50] These anxiogenic effects of CRH are reversed by administration of CRH antagonists.[50] As noted earlier, findings from animal and human studies have supported a role for CRH in mediating some effects of drugs of abuse, including stress- or priming-induced relapse to drug self-administration and symptoms of withdrawal.[27,28,32–34] Thus, elevated levels of CRH in the brain in PTSD may mediate the symptoms of hyperarousal as well as the increased risk for substance abuse and dependence seen in this disorder. More specifically, elevated levels of CRH in the brain in PTSD may enhance the euphorigenic properties of certain drugs, such as stimulants, and may worsen the severity of withdrawal symptoms, thereby prompting patients to relapse to drug use. Conversely, brain CRH elevations induced by withdrawal from substance use may exacerbate symptoms of hyperarousal, which could trigger other symptoms of PTSD, prompting relapse to substance use.

Noradrenergic System in PTSD and Addiction

During chronic uncontrollable stress, norepinephrine turnover increases in specific brain regions, including the locus ceruleus, hypothalamus, hippocampus, amygdala, and cerebral cortex.[51] Evidence for noradrenergic dysregulation in patients with PTSD has included elevated 24-hour urinary epinephrine and norepinephrine excretion, a lower than normal number of platelet $alpha_2$-adrenergic receptors, elevated 24-hour plasma norepinephrine, and exaggerated cardiovascular and 3-methoxy-4-hydroxy-phenylglycol (MHPG, a norepinephrine metabolite) responses to intravenous yohimbine.[52] Noradrenergic dysregulation has also been reported during states of withdrawal from chronic self-administration of alcohol and other abused substances. The levels of noradrenaline, norepinephrine, and MHPG in both plasma and CSF have been found to be increased and the number of platelet $alpha_2$-adrenergic receptors decreased in alcoholics during acute withdrawal.[53,54] The severity of alcoholic withdrawal symptoms has been positively correlated with the concentration of MHPG in CSF.[54] Evidence for noradrenergic dysregulation in opiate withdrawal has included findings of elevated plasma MHPG in humans and elevated plasma and brain MHPG in animals.[55,56] The level of noradrenergic activity in animals was significantly correlated with the severity of withdrawal symptoms.[56] These findings have prompted the use of the $alpha_2$-adrenergic receptor agonist clonidine in the treatment of both opiate withdrawal symptoms and PTSD.[57,58]

Noradrenergic System/HPA Axis Interactions

Evidence that brain CRH and noradrenergic systems modulate each other has been reported. Stress has been shown to increase CRH levels in the locus ceruleus,[59] a primary source of noradrenergic projections to all cortices as well as to the thalamus and hypothalamus, while intraventricular administration of CRH has been found to increase the discharge rates of locus ceruleus neurons and to increase norepinephrine turnover in the hippocampus, hypothalamus, and prefrontal cortex.[60–62] Conversely, stress-induced activation of the locus ceruleus has been blocked by administration of CRH antagonists.[63] Similar evidence exists for the interaction of the CRH and noradrenergic systems in the hypothalamus[64] and the amygdala, where stress induces increases in both CRH and norepinephrine.[65] Furthermore, norepinephrine in the amygdala appears to stimulate release of CRH.[66]

These observations have prompted the proposal by Koob[20] that interactions of the CRH and noradrenergic systems in the brain may function as a feed-forward system under some conditions, leading to the progressive augmentation of the stress response with repeated stress exposure that is characteristic of PTSD. This progressive augmentation of response with repeated stress has previously been conceptualized as kindling.[67] A feed-forward interaction between the CRH and noradrenergic systems may represent one neurobiologic underpinning of both PTSD and substance use disorders. More specifically, stress, including stress related to self-administration of or withdrawal from substances, may stimulate CRH release in the locus ceruleus, leading to activation of the locus ceruleus and release of norepinephrine in the cortex, which in turn may stimulate the release of CRH in the hypothalamus and amygdala.[20] Such an interaction between the brain noradrenergic and CRH systems may mediate the symptoms of hyperarousal seen in PTSD, including exaggerated startle response. The proclivity toward misuse of CNS depressants by patients with PTSD may reflect an attempt to interrupt this feed-forward interaction by suppressing activity of the locus ceruleus with these agents.[68]

CONCLUSIONS

Clinical and epidemiologic studies confirm that comorbidity of PTSD with substance use disorders is common and that the symptoms of patients with this comorbidity tend to be more severe and more refractory to treatment than those of patients suffering from either disorder alone. Despite the frequency with which patients with both diagnoses present for treatment, no systematic treatment approach of proven efficacy has been developed for this population. Furthermore, little is known about the impact on substance use disorder outcomes of the medications and psychosocial interventions commonly used to treat PTSD, or vice versa.

These limitations notwithstanding, the research conducted to date can inform both clinical practice and future clinical and preclinical research. For example, clinical research suggests that PTSD patients with substance dependence, particularly those who are addicted to CNS depressants, may find the physiologic arousal resulting from substance withdrawal intolerable due to additive effects with preexisting arousal symptoms related to PTSD. Successful detoxification of these patients may thus require inpatient admission to permit vigorous control of withdrawal and PTSD-related arousal symptoms.

Neurobiologic research indicates that high levels of CRH in the brain, particularly in the amygdala, may be common to both PTSD and to substance withdrawal states. Further, CRH antagonists reduce both the anxiety and the enhanced response to illicit substances (sensitization) that are induced by higher levels of brain CRH. These observations suggest that CRH antagonists could potentially have a role in the treatment of patients with PTSD and comorbid substance dependence. Although no CRH antagonist has been approved for human use at present, a series of CRH antagonists that can be administered peripherally have been developed and have been shown to cross the blood-brain barrier.[34,69] These agents will be important tools for further defining the potential role of CRH antagonism in the treatment of patients with PTSD and substance dependence and will hopefully lead to the development of orally active preparations.

Evidence of noradrenergic dysregulation in both PTSD and in withdrawal from CNS depressants has prompted the use of the $alpha_2$-adrenoceptor agonist clonidine in both disorders.[57,58] Data from both preclinical and clinical research suggest that this agent, as well as the selective $alpha_2$-adrenoceptor agonist guanfacine, would be effective in reducing noradrenergic hyperactivity in patients with PTSD and comorbid substance dependence. Guanfacine, given its greater selectivity, may offer a more favorable side effect profile. Given the dearth of established treatments for this patient population, controlled clinical trials to establish the efficacy of these agents are clearly indicated.

Finally, although preclinical work has resulted in considerable progress toward delineating the contributions of the HPA axis and noradrenergic systems to the pathophysiologic underpinnings of PTSD with comorbid substance dependence, few neurobiologic studies have been conducted in this patient population. The inclusion of subjects with this comorbidity may render such studies more complicated, but the data emerging from this work would better inform the clinical management of the difficult-to-treat symptoms of these frequently encountered patients. At the minimum, patients who participate in PTSD or substance dependence studies must be thoroughly evaluated for the presence of this comorbidity to permit adequate control of the effects of the comorbid condition on the neurobiologic processes under study.

REFERENCES

1. Kessler RC, Sonnega A, Bromet E, Hughes M, Nelson CB. Post-traumatic stress disorder in the National Comorbidity Survey. *Arch Gen Psychiatry* 1995;2:1048–1060.
2. Kulka RA, Schlenger WE, Fairbank JA, Hough RL, Jordan BK, Marmar CR, Weiss DS. *Trauma and the Vietnam War Generation: Report of Findings From the National Vietnam Veterans Readjustment Study.* New York: Brunner/Mazel, 1990.
3. Breslau N, Davis GC, Andreski P, Peterson E. Traumatic events and posttraumatic stress disorder in an urban population of young adults. *Arch Gen Psychiatry* 1991;48:216–222.
4. Breslau N, Davis GC, Peterson EL, Schultz L. Psychiatric sequelae of posttraumatic stress disorder in women. *Arch Gen Psychiatry* 1997;54:81–87.
5. Cottler LB, Compton WM III, Mager D, Spitznagel EL, Janca A. Posttraumatic stress disorder among substance users from the general population. *Am J Psychiatry* 1992;149:664–670.

6. Dansky BS, Saladin ME, Brady KT, Kilpatrick DG, Resnick HS. Prevalence of victimization and posttraumatic stress disorder among women with substance use disorders: comparison of telephone and in-person assessment samples. *Int J Addict* 1995;30:1079–1099.

7. Thompson MP, Kingree JB. The frequency and impact of violent trauma among pregnant substance abusers. *Addict Behav* 1998;23:257–262.

8. Deykin EY, Buka SL. Prevalence and risk factors for posttraumatic stress disorder among chemically dependent adolescents. *Am J Psychiatry* 1997;154:752–757.

9. Najavits LM, Gastfriend DR, Barber JP, Reif S, Muenz LR, Blaine J, Frank A, Crits-Christoph P, Thase M, Weiss RD. Cocaine dependence with and without PTSD among subjects in the National Institute on Drug Abuse Collaborative Cocaine Treatment Study. *Am J Psychiatry* 1998;155:214–219.

10. Saladin ME, Brady KT, Dansky BS, Kilpatrick DG. Understanding comorbidity between PTSD and substance use disorders: two preliminary investigations. *Addict Behav* 1995;20:643–655.

11. Ouimette PC, Brown PJ, Najavits LM. Course and treatment of patients with both substance use and posttraumatic stress disorders. *Addict Behav* 1998;23:785–795.

12. Brady KT, Dansky BS, Sonne SC, Saladin ME. Posttraumatic stress disorder and cocaine dependence. *Am J Addict* 1998;7:128–135.

13. Aouizerate B, Schluger JH, Perret G, McClary K, Ho A, Piazza PV, Kreek MJ. Enhanced sensitivity to negative glucocorticoid feedback in methadone patients with ongoing cocaine dependence. In: *Proceedings of the College on Problems of Drug Dependence Annual Meeting*. Bethesda, MD: National Institute on Drug Abuse, CPDD; 1998, p 3.

14. Bremner JD, Southwick SM, Darnell A, Charney DS. Chronic PTSD in Vietnam combat veterans: course of illness and substance abuse. *Am J Psychiatry* 1996;153:369–375.

15. van der Kolk B, Greenberg M, Boyd H, Krystal J. Inescapable shock, neurotransmitters, and addiction to trauma: toward a psychobiology of post traumatic stress. *Biol Psychiatry* 1985;20:314–325.

16. Hutchison KE, Rohsenow D, Monti P, Palfai T, Swift R. Prepulse inhibition of the startle reflex: preliminary study of the effects of a low dose of alcohol in humans. *Alcohol Clin Exp Res* 1997;21:1312–1319.

17. Mirin SM, McKenna GJ. Combat zone adjustment: the role of marihuana use. *Mill Med* 1975;140:482–485.

18. Keane TM, Gerardi RJ, Lyons JA, Wolfe J. The interrelationship of substance abuse and posttraumatic stress disorder: epidemiological and clinical considerations. *Recent Dev Alcohol* 1988;6:27–48.

19. Chilcoat HD, Breslau N. Posttraumatic stress disorder and drug disorders: testing causal pathways. *Arch Gen Psychiatry* 1998;55:913–917.

20. Koob GF. Corticotropin-releasing factor, norepinephrine, and stress. *Biol Psychiatry* 1999;46:1167–1180.

21. Brewer DD, Catalano RF, Haggerty K, Gainey RR, Fleming CB. A meta-analysis of predictors of continued drug use during and after treatment for opiate addiction. *Addiction* 1998;93:73–92.

22. Sinha R, Catapano D, O'Malley S. Stress-induced craving and stress response in cocaine dependent individuals. *Psychopharmacology* 1999;142:343–351.

23. Shaham Y, Stewart J. Stress reinstates heroin-seeking in drug-free animals: an effect mimicking heroin, not withdrawal. *Psychopharmacology* 1995;119:334–341.

24. Erb S, Shaham Y, Stewart J. Stress reinstates cocaine-seeking behavior after prolonged extinction and a drug-free period. *Psychopharmacology* 1996;128:408–412.

25. Piazza PV, Deminiere JM, Le Moal M, Simon H. Stress- and pharmacologically-

induced behavioral sensitization increases vulnerability to acquisition of amphetamine self-administration. *Brain Res* 1990;514:22–26.

26. Deroche V, Marinelli M, LeMoal M, Piazza PV. Glucocorticoids and behavioral effects of psychostimulants, II: cocaine intravenous self-administration and reinstatement depend on glucocorticoid levels. *J Pharmacol Exp Ther* 1997;281:1401–1407.

27. Cador M, Cole BJ, Koob GF, Stinus L, Le Moal M. Central administration of corticotropin releasing factor induces long-term sensitization to d-amphetamine. *Brain Res* 1993;606:181–186.

28. Cole BJ, Cador M, Stinus L, Rivier J, Vale W, Koob GF, Le Moal M. Central administration of a CRF antagonist blocks the development of stress-induced behavioral sensitization. *Brain Res* 1990;512:343–346.

29. Sarnyai Z, Hohn J, Szabo G, Penke B. Critical role of endogenous corticotropin-releasing factor (CRF) in the mediation of the behavioral action of cocaine in rats. *Life Sci* 1992;51:2019–2024.

30. Sarnyai Z, Biro E, Gardi J, Vecsernyes M, Julesz J, Telegdy G. Brain corticotropin-releasing factor mediates "anxiety-like" behavior induced by cocaine withdrawal in rats. *Brain Res* 1995;675:89–97.

31. Merlo-Pich E, Koob GF, Heilig M, Menzaghi F, Vale W, Weiss F. Corticotropin-releasing factor release from mediobasal hypothalamus of the rat as measured by microdialysis. *Neuroscience* 1993;55:695–707.

32. Adinoff B, Anton R, Linnoila M, Guidotti A, Nemeroff CB, Bissette G. Cerebrospinal fluid concentrations of corticotropin-releasing hormone (CRH) and diazepam-binding inhibitor (DBI) during alcohol withdrawal and abstinence. *Neuropsychopharmacology* 1996;15:288–295.

33. Shaham Y, Funk D, Erb S, Brown TJ, Walker C-D, Stewart J. Corticotropin-releasing factor, but not corticosterone, is involved in stress-induced relapse to heroin-seeking in rats. *J Neurosci* 1997;17:2605–2614.

34. Shaham Y, Erb S, Leung S, Buczek Y, Stewart J. CP-154,526, a selective, non-peptide antagonist of the corticotropin-releasing factor 1 receptor attenuates stress-induced relapse to drug seeking in cocaine- and heroin-trained rats. *Psychopharmacology* 1998;137:184–190.

35. Maes M, Lin A, Bonaccorso S, van Hunsel F, Van Gastel A, Delmeire L, Biondi M, Bosmans E, Kenis G, Scharpe S. Increased 24-hour urinary cortisol excretion in patients with post-traumatic stress disorder and patients with major depression, but not in patients with fibromyalgia. *Acta Psychiatr Scand* 1998;98:328–335.

36. Mason JW, Giller EL, Kosten TR, Ostroff RB, Podd L. Urinary free cortisol levels in posttraumatic stress disorder patients. *J Nerv Ment Dis* 1986;174:145–149.

37. Baker DG, West SA, Nicholson WE, Ekhator NN, Kasckow JW, Hill KK, Bruce AB, Orth DN, Geracioti TD Jr. Serial CSF corticotropin-releasing hormone levels and adrenocortical activity in combat veterans with posttraumatic stress disorder. *Am J Psychiatry* 1999;156:585–588.

38. Yehuda R, Lowy MT, Southwick SM, Shaffer D, Giller EL Jr. Lymphocyte glucocorticoid receptor number in posttraumatic stress disorder. *Am J Psychiatry* 1991;148:499–504.

39. Yehuda R, Boisoneau D, Lowy MT, Giller EL. Dose-response changes in plasma cortisol and lymphocyte glucocorticoid receptors following dexamethasone administration in combat veterans with and without posttraumatic stress disorder. *Arch Gen Psychiatry* 1995;52:583–593.

40. Yehuda R, Levengood RA, Schmeilder J, Wilson S, Guo LS, Gerber D. Increased pituitary activation following metyrapone administration in post-traumatic stress disorder. *Psychoneuroendocrinology* 1996;21:1–16.

41. Kant GJ, Bauman RA, Anderson SM, Mougey EH. Effects of controllable vs uncon-

trollable chronic stress on stress-responsive plasma hormones. *Physiol Behav* 1992;51:1285–1288.

42. Irwin J, Ahluwalia P, Zacharko RM, Anisman H. Central norepinephrine and plasma corticosterone following acute and chronic stressors: influence of social isolation and handling. *Pharmacol Biochem Behav* 1986;24:1151–1154.

43. Gamallo A, Villanua A, Trancho G, Fraile A. Stress adaptation and adrenal activity in isolated and crowded rats. *Physiol Behav* 1986;36:217–221.

44. Young EA, Akana S, Dallman MF. Decreased sensitivity to glucocorticoid fast feedback in chronically stressed rats. *Neuroendocrinology* 1990;51:536–542.

45. Liberzon I, Krstov M, Young EA. Stress-restress: effects on ACTH and fast feedback. *Psychoneuroendocrinology* 1997;22:443–453.

46. Schulkin J, Gold PW, McEwen BS. Induction of corticotropin-releasing hormone gene expression by glucocorticoids: implication for understanding the states of fear and anxiety and allostatic load. *Psychoneuroendocrinology* 1998;23:219–243.

47. Makino S, Gold PW, Schulkin J. Corticosterone effects on corticotropin-releasing hormone mRNA in the central nucleus of the amygdala and the parvocellular region of the paraventricular nucleus of the hypothalamus. *Brain Res* 1994;640:105–112.

48. Makino S, Gold PW, Schulkin J. Effects of corticosterone on CRH mRNA and content in the bed nucleus of the stria terminalis: comparison with the effects in the central nucleus of the amygdala and the paraventricular nucleus of the hypothalamus. *Brain Res* 1994;657:141–149.

49. Bremner JD, Licinio J, Darnell A, Krystal JH, Owens MJ, Southwick SM, Nemeroff CB, Charney DS. Elevated CSF corticotropin-releasing factor concentrations in posttraumatic stress disorder. *Am J Psychiatry* 1997;154:624–629.

50. Swerdlow NR, Britton KT, Koob GF. Potentiation of acoustic startle by corticotropin-releasing factor (CRF) and by fear are both reversed by alpha-helical CRF (9–41). *Neuropsychopharmacology* 1989;2:285–292.

51. Tanaka T, Yokoo H, Mizoguchi K, Yoshida M, Tsuda A, Tanaka M. Noradrenaline release in the rat amygdala is increased by stress: studies with intracerebral microdialysis. *Brain Res* 1991;544:174–176.

52. Southwick SM, Bremner JD, Rasmusson A, Morgan CA, Arnsten A, Charney DS. Role of norepinephrine in the pathophysiology and treatment of posttraumatic stress disorder. *Biol Psychiatry* 1999;46:1192–1204.

53. Smith AJ, Brent PJ, Henry DA, Foy A. Plasma noradrenaline, platelet alpha 2-adrenoceptors, and functional scores during ethanol withdrawal. *Alcohol Clin Exp Res* 1990;14:497–502.

54. Hawley RJ, Major LF, Schulman EA, Linnoila M. Cerebrospinal fluid 3-methoxy-4-hydroxyphenylglycol and norepinephrine levels in alcohol withdrawal: correlations with clinical signs. *Arch Gen Psychiatry* 1985;42:1056–1062.

55. Charney DS, Redmond DE, Galloway MP, Kleber HD, Heninger GR, Murberg M, Roth RH. Naltrexone precipitated opiate withdrawal in methadone addicted human subjects: evidence for noradrenergic hyperactivity. *Life Sci* 1984;35:1263–1272.

56. Swann AC, Elsworth JD, Charney DS, Jablons DM, Roth RH, Redmond DE, Maas JW. Brain catecholamine metabolites and behavior in morphine withdrawal. *Eur J Pharmacol* 1982;86:167–175.

57. Agren H. Clonidine treatment of the opiate withdrawal syndrome: a review of clinical trials of a theory. *Acta Psychiatr Scand Suppl* 1986;327:91–113.

58. Harmon RJ, Riggs PD. Clonidine for posttraumatic stress disorder in preschool children. *J Am Acad Child Adolesc Psychiatry* 1996;35:1247–1249.

59. Chappell PB, Smith MA, Hilts CD, Bissette G, Ritchie J, Andersen C, Nemeroff CB. Alterations in corticotropin-releasing factor-like immunoreactivity in discrete rat brain regions after acute and chronic stress. *J Neurosci* 1986;10:2908–2916.

60. Valentino RJ, Foote SL, Aston-Jones G. Corticotropin-releasing factor activates noradrenergic neurons of the locus coeruleus. *Brain Res* 1983;270:363–367.
61. Zhang JJ, Swiergiel AH, Palamarchouk VS, Dunn AJ. Intracerebroventricular infusion of CRF increases extracellular concentrations of norepinephrine in the hippocampus and cortex as determined by in vivo voltametry. *Brain Res Bull* 1998;47:277–284.
62. Lavicky J, Dunn AJ. Corticotropin-releasing factor stimulates catecholamine release in hypothalamus and prefrontal cortex in freely moving rats as assessed by microdialysis. *J Neurochem* 1993;60:602–612.
63. Valentino RJ, Page ME, Curtis AL. Activation of noradrenergic locus coeruleus neurons by hemodynamic stress is due to local release of corticotropin-releasing factor. *Brain Res* 1991;555:25–34.
64. Pacak K, Palkovits M, Kopin IJ, Goldstein DS. Stress-induced norepinephrine release in the hypothalamic paraventricular nucleus and pituitary-adrenocortical and sympathoadrenal activity: in vivo microdialysis studies. *Front Neuroendocrinol* 1995;16:89–150.
65. Pich EM, Lorang M, Yeganeh M, Rodriquez de Fonseca F, Raber J, Koob GF, Weiss F. Increase of extracellular corticotropin-releasing factor-like immunoreactivity levels in the amygdala of awake rats during restraint stress and ethanol withdrawal as measured by microdialysis. *J Neurosci* 1995;15:5439–5447.
66. Raber J, Koob GF, Bloom FE. Interleukin-2 (IL-2) induces corticotropin-releasing factor (CRF) release from the amygdala and involves a nitric oxide-mediated signaling: comparison with the hypothalamic response. *J Pharmacol Exp Ther* 1995;272:815–824.
67. Post RM, Weiss SRB, Smith M, Li H, McCann U. Kindling versus quenching; implications for the evolution and treatment of posttraumatic stress disorder. *Ann NY Acad Sci* 1997;821:285–295.
68. Kosten TR, Krystal J. Biological mechanisms in posttraumatic stress disorder: relevance for substance abuse. *Recent Dev Alcohol* 1988;6:49–68.
69. Arai K, Ohata H, Shibasaki T. Non-peptidic corticotropin-releasing hormone receptor type 1 antagonist reverses restraint stress-induced shortening of sodium pentobarbital-induced sleeping time of rats: evidence that an increase in arousal induced by stress is mediated through CRH receptor type 1. *Neurosci Lett* 1998;255:103–106.

Social Functioning, Psychopathology, and Medication Side Effects in Relation to Substance Use and Abuse in Schizophrenia

Michelle P. Salyers
Kim T. Mueser

INTRODUCTION

Substance use disorder is common in persons with schizophrenia. The Epidemiological Catchment Area (ECA) study found rates of lifetime substance use disorder to be 47% among people with schizophrenia, compared with only 16.7% in the general population (Regier et al., 1990). Similar lifetime prevalence rates have been reported by others (Mueser et al., 1990, 1992, 2000). Rates of current substance use disorder are lower but still substantial, with most estimates between 25% and 35% (Mueser et al., 1995). Substance use disorder in schizophrenia has been associated with a wide range of negative outcomes, including psychiatric relapse and rehospitalization (Drake et al., 1989), homelessness (Caton et al., 1994), and greater service utilization and costs (Bartels et al., 1993).

Given the high rate of substance use disorder and its negative impact among persons with schizophrenia, there is a need to be able to identify which patients are most likely to use alcohol and other drugs, and who is most likely to experience problems with that use (i.e., substance abuse). Specific areas that may be important in this regard include demographic characteristics and psychiatric history, psychopathology, medication side effects, social adjustment, and family adjustment. Although some work has been done in each of these areas to examine correlates of substance use *disorder* among people with schizophrenia, few studies have examined correlates of substance *use* itself.

However, it is possible that correlates of substance use and substance use disorder in schizophrenia are quite similar. Mueser et al. (1998) have posited that the high prevalence of substance use disorder in patients with schizophrenia and other severe mental illnesses is partly due to the psychobiological vulnerability that characterizes those disorders. This vulnerability increases sensitivity to the effects of alcohol and drugs, which leads to negative consequences at relatively low amounts of substance use. Thus, few patients with schizophrenia are able to sustain "controlled" use of substances without eventually developing a substance use disorder (Drake and Wallach, 1993).

As the focus of this study is on the correlates of substance use in patients with schizophrenia, we provide a brief summary of prior research on this topic.

Demographic Variables and Premorbid Functioning

Demographic predictors of substance use disorders among persons with schizophrenia have been fairly consistent and parallel those in the general population. In general, males, younger people, and people with lower levels of education are more likely to have alcohol and drug use disorders (e.g., Mueser et al., 2000). A few studies have examined the relationship between psychiatric history and substance use disorder and have generally found that better premorbid functioning is associated with substance abuse (Arndt et al., 1992; Breakey et al., 1974; Dixon et al., 1991; Tsuang et al., 1982). Although this finding may seem counterintuitive, a plausible explanation is that a certain level of social skill is needed to acquire and use drugs and alcohol (Cohen and Klein, 1970). That is, because substance use is often socially mediated (Becker, 1953), people with better social functioning may have more opportunities to use substances and to develop substance use disorders.

Psychopathology

The majority of prior work has examined the relationship between symptoms and substance abuse among persons with schizophrenia, exploring self-medication or symptom exacerbation hypotheses. As reviewed by Brunette et al. (1997), correlational findings in this area have been mixed, particularly regarding positive symptoms (e.g., hallucinations, delusions) of schizophrenia. Depression and dysphoria have had somewhat greater consistency as correlates of increased substance use and abuse (e.g., Drake et al., 1989), although this has not been reported in other studies (e.g., Mueser et al., 1990). Blanchard et al. (1999) found stable negative affect to be associated with alcohol-related problems and using substances to cope with stress, lending further support to the alleviation of dysphoria model of comorbid substance use disorders (Mueser et al., 1998). In addition, fewer negative symptoms of schizophrenia are generally associated with greater substance abuse (Buckley et al., 1994; Dixon et al., 1991; Kirkpatrick et al., 1996; Lysaker et al., 1994; Mueser et al., 1990; Serper et al., 1995) but not always (Cleghorn et al., 1991; Linszen et al., 1994; Sevy et al., 1990). Similar to the findings for premorbid functioning, it is likely that negative symptoms interfere with socially based alcohol and drug use.

Medication Side Effects

In addition to psychiatric symptoms, some have speculated that medication side effects may be related to substance use (Dixon et al., 1991); however, the few studies in this area have had mixed results. Increased extrapyramidal side effects have been associated with a lifetime diagnosis of alcohol abuse (Dixon et al., 1992) but not cocaine abuse (Dhopesh et al., 1997). Duke et al. (1994) found that severity of alcohol abuse did not correlate with global measures of tardive dyskinesia or subjective awareness of dyskinesia but was associated with greater levels of akathisia. Finally, dysphoria related to medication side effects has been shown to be related to subsequent alcohol abuse (Voruganti et al., 1997). Although it appears that alcohol use is associated with some side effects, it is unclear whether side effects contribute to increased alcohol use. For example, the only study to examine alcohol abuse following assessment of side effects did so through chart review and assessed perceptions of dysphoria rather than the actual side effects (Voruganti et al., 1997). In addition, studies of medication side effects have been hampered by their relatively small sample sizes (e.g., Dhopesh et al., 1997).

Social Functioning

Social adjustment has generally been neglected as a correlate of substance use in schizophrenia. Aside from measures of overall functioning, such as the Global Assessment Scale (Endicott et al., 1976), little systematic work has been done in this area. However, given the importance of impairment in social adjustment as a defining feature of both schizophrenia and substance abuse, this is an important topic to examine. Similarly, family adjustment, both as a predictor and an outcome of substance use, has been rarely studied, although there is some evidence that family-related problems are more common in persons with severe mental illness who also abuse alcohol or drugs (Alterman et al., 1980; Dixon et al., 1995; Kashner et al., 1991).

Aside from demographic variables, reliable clinical correlates of substance use and abuse have not been identified. Further, the majority of prior studies have been limited by their small sample size, lack of rigorous psychiatric diagnosis and comprehensive assessment of predictors, cross-sectional and often retrospective assessment of substance use, and use of single-site data collection. The current study sought to overcome these problems by examining the association between substance use and problems associated with use, assessed longitudinally, and a wide variety of clinical aspects of schizophrenia in a large sample of patients participating in a multisite study.

Based on prior research, we hypothesized that demographic correlates of younger age, being male, and having lower levels of education would be associated with greater substance use. We expected greater negative symptoms, but not positive symptoms, to be associated with less substance use. We also expected that substance use and abuse would be related to greater problems in family relationships. Because relationships between substance use and medication side effects have had mixed results in prior research, we conducted exploratory analyses without directional hypotheses. We also explored relationships between substance use and current social functioning, aside from family relations. On one hand, substance use may be associated with fewer negative symptoms and therefore with better social functioning. On the other hand, diagnostic criteria for substance use disorders include social impairments; thus, substance use in this sample could be related to poorer social functioning.

METHOD

Participants

Participants were subjects in the Treatment Strategies in Schizophrenia (TSS) study (Schooler et al., 1997), a large, multisite, randomized clinical trial that examined the efficacy of family intervention and medication maintenance dosage in five urban areas. Patients were recruited following a symptom exacerbation and medicated with fluphenazine decanoate (FPZ) and supplemental medications during a stabilization period usually lasting 3 to 6 months.

Inclusion criteria were (1) age between 18 and 55 years; (2) willing to take FPZ injections and not receive other major psychotropic medications; (3) maintaining contact with family of origin or legal guardian at least 4 hours per week; (4) willing to give consent for both the medication dosage and family intervention aspects of the study and have at least one relative participating in family intervention; and (5) had a psychiatric hospitalization or symptom exacerbation in the past 3 months. Exclusion criteria were (1) transient and likely to leave the area; (2) known liver damage; (3) organic brain syndrome; (4) epilepsy as an adult; (5) current physical dependence on alcohol, opiates, benzodiazepines, barbiturates, or stimulants; (6) current drug-related psychosis; and (7) current pregnancy. Of the 6,012 subjects initially screened for the TSS study, 7% were excluded for physical dependence on substances of abuse and 2% were excluded for current drug-related psychosis (Robinson et al., 1996).

We limited our analyses to patients who had at least 3 monthly ratings of substance use during the stabilization period. This resulted in reducing the sample size from 528 to 404 participants. We compared these 404 patients to the 124 excluded and found that the two groups did not differ significantly on age, gender, marital status, diagnosis, or educational level. However, the two groups differed significantly on race. Patients who were excluded were more likely to be Caucasian (56%) than patients included (39%), χ^2 ($df = 1$, $N = 528$) = 10.59, $p < 0.001$.

The mean age of the sample was 29.5 ($SD = 7.5$) years and the majority of patients were male (67%). Most had never been married (83%); 13% were divorced, widowed, or separated; and 4% were currently married. Racial composition was Caucasian, 39%; African-American, 51%; Asian, 2%; Hispanic, 3%; and other, 6%. Diagnoses were based on the Structured Clinical Interview for *DSM-III-R* (SCID; Spitzer et al., 1988) and included schizophrenia (78%), schizoaffective disorder (16%), and schizophreniform disorder (6%).

Measures

We examined several sets of variables from the clinical domain, including symptoms, distress, medication side effects, and social functioning. We also examined psychiatric history, including indices of premorbid functioning and hospitalization history. We included all standardized instruments from the parent TSS study.

Symptoms

Brief Psychiatric Rating Scale (BPRS; Overall and Gorham, 1962). The anchored version of BPRS (Woerner et al., 1988) was used to rate symptoms for the previous week, using behavioral anchors on a 7-point scale based on clinical interviews by the treating psychiatrist. Interrater reliability for the BPRS items was high based on independent interviews conducted by separate raters (Mueser et al., 1997). Following Mueser et al. (1997), we used the 4-factor model of the BPRS: thought disturbance, anergia, affect, and disorganization. Mean scores for each of these subscales were calculated for the baseline assessment.

Scale for the Assessment of Negative Symptoms (SANS; Andreason, 1984). SANS was administered during a clinical interview by a psychiatrist. Interrater reliability was satisfactory for the SANS based on multiple raters of videotaped SANS interviews (Mueser et al., 1994). We examined negative symptoms using the 3-factor model identified by Sayers et al. (1996): diminished expression, inattention-alogia, and social amotivation. As with the BPRS, we used the mean score for each of the subscales at baseline.

Distress

Symptom Checklist-90 (SCL-90; Derogatis, 1977). Trained research assistants administered the SCL-90. We used the overall mean score at baseline to assess general distress.

Family Symptom Checklist (Family SCL). We used a variant of SCL-90 developed specifically for the TSS study to assess family members' perceptions of the patient's distress. This questionnaire consisted of 49 items from SCL-90 with the wording changed to read "How much has ____ been bothered by ____" rather than "How much were you bothered by ____." Items that assessed internal thoughts or perceptions were dropped from the scale. Research assistants administered the Family SCL. We used the mean overall score at baseline to assess family members' perceptions of patients' distress.

Side Effects

Abnormal Involuntary Movement Scale (AIMS; Guy, 1976). AIMS is a 12-item scale administered by nurses to assess tardive dyskinesia on a 5-point scale. Ratings range from 1 = none to 5 = severe. We used the baseline rating of the AIMS.

Neurological Rating Scale—Revised (NRS; Simpson and Angus, 1970). A revised version of NRS (Simpson, 1985) assessed the presence and severity of 10 extrapyramidal side effects on a 5-point scale, with higher numbers indicating greater severity. NRS was administered by nurses along with AIMS. Because of the importance of akathisia as a particularly troublesome side effect (Drake and Ehrlich, 1985; Van Putten, 1975), we also examined this item separately.

Social Functioning

Patient-Rated and Family-Rated Social Adjustment Scales. Patient social functioning was assessed from both the patient's and the key relative's perspectives using modified versions of the Social Adjustment Scale–II (SAS; Schooler et al., 1979). Research assistants administered the Patient and Family SAS. Monthly conference calls to review issues related to SAS ratings were conducted with the research assistants from all the sites. The Patient SAS contains several domains of social adjustment, including instrumental role functioning, finances, family relations, extended family relations, social leisure, interpersonal relations, romantic involvement, sexual adjustment, and personal well-being. Items are rated on 5-point scales, with 5 representing poorest adjustment. In order to decrease the number of variables, we conducted an exploratory factor analysis with principal axis extraction and varimax rotation on the Patient SAS items. Based on the scree plots and the interpretability of factor loadings, four factors were extracted, accounting for 28.4% of the total variance: social leisure, interpersonal/family relations, romantic/sexual, and self-efficacy.

The Family SAS contains items tapping parallel domains of the Patient SAS; however, the items were not identical to those of the Patient SAS. Thus, we conducted a separate exploratory factor analysis on the Family SAS items using principal axis extraction and varimax rotation. Three factors were extracted, accounting for 29.0% of the total variance, including family burden, social leisure, and self-care.

Patient rejection. Rejecting attitudes by key family members were assessed using the Patient Rejection Scale (Kreisman et al., 1988), which was administered following the Family SAS. Items are rated on a 7-point scale, with higher scores indicating more negative family attitudes toward the patient. Internal consistency was good, with Cronbach's alpha of 0.90.

Social Adjustment Scale–Interim Patient (SAS-IP). Every 4 weeks throughout the study, nurses completed assessments of patient functioning based on four items drawn from the SAS: friction in the household, problems in leisure activities, infrequent social contacts, and problems in self-appraisal. Ratings were made on a 5-point scale, with higher numbers indicating greater severity of problems in each area. Because these ratings were conducted every 4 weeks, we used the mean score for the first six ratings to coincide with the time period in which substance use ratings were obtained. The intraclass correlation coefficient (ICC; Shrout and Fleiss, 1979) for the mean of the ratings across all six assessments was 0.83 for friction, 0.86 for leisure activities, 0.83 for social contacts, and 0.80 for self-appraisal.

Psychiatric History

In addition to the aforementioned scales, we examined several items from the baseline clinical interview. The baseline interview was completed by a trained research assistant based on interviews with the patient and a key relative, and chart review. No information on reliability of these ratings was available from the parent TSS study. *Premorbid functioning* included age of onset of illness, age the patient last behaved like his or her peers, and age first hospitalized. In addition, a single item of premorbid functioning (1 = very well to 3 = poorly) and an item assessing the presence of behavioral problems as a child (1 = yes, 0 = no) were included. *Hospitalization history* included the number of months hospitalized prior to the index hospitalization and the number of admissions in the 2 years prior to index hospitalization. Finally, *patient background variables* included age, gender (male), race (Caucasian), marital status (ever married), and patient educational level (0 = no schooling to 8 = completed postgraduate training).

Substance Use and Problems

Substance Use

Standardized assessments of substance use disorder were not part of the TSS parent study. However, patient-reported substance use was assessed during the monthly interviews by the nurse. Patients were asked to rate the frequency of alcohol use over the past month on a 5-point scale (1 = none to 5 = most days or daily). Stability of the ratings was examined over the first six assessments, with an ICC for mean ratings of 0.89. Similarly, patients were asked to rate the frequency of use of other drugs during the past month (1 = none to 5 = every day). The mean substance use ratings were also relatively stable (ICC = 0.85).

In order to characterize consistent substance use, we formed three groups of patients based on the frequency of reported use of alcohol and other drugs over time. We created categories, rather than using a continuous variable, because of the skewed distribution in substance use. For example, over 25% of the sample reported no alcohol use over the 6-month period. Thus, we created rationally derived categories to reflect "consistent" users. Given findings by Drake and Wallach (1993) that people with schizophrenia are usually not able to sustain low levels of use over time without experiencing negative consequences, we liberally defined consistent users as those who used at least once per month for at least 2 months. Thus, patients who reported using alcohol once a month or less, or who used alcohol more frequently for only 1 month but did not report using other substances for more than 1 month, were classified in the No/Low Alcohol group (N = 236); of these patients, 130 (55%) reported no alcohol use during the 6-month assessment period. Patients who reported using alcohol more than once a month for at least 2 months but did not report using other substances for more than 1 month were classified in the Alcohol Only group (N = 127). On average, the Alcohol Only group reported using alcohol two to three times per month. Patients who reported using drugs (including alcohol or not) at least once a month for at least 2 months were classified in the Drug Use group (N = 41). Of these patients, 34 (83%) reported using both alcohol and other substances on a consistent basis; only 2 (5%) reported never using alcohol during the first 6 months For the Drug Use group, the primary drug used was cannabis, with 39 (95%) reporting some use during the 6 months. Other substances included cocaine (27%), hallucinogens (5%), amphetamines (5%), and narcotics (2%). On average, the Drug Use group reported using alcohol two to three times per month and using drugs once a week or less.

Problems

We also examined correlates of reported problems with alcohol use. During the monthly interview with the nurse, patients rated their problems with alcohol over the past month on a 5-point scale (1 = none to 5 = extreme problems): "If yes (i.e., patient has been drinking), has drinking caused any problems with your health, your work, or with other people?" Problems related to drug use were not assessed. Problems related to alcohol use were relatively stable over time (ICC = 0.79).

As with the substance use groups, we formed three groups of patients based on the consistency of their reports of problems over time. Patients who reported no alcohol use throughout the 6-month period (N = 132) were excluded from the problem analyses. Patients who reported that they did not have alcohol-related problems at all during the first 6 months were in the No Problem group ($N = 151$); patients who reported that they had slight or more severe problems with alcohol use for only 1 month were classified in the Infrequent Problem group ($N = 42$); and patients who reported having slight or more severe problems for at least 2 of the 6 months were grouped into the Frequent Problem group ($N = 42$).

Data Analysis

In order to examine correlates of substance use and problems related to alcohol use, we first compared the groups described above on demographic and diagnostic variables. For continuous variables (e.g., age) we used one-way analyses of variance (ANOVAs); for categorical variables (e.g., gender) we used chi-square tests. Groups were then compared on symptoms (BPRS, SANS), distress (SCL-90, SCL-Family), side effects (AIMS, NRS), and social functioning (Patient SAS, Family SAS, SAS-IP). Groups were also compared on the psychiatric history variables. Each of these sets of correlates was examined with multivariate analyses of variance (MANOVAs) and, where the overall comparison was significant, univariate tests and post hoc group comparisons (Tukey's honestly significant difference) were conducted. When background or other potentially confounding variables (e.g., site differences) were related, multivariate analyses of covariance were performed, controlling for the confounding variables. In addition, we calculated effect sizes for significant findings so as not to overinterpret statistical significance in the absence of clinical significance. We calculated the effect size as the difference in mean scores divided by the pooled standard deviation of the two groups being compared. We used Lipsey's (1990) criteria of 0.33 to 0.55 as moderate and 0.56 or above as large effects.

RESULTS

Correlates of Substance Use*

Demographics

Substance use groups differed significantly on three of seven background variables. As shown in Table 11.1, there were graduated differences between groups on age, gender, and education level in the hypothesized direction. Of all three groups,

---

*We split the No/Low Alcohol group into No Alcohol ($n = 130$) and Some Use ($n = 106$) and compared them on background and clinical variables. The two groups differed on gender, with males being more likely to be in the Some Use group, and they differed on number of hospitalizations in prior 2 years: Some Use had more admissions ($M = 1.0$, $SD = 1.7$) than No Alcohol ($M = 0.6$, $SD = 1.0$), $t = 2.18$, $p < 0.05$. The two groups did not differ significantly on any other clinical or premorbid functioning variable, which generally supports grouping them together.

TABLE 11.1. Sample Characteristics of Substance Use Groups

	No/Low Alcohol (N = 236)	Alcohol Only (N = 127)	Drug Use (N = 41)	Test of Significance
Mean age (SD)	30.1 (7.9)	29.4 (7.1)	26.3 (5.1)	$F = 4.57$**
Gender				
Male	145 (61.4%)	92 (72.4%)	34 (82.9%)	$\chi^2 = 9.71$**
Female	91 (38.6%)	35 (27.6%)	7 (17.1%)	
Race				
Caucasian	95 (40.3%)	49 (38.6%)	14 (34.1%)	$\chi^2 = 0.57$
Other	141 (59.7%)	78 (61.4%)	27 (65.9%)	
Marital status				
Ever married	46 (19.5%)	21 (16.5%)	2 (4.9%)	$\chi^2 = 5.31$
Never married	190 (80.5%)	106 (83.5%)	39 (95.1%)	
Diagnosis				
Schizophrenia	181 (76.7%)	102 (80.3%)	31 (75.6%)	$\chi^2 = 0.74$
Schizoaffective/ schizophreniform	55 (23.3%)	25 (19.7%)	10 (24.4%)	
Mean educational level (SD)[a]	4.3 (1.0)	4.0 (1.1)	3.9 (0.9)	$F = 3.56$*

*$p < 0.05$; **$p < 0.01$; ***$p < 0.001$.
[a]Ranges from 0 = no schooling to 8 = complete postgraduate education.

drug users were the youngest, most likely to be male, and had the lowest levels of education. The three groups did not differ on race, marital status, or diagnosis.

Symptoms and Distress

As shown in Table 11.2, the three groups differed significantly on the SANS subscales but not on the BPRS ratings or the SCL ratings of distress. As hypothesized, the general pattern was for the No/Low Alcohol Use group to have the most severe negative symptoms (Table 11.2). Tukey's post hoc comparisons revealed that patients in the No/Low Alcohol group had significantly greater levels of diminished expression than drug users and greater levels of social amotivation than the Alcohol Only group ($p < 0.05$). Both differences were of moderate magnitude with an effect size of 0.45.

Medication Side Effects

As shown in Table 11.2, the groups did not differ significantly on either measure of medication side effects or on akathisia.

TABLE 11.2. Comparisons of Substance Use Groups on Clinical Variables

	a No/Low Alcohol (N = 236)	b Alcohol Only (N = 127)	c Drug Use (N = 41)	Significance	Post Hoc[a]
Symptoms					
BPRS Scales[b]				$F(8,758) = 1.18$	
Affect	2.2 (1.0)	2.2 (0.9)	2.3 (0.9)	$F(2,381) = 0.15$	
Anergia	2.3 (0.9)	2.1 (1.0)	2.0 (0.9)	$F(2,381) = 2.23$	
Disorganization	2.0 (0.9)	2.0 (0.9)	1.9 (0.8)	$F(2,381) = 0.00$	
Thought Disturbance	2.7 (1.4)	2.6 (1.3)	3.1 (1.4)	$F(2,381) = 2.04$	
SANS Scales[c]				$F(6,662) =$ **3.41****	
Diminished Expression	2.3 (0.9)	2.1 (0.9)	0.9 (0.8)	$F(2,332) =$ 4.27*	a > c
Inattention-Alogia	1.7 (0.6)	1.7 (0.6)	1.7 (0.6)	$F(2,332) = 0.05$	
Social Amotivation	2.6 (0.9)	2.2 (0.8)	2.2 (0.8)	$F(2,332) =$ 7.85***	a > b
Baseline distress[d]				$F(4,502) = 2.05$	
SCL-90 self-report	1.7 (0.7)	1.7 (0.6)	1.9 (0.7)	$F(2,251) = 2.64$	
Family SCL report	1.6 (0.5)	1.8 (0.6)	1.7 (0.7)	$F(2,251) = 1.17$	
	(n = 153)	(n = 78)	(n = 23)		
Baseline side effects[e]				$F(4,736) = 2.03$	
AIMS	1.3 (0.4)	1.4 (0.4)	1.3 (0.3)	$F(2,368) = 1.26$	
EPS ratings	1.5 (0.4)	1.4 (0.4)	1.4 (0.3)	$F(2,368) = 1.93$	
	(n = 221)	(n = 117)	(n = 33)		
Social Adjustment Problems[e]					
Patient ratings				$F(6,724) =$ **2.18***	
Social leisure	2.8 (0.6)	2.8 (0.6)	2.8 (0.7)	$F(2,363) = 0.08$	
Interpersonal/ fam. rel.	1.8 (0.6)	2.0 (0.7)	2.1 (0.9)	$F(2,363) =$ 4.36*	c > a
Self-efficacy	1.9 (0.5)	2.0 (0.5)	2.0 (0.5)	$F(2,363) = 2.02$	
Romantic/ sexual rel.	3.0 (1.0)	2.7 (0.9)	2.7 (0.9)	$F(2,205) = 2.28$	
Family ratings				$F(8,584) =$ **2.05***	
Family burden	2.2 (0.6)	2.3 (0.7)	2.2 (0.6)	$F(2,294) = 0.35$	
Social leisure	3.1 (0.8)	2.9 (0.8)	2.7 (0.6)	$F(2,294) =$ 3.52*	No diff.
Self-care	1.8 (0.7)	2.0 (0.9)	2.1 (0.8)	$F(2,294) = 2.30$	
Patient rejection	58.7 (21.6)	62.5 (21.1)	64.6 (21.6)	$F(2,294) = 1.15$	

(Continued)

TABLE 11.2. Continued

	a No/Low Alcohol (N = 236)	b Alcohol Only (N = 127)	c Drug Use (N = 41)	Significance	Post Hoc[a]
Nurse ratings[f]				$F(8,798) =$ **5.76*****	
Friction in household	1.7 (0.8)	1.7 (0.8)	2.2 (0.9)	$F(2,402) =$ 7.13***	c > a,b
Problems in leisure	3.8 (0.9)	3.5 (1.0)	3.8 (0.8)	$F(2,402) =$ 3.15*	a > b
Infrequent social contacts	2.6 (1.0)	2.3 (1.1)	2.2 (0.9)	$F(2,402) =$ 5.95**	a > b,c
Problems in self-appraisal	2.4 (0.7)	2.6 (0.8)	2.7 (0.6)	$F(2,402) =$ 5.00**	b > a

$*p < 0.05; **p < 0.01; ***p < 0.001.$
[a]Tukey's HSD at $p < 0.05$.
[b]Ranges from 1 to 7, with higher numbers indicating greater severity.
[c]Ranges from 1 to 5, with higher numbers indicating greater severity.
[d]Ranges from 0 to 4, with higher numbers indicating greater severity.
[e]Ranges from 1 to 5, with higher numbers indicating greater problems in social adjustment.
[f]Mean of six monthly ratings.

Social Functioning

As shown in Table 11.2, the groups differed significantly on social adjustment as rated by patients, family, and nurses. Patients in the Drug Use group reported the greatest problems in interpersonal and family relationships, significantly more than the No/Low Alcohol Use group (Tukey's $p < 0.05$). Family ratings of social leisure showed a significant univariate effect, with the greatest problems reported for No/Low Alcohol Use. However, no two groups differed significantly at $p < 0.05$. Finally, each of the nurse ratings of social adjustment was significantly different across groups. Drug Users were rated as having the greatest amount of friction in their households (compared with both No/Low Alcohol and Alcohol Only groups, p values < 0.05). Patients in the No/Low Alcohol group were rated as having the most severe problems in leisure activities (compared with Alcohol Only, $p < 0.05$), as well as the most infrequent social contacts (compared to both Alcohol Only and Drug Users, p values < 0.05). However, the No/Low Alcohol group was rated as having the fewest problems in self-appraisal (compared with Alcohol Only, $p < 0.05$). Between-group comparisons revealed moderate to large effects, with effect sizes ranging from 0.32 to 0.62.

TABLE 11.3. Comparisons of Substance Use Groups on Psychiatric History

	a No/Low Alcohol ($N = 236$)	b Alcohol Only ($N = 127$)	c Drug Use ($N = 41$)	Significance	Post Hoc[a]
Premorbid functioning				$F(10,772) =$ **1.86***	
Age onset	20.7 (5.9)	20.9 (5.7)	19.6 (2.6)	$F(2,389) = 0.87$	
Age behaved like peers	18.5 (6.9)	18.8 (6.6)	16.9 (4.4)	$F(2,389) = 1.32$	
Age first hospitalized	23.7 (5.8)	23.8 (5.5)	20.9 (2.9)	$F(2,389) =$ 4.48*	c < a,b
Problems in premorbid functioning[b]	1.6 (0.7)	1.5 (0.7)	1.3 (0.6)	$F(2,389) = 2.51$	
Behavior problems as child[c]	0.24 (0.43)	0.24 (0.43)	0.32 (0.47)	$F(2,389) = 0.57$	
Hospital history				$F(4,796) =$ **2.88***	
No. of months hospitalized	6.8 (14.8)	5.6 (10.7)	9.0 (20.3)	$F(2,398) = 0.89$	
No. of admissions prior 2 years	0.8 (1.4)	1.1 (1.5)	1.5 (1.8)	$F(2,398) =$ 4.73**	c > a

$*p < 0.05; **p < 0.01; ***p < 0.001.$
[a]Tukey's HSD at $p < 0.05$.
[b]Ranges from 1 to 3, with higher numbers indicating greater problems.
[c]Ranges from 1 to 100, with higher numbers indicating greater problems.

Psychiatric History

As shown in Table 11.3, the three groups also differed significantly on indices of premorbid functioning and hospital history. Post hoc analyses revealed that the Drug Use group had the earliest age at first hospitalization (compared with both Low Use and Alcohol Only groups). The Drug Use group also had significantly more hospital admissions in the 2 years prior to the study, compared with the No/Low Alcohol Use group. Again, the effect sizes were in the moderate range: 0.52 for age first hospitalized and 0.47 for number of hospital admissions.

Control Analyses

Because the groups differed significantly on several demographic variables, the above analyses were repeated controlling for age, gender, and education level (MANCOVAs). After controlling for these background variables, group differences remained significant on all of the above variables, except for family ratings of social adjustment and indices of premorbid functioning, which were marginally significant, $F(8,578) = 1.82, p = 0.07$ and $F(10,766) = 1.78, p = 0.06$, respectively.

Correlates of Self-Reported Problems with Alcohol

Preliminary Analyses

Prior to examining the correlates of problems with alcohol, we examined the overlap between the use and problem groupings. Of the No Problem group, 44% were in the No/Low Alcohol group, 46% were in the Alcohol Only group, and 9% were in the Drug Use group. Of patients in the Infrequent Problem group, 26% were in the No/Low Alcohol group, 55% were in the Alcohol Only group, and 19% were in the Drug Use group. Few patients in the Frequent Problem group were classified as No/Low Alcohol users (4%); most were in the Alcohol Only group (64%) or the Drug Use group (29%). Overall, the differences between classification were significant, χ^2 ($df = 4, N = 235$) $= 25.64, p < 0.001$.

Mean ratings of substance use also differed significantly across problem groups. Patients in the Frequent Problem group reported the greatest amount of alcohol use ($M = 3.0, SD = 0.9$), followed by patients in the Infrequent Problem group ($M = 2.6, SD = 0.9$) and the No Problem group ($M = 2.3, SD = 1.0$), $F(2,232) = 9.60, P0 < 0.001$. Tukey's post hoc test indicated that the Frequent Problem group was significantly different from the No Problem group ($p < 0.05$). Problem groups also differed significantly on reported drug use: Frequent Problem ($M = 1.4, SD = 0.8$), Infrequent Problem ($M = 1.2, SD = 0.6$), and No Problem ($M = 1.1, SD = 0.4$), $F(2,232) = 3.79, p < 0.05$. Again, post hoc analyses revealed that the Frequent Problem group was significantly different from the No Problem group ($p < 0.05$).

Demographics

The problem groups were compared on background characteristics and did not differ significantly on any of the variables examined (age, gender, race, marital status, diagnosis, and educational level).

Symptoms and Distress

The problem groups did not differ on any measure of symptoms or distress.

Medication Side Effects

The problem groups did not differ on overall side effects. However, akathisia did differ between problem groups, with those reporting frequent problems having the most severe akathisia, $M = 2.2$ ($SD = 1.1$) vs. $M = 1.7$ ($SD = 1.0$) for both of the other groups, $F(2,209) = 3.52$, $p < 0.05$. This difference is a moderate effect size of 0.50.

Social Functioning

As shown in Table 11.4, alcohol problem groups differed significantly on patient- and nurse-rated social adjustment. However, the groups did not differ significantly on family ratings of social adjustment. Patients in the Frequent Problem group rated themselves as having the highest levels of problems with interpersonal/family adjustment, as well as problems in self-efficacy. Post hoc analyses revealed that the Frequent Problem group reported significantly more interpersonal/family difficulties than both the Infrequent Problem and No Problem groups. The Frequent Problem group also reported significantly more problems in self-efficacy compared with the No Problem group but did not differ significantly from the Infrequent Problem group. These were large effects, ranging from 0.58 to 0.77.

Nurse ratings of social adjustment problems revealed a similar pattern (see Table 11.4). Nurses rated patients in the Frequent Problem group as having the

TABLE 11.4. Significant Differences Between Problem Groups on Social Functioning

	a No Problem ($N = 151$)	b Infrequent Problem ($N = 42$)	c Frequent Problem ($N = 42$)	Significance	Post Hoc[a]
Social Adjustment Problems					
Patient ratings				$F(6,422) =$ 2.79**	
Social leisure	2.8 (0.6)	2.8 (0.6)	2.9 (0.6)	$F(2,212) = 0.96$	
Interpersonal/family relations	1.9 (0.6)	1.8 (0.6)	2.3 (0.7)	$F(2,212) =$ 5.40**	c > a, b
Self-efficacy	1.9 (0.5)	2.1 (0.5)	2.2 (0.6)	$F(2,212) =$ 4.58**	c > a
Nurse ratings[b]				$F(8,460) =$ **2.92***	
Friction in household	1.7 (0.9)	1.8 (0.8)	2.2 (0.9)	$F(2,232) =$ 4.48**	c > a
Problems in leisure activities	3.5 (1.0)	3.6 (0.9)	3.8 (0.8)	$F(2,232) = 1.34$	
Infrequent social contacts	2.4 (1.0)	2.3 (1.0)	2.1 (0.9)	$F(2,232) = 1.10$	
Problems in self-appraisal	2.5 (0.7)	2.6 (0.6)	2.9 (0.7)	$F(2,232) =$ 6.15**	c > a

*$p < 0.05$; **$p < 0.01$; ***$p < 0.001$.
[a]Tukey's HSD at $p < 0.01$.
[b]Mean of six monthly ratings.

greatest amount of friction in their households and the greatest problems in self-appraisal. For both variables, post hoc analyses revealed that the significant differences were between the Frequent Problem and No Problem groups. Effects were large (0.56 and 0.57).

Psychiatric History

The problem groups did not differ on indices of premorbid functioning or hospital history.

Control Analyses

Because the problem groups differed in amount of alcohol and drug use, we examined group differences on the significant variables above, controlling for alcohol and drug use with MANCOVAs. The problem groups still differed significantly on overall patient-rated social adjustment, $F(6,418) = 2.48$, $p < 0.05$; univariate tests remained significant for both interpersonal/family problems and self-efficacy. Overall differences for the nurse-rated social adjustment, however, were only marginally significant, $F(8,456) = 1.85$, $p = 0.07$. In this set, the univariate test for self-appraisal was still significant, $F(2,230) = 4.91$, $p < 0.01$, and household friction was marginally significant, $F(2,230) = 2.53$, $p = 0.08$.

DISCUSSION

A wide range of demographic and clinical correlates of self-reported substance use and abuse were examined. Patients with schizophrenia who reported consistent substance use were younger, had lower levels of education, and were more likely to be male. These same correlates have been associated with substance use disorder in other studies of psychiatric patients (e.g., Mueser et al., 2000). Thus, age, education level, and gender continue to serve as important indicators of who may use or abuse alcohol and other drugs. Psychiatric history was also found to be a correlate, particularly of drug use, as drug users had an earlier age at first hospitalization and the most hospital admissions prior to the study.

Consistent with some prior research on negative symptoms and premorbid functioning (e.g., Dixon et al., 1991), patients with little or no alcohol use were the most impaired in terms of social functioning. They had the most severe negative symptoms, the fewest social contacts, and the most problems in social leisure adjustment. Conversely, although consistent substance users had better functioning in these areas, they reported the greatest problems in their family relationships and the most negative self-appraisal.

These findings, taken together with prior research, support an emerging pattern between social adjustment and substance use. On one hand, substance use is associated with better social and leisure functioning and fewer negative symptoms. It may be that patients who have a stronger social drive, including better social skills, and the desire to be with others are more likely to be exposed to substances through their social contacts, and hence to use those substances. Substance use in social situations could facilitate social functioning and decrease negative symptoms by providing a convenient, easily accessible, shared recreational activity. This social facilitation may account for some of the difficulty patients have when they try to reduce or stop their substance use. When patients try to stop using substances, they are either confronted with managing relationships in which substance use has formerly played an important role or with seeking out new relationships that do not involve substance use. The hypothesized importance of social relationships with other substance users is consistent with evidence that dually diagnosed patients with more people in their social networks who use substances have worse outcomes from integrated dual-disorder treatment (Trumbetta et al., 1999).

On the other hand, while substance use may facilitate some aspects of social functioning, there are clear costs to this use as well. Patients who reported consistent substance use were more likely to have problems in self-appraisal and interpersonal relationships, even after controlling for demographic variables. In particular, family relationships appear disrupted both in this sample and in others (Alterman et al., 1980; Dixon et al., 1995; Kashner et al., 1991). Furthermore, substance use was associated with increased psychiatric hospitalization, as has been found in other studies (e.g., Drake et al., 1989).

Our examination of correlates of problems associated with alcohol use found that among alcohol users we could not distinguish those who reported problems from those who did not on demographic variables, psychiatric history, symptoms, or most medication side effects. The problem groups differed primarily on indices of social adjustment, which likely reflect the areas that the alcohol was affecting. Patients who reported problems with alcohol also reported problems in interpersonal and family relationships, had more friction at home, and had poorer self-appraisal. Most of these associations remained significant after controlling for substance use, thereby supporting the validity of our measure of perceived problems. That is, correlates of alcohol problems were relatively independent of amount of use.

As expected, the substance use problem groups differed on frequency of substance use, with those having frequent problems with alcohol reporting greater amounts of both alcohol and other drug use. Thus, the frequency of substance use appeared to be the primary determinant of which patients had problems with alcohol. While some substance use was not associated with impairment in the areas we assessed, more frequent use of alcohol and drugs was detrimental to relationships and to self-appraisal. The threshold at which alcohol becomes problematic, however, cannot be determined from this study.

These findings did not support the hypothesis that patients use substances to either self-medicate their psychiatric symptoms or to deal with side effects. Symptom severity was not related to increased substance use. Where group differences in symptomatology were found (diminished expression and social amotivation), those patients with the greatest symptoms reported using the least amount of alcohol and other substances. Further, the alleviation of dysphoria model—that people with schizophrenia may use substances to alleviate general dysphoria (see Mueser et al., 1998)—was not supported; substance use groups did not differ on ratings of distress or affective symptoms. However, our assessment of mood was limited to clinical measures administered at baseline. In contrast, Blanchard et al. (1999) reported that trait levels of negative affect measured longitudinally were associated with substance use among people with schizophrenia.

There were no differences in side effects among the substance use groups. Side effects were rated by nurse observation rather than patient report. In addition, the majority of side effects assessed were primarily motor-related symptoms. It is possible that the subjective experience of side effects (Voruganti et al., 1997), or other side effects such as drowsiness or anticholinergic problems (e.g., dry mouth), would be more potent predictors of substance use. Somewhat surprisingly, problems due to alcohol, but not alcohol or drug use per se, were related to higher levels of akathisia. This is consistent with Duke et al. (1994), who found akathisia to be associated with problem drinking and dependence on alcohol. This suggests that problem drinking may lead to greater levels of akathisia. Alternatively, patients or clinicians may misinterpret problems related to alcohol abuse, such as cravings, for akathisia.

The lack of relationships between substance use and psychiatric symptoms or side effects may be due to a methodological artifact of our sample. The sample was restricted to patients without physical dependence on alcohol or other drugs, limiting the range of use examined. Although relatively few patients (7%) were screened out of the study on this basis, the sample may have been further limited by the requirement of having regular family contact and family members willing to participate. Substance abuse in schizophrenia is related to the loss of family support and homelessness (Caton et al., 1994, 1995). Thus, patients with the heaviest substance abuse may have had less frequent contact with family members and were less likely to be included in the study. A consequence of excluding the most extreme cases of substance abuse is that the range of substance abuse severity was restricted to the patients studied here. Given this restricted range, where significant relationships were identified, we may be reasonably confident that they exist. However, the absence of findings is not strong evidence against any hypothesized associations and may be due to the restricted range in substance use.

The sampling criteria in the TSS parent study may have restricted our sample in other ways. For example, because of the requirement of regular contact with family members, the sample is likely to be younger and to have a higher level of education than other samples of people with schizophrenia in treatment. Although age and education were still found to be correlates of substance use in this sample, there may have been other effects of the sampling that are not readily apparent.

An important limitation of this study is that the amount of substance use was based solely on self-report, and patients typically underreport the amount of substances used (Drake et al., 1996). On the other hand, longitudinal assessments of substance use over time allowed us to identify subgroups of consistent users without relying on long-term, retrospective accounts of substance use, such as the time-line follow-back calendar (Sobell et al., 1980). Ideally, substance use and abuse should be assessed through multiple sources over time when possible (Drake et al., 1996). For example, in addition to self-reported use, objective measures (e.g., urine samples) and informant ratings (e.g., case managers, family members) of substance use would be important. In addition, although substance use and problems were assessed over time and subsequent to the baseline measures, we did not have information pertaining to prior substance use. Thus, the analyses were essentially cross-sectional and correlational, and we cannot address issues of directionality among the observed relationships in this study.

It should be noted that differences between substance use groups were most pronounced on the nurse ratings on SAS-IP, compared with family and symptom ratings. To some extent, this finding likely reflects method variance. That is, the monthly nurse ratings and the reports of substance use were completed at the same time with the same informant, namely the patient. Conversely, family and patient ratings of SAS and symptom ratings were all done at baseline. In the case of the Family SAS, the informant was a family member. Thus, the stronger relationships found for the nurse ratings may be partially due to the method of monthly interviews with the patient to obtain both forms of information. Notably, nurse ratings of friction, leisure, and social contacts were rated *before* self-reported substance use in the interview. Thus, the possibility that these ratings were biased by known substance use may have been reduced.

Despite these limitations, this study replicates earlier findings concerning demographics, psychiatric history, and negative symptoms as correlates of substance use, supporting the validity of our substance use ratings. Moreover, this study extends prior research by suggesting that substance use may be differentially related to separate dimensions of social functioning, including social leisure and family relationships. The findings suggest that substance use and abuse may in part be maintained by the social and recreational functions it serves, but may also contribute to stress and tension in family relationships, increasing the risk of losing family support. Effective interventions for such dual disorders may need to address the social factors that maintain substance use and buffer families against the negative effects of patients' substance abuse. Ultimately, collaborative work between professionals and families, including patients, may be required if improvements in substance use problems are to take place without the loss of family support.

ACKNOWLEDGMENTS

The Treatment Strategies in Schizophrenia (TSS) Cooperative Agreement Program was a multicenter clinical trial carried out by five research teams in collaboration with the Division of Clinical Research of the National Institute of Mental Health (NIMH), Rockville, MD. NIMH principal collaborators were Nina R. Schooler, Ph.D., Samuel J. Keith, M.D., Joanne B. Severe, B.A., and Susan M. Matthews, M.A. The principal investigators at the five sites and grant numbers were Albert Einstein School of Medicine and Hillside Hospital–Long Island Jewish Medical Center, Glen Oaks, NY, UO1-MH39992 (John M. Kane, M.D.); Medical College of Pennsylvania and Eastern Pennsylvania Psychiatric Institute, Philadelphia, PA, UO1-MH39998 (Alan S. Bellack, Ph.D.); Cornell University Medical College and Payne Whitney Clinic, New York, NY, UO1-MH40007 (Ira D. Glick, M.D.); University of California at San Francisco and San Francisco General Hospital, San Francisco, CA, UO1-MH40042 (William A. Hargreaves, Ph.D.); and Emory University and Grady Memorial Hospital, Atlanta, GA, UO1-MH40597 (Philip T. Ninan, M.D.). We would like to thank Robert E. Drake, M.D., Ph.D., and Nina R. Schooler, Ph.D., for their helpful comments on earlier drafts of this chapter.

REFERENCES

1. Alterman AI, Erdlen, FR, McLellan, AT, Mann, SC. Problem drinking in hospitalized schizophrenic patients. *Addict Behav* 1980;5:273–276.
2. Andreason, NC. *Modified Scale for the Assessment of Negative Symptoms.* Bethesda, MD: Department of Health and Human Services; 1984.
3. Arnd, S, Tyrrell G, Flaum M, Andreasen, NC. Comorbidity of substance abuse and schizophrenia: the role of pre-morbid adjustment. *Psychol Med* 1992;22:379–388.
4. Bartels SJ, Teague GB, Drake RE, Clark RE, Bush PW, Noordsy DL. Substance abuse in schizophrenia: service utilization and costs. *J Nerv Ment Dis* 1993;181: 227–232.
5. Becker HS. Becoming a marijuana user. *Am J Sociol* 1953;59:235–242.
6. Blanchard JJ, Squires D, Henry T, Horan WP, Bogenschutz M, Lauriello J, Bustillo J. Examining an affect regulation model of substance abuse in schizophrenia: the role of traits and coping. *J Nerv Ment Dis* 1999;187:72–79.
7. Breakey WR, Goodell H, Lorenz PC, McHugh PR. Hallucinogenic drugs as precipitants of schizophrenia. *Psychol Med* 1974;4:255–261.
8. Brunette MF, Mueser KT, Xie H., Drake RE. Relationships between symptoms of schizophrenia and substance abuse. *J Nerv Ment Dis* 1997;185:13–20.
9. Buckley P, Thompson P, Way L, Meltzer HY. Substance abuse among patients with treatment-resistant schizophrenia: characteristics and implications for clozapine therapy. *Am J Psychiatry* 1994;151:385–389.
10. Caton CLM, Shrout PE, Dominguez B, Eagle PF, Opler LA, Cournos F. Risk factors for homelessness among women with schizophrenia. *Am J Public Health* 1995;85:1153–1156.
11. Caton CL, Shrout PE, Eagle PF, Opler LA, Felix AF, Dominguez B.. Risk factors for homelessness among schizophrenic men: a case-control study. *Am J Public Health* 1994;84:265–270.
12. Cleghorn JM, Kaplan RD, Szechtman B, Szechtman H, Brown GM, Franco S. Substance abuse and schizophrenia: effect on symptoms but not on neurocognitive function. *J Clin Psychiatry* 1991;52:26–30.

13. Cohen M, Klein DF. Drug abuse in a young psychiatric population. *Am J Orthopsychiatry* 1970;40:448–455.
14. Derogatis LR. *SCL-90-R (Revised)*. Baltimore, MD: Johns Hopkins University School of Medicine; 1977.
15. Dhopesh V, Macfadden A, Maany I, Gamble, G. Absence of parkinsonism among patients in long-term neuroleptic therapy who abuse cocaine. *Psychiatr Serv* 1997;48:95–97.
16. Dixon L, Haas G, Weiden PJ, Sweeney J, Frances AJ. Drug abuse in schizophrenic patients: clinical correlates and reasons for use. *Am J Psychiatry* 1991;148:224–230.
17. Dixon L, McNary S, Lehman A. Substance abuse and family relationships of persons with severe mental illness. *Am J Psychiatry* 1995;152:456–458.
18. Dixon L, Weiden PJ, Haas G, Sweeney J, Frances A. . Increased tardive dyskinesia in alcohol-abusing schizophrenic patients. *Compr Psychiatry* 1992;33:121–122.
19. Drake RE, Ehrlich J. Suicide attempts associated with akathisia. *Am J Psychiatry* 1985;142:499–501.
20. Drake RE, Osher FC, Wallach M. Alcohol use and abuse in schizophrenia: a prospective community study. *J Nerv Ment Dis* 1989;177:408–414.
21. Drake RE, Rosenberg SD, Mueser KT. Assessing substance use disorder in persons with severe mental illness. In: Drake RE, Mueser KT, eds. *New Directions for Mental Health Services,* vol. 70. San Francisco: Jossey-Bass; 1996, pp 3–17.
22. Drake RE., Wallach MA. Moderate drinking among people with severe mental illness. *Hosp Community Psychiatry* 1993;44:780–782.
23. Duke PJ, Pantelis C, Barnes TRE. South Westminster schizophrenia survey: alcohol use and its relationship to symptoms, tardive dyskinesia and illness onset. *Br J Psychiatry* 1994;164:630–636.
24. Endicott J, Spitzer RL, Fleiss JL, Cohen J. The Global Assessment Scale: a procedure for measuring overall severity of psychiatric disturbance. *Arch Gen Psychiatry* 1976;33:766–771.
25. Guy W. *ECDEU Assessment Manual for Psychopharmacology, Revised.* Rockville, MD: U.S. Department of Health and Human Services, DHEW Publication No. ADM 76–338; 1976.
26. Kashner M, Rader L, Rodell D, Beck C, Rodell L, Muller K. Family characteristics, substance abuse, and hospitalization patterns of patients with schizophrenia. *Hosp Community Psychiatry* 1991;42:195–197.
27. Kirkpatrick B, Amador XF, Flaum M, Yale SA, Gorman JM, Carpenter Jr, WT, Tohen M., McGlashan T. The deficit syndrome in the DSM-IV field trial: I. Alcohol an other drug abuse. *Schizophr. Res* 1996;20:69–77.
28. Kreisman D, Blumenthal R, Borenstein M, Woerner M, Kane J, Rifkin A, Reardon, G. Family attitudes and patient social adjustment in a longitudinal study of outpatient schizophrenics receiving low-dose neuroleptics: the family's view. *Psychiatry* 1988;51:3–13.
29. Linszen D, Dingemans P, Lenior M. Cannabis abuse and the course of recent-onset schizophrenic disorders. *Arch Gen Psychiatry* 1994;51:273–279.
30. Lipsey ML. *Design Sensitivity: Statistical Power for Experimental Research.* Newbury Park, CA: Sage; 1990.
31. Lysaker P, Bell M, Beam-Goulet J, Milstein R. Relationship of positive and negative symptoms to cocaine abuse in schizophrenia. *J Nerv Ment Dis* 1994;82:109–112.
32. Mueser KT, Bennett M, Kushner MG. Epidemiology of substance abuse among persons with chronic mental disorders. In: Lehman AF, Dixon L, eds. *Double Jeopardy: Chronic Mental Illness and Substance Abuse.* New York: Harwood Academic; 1995, pp 9–25.

33. Mueser KT, Curran PJ, McHugo, GJ. Factor structure of the Brief Psychiatric Rating Scale in schizophrenia. *Psychol Assess* 1997;9:196–204.

34. Mueser K, Drake R, Wallach M. Dual diagnosis: a review of etiological theories. *Addict Behav* 1998;23:717–734.

35. Mueser KT, Sayers SL, Schooler NR, Mance RM, Haas GL. A multisite investigation of the reliability of the Scale for the Assessment of Negative Symptoms. *Am J Psychiatry* 1994;151:1453–1462.

36. Mueser KT, Yarnold PR, Bellack AS. Diagnostic and demographic correlates of substance abuse in schizophrenia and major affective disorder. *Acta Psychiatr Scand* 1992;85:48–55.

37. Mueser KG, Yarnold PR, Levinson DF, Singh H, Bellack AS, Kee K, Morrison RL, Yadalam KG. Prevalence of substance abuse in schizophrenia: demographic and clinical correlates. *Schizophr Bull* 1990;16:31–56.

38. Mueser KT, Yarnold PR, Rosenberg SD, Swett C, Miles KM, Hill D. Substance use disorder in hospitalized severely mentally ill psychiatric patients: prevalence, correlates, and subgroups. *Schizophr Bull* 2000;24(1):179–192.

39. Overall JE, Gorham DR. The Brief Psychiatric Rating Scale. *Psychol Rep* 1962;10:799–812.

40. Regier DA, Farmer ME, Rae DS, Locke BZ, Keith SJ, Judd LL, Goodwin FK. Comorbidity of mental disorders with alcohol and other drug abuse: results from the Epidemiologic Catchment Area (ECA) study. *J Am Med Assoc* 1990;264:2511–2518.

41. Robinson D, Woerner MG, Pollack S, Lerner G. Subject selection biases in clinical trials: data from a multicenter schizophrenia treatment study. *J Clin Psychopharmacol* 1996;16:170–176.

42. Sayers SL, Curran PJ, Mueser KT. Factor structure and construct validity of the Scale for the Assessment of Negative Symptoms. *Psychol Assess* 1996;8:269–280.

43. Schooler, N, Hogarty G, Weissman M. Social Adjustment Scale II (SAS-II). In: Hargreaves, WA, Atkisson CC, Sorenson JE, eds. *Resource Materials for Community Mental Health Program Evaluations*. Rockville, MD: NIHM; 1979, pp 209–303.

44. Schooler NR, Keith SJ, Severe JB, Matthews SM, Bellack AS, Glick, ID, Hargreaves WA, Kane, JM, Ninan, PT, Frances A, et al. Relapse and rehospitalization during maintenance treatment of schizophrenia: the effects of dose reduction and family treatment. *Arch Gen Psychiatry* 1997;54:453–463.

45. Serper MR, Alpert M, Richardson NA, Dickson S, Allen MH, Werner A. Clinical effects of recent cocaine use on patients with acute schizophrenia. *Am J Psychiatry* 1995;152:1464–1469.

46. Sevy S, Kay SR, Opler L, van Praag HM. Significance of cocaine history in schizophrenia. *J Nerv Ment Dis* 1990;178:642–648.

47. Shrout PE, Fleiss JL. Intraclass correlations: uses in assessing rate reliability. *Psychol Bull* 1979;86:420–428.

48. Simpson GM. Neurological Rating Scale, vol. ADM 9-101. DHHS/Public Health Service—Alcohol Drug Abuse and Mental Health Administration NIMH Treatment Strategies in Schizophrenia Study; 1985.

49. Simpson GM, Angus JWS. A rating scale for extrapyramidal side effects. *Acta Psychiatr Scand* 1970;12(Suppl.):11–19.

50. Sobell MB, Maisto SA, Sobell LC, Copper AM, Sanders B. Developing a prototype for evaluating alcohol treatment effectiveness. In: Sobell LC, Sobell MB, Ward E, eds. *Evaluating Alcohol and Drug Abuse Treatment Effectiveness*. New York: Pergamon; 1980, pp 129–150.

51. Spitzer R, Williams J, Gibbon M, First M. Structured *Clinical Interview for DSM-III-R—Patient Version (SCID-P)*. New York: Biometrics Research Department, New York State Psychiatric Institute; 1988.

52. Trumbetta SL, Mueser K, Quimby E, Bebout R, Teague GB. Social networks and clinical outcomes of dually diagnosed homeless persons. *Behav Ther* 1999;30:389–406.
53. Tsuang MT, Simpson JC, Kronfol Z. Subtypes of drug abuse with psychosis. *Arch Gen Psychiatry* 1982;39:141–147.
54. Van Putten T. The many faces of akathisia. *Compr Psychiatry* 1975;16:43–47.
55. Voruganti LNP, Heslegrave RJ, Awad AG. Neuroleptic dysphoria may be the missing link between schizophrenia and substance abuse. *J Nerv Ment Dis* 1997;185:463–465.
56. Woerner MG, Mannuzza S, Kane JM. Anchoring the BPRS: an aid to improved reliability. *Psychopharmacol Bull* 1988;24:112–117.

Chapter 12

Personality and Substance Use Disorders

A Prospective Study

Kenneth J. Sher
Bruce D. Bartholow
Mark D. Wood

The personality systems of Cloninger (as measured by the Tridimensional Personality Questionnaire [TPQ]) and Eysenck (as measured by the Eysenck Personality Questionnaire [EPQ]) both have been linked to substance use and abuse. The current study examined the predictive utility of both systems for substance use disorder (SUD) diagnoses, both cross-sectionally and prospectively. Participants (N = 489 at baseline) completed the EPQ and TPQ and were assessed via structured diagnostic interviews at baseline and 6 years later (N = 457 at follow-up). Both the EPQ and TPQ scales demonstrated bivariate cross-sectional and prospective associations with SUDs. Within each system, those dimensions marking a broad impulsive sensation-seeking or behavioral disinhibition trait were the best predictors prospectively, although the 2 systems were differentially sensitive to specific diagnoses. These relations remained significant even with autoregressivity, other concurrent SUD diagnoses, and multiple personality dimensions statistically controlled.

Preparation of this chapter was supported in part by grants R37 AA7231 and P50 AA11998 from the National Institute on Alcohol Abuse and Alcoholism. We thank Marvin Zuckerman and Matt McGue for their helpful comments on a previous version of this chapter and the members of the Alcohol, Health, and Behavior Project at the University of Missouri for their assistance with the research.

Personality traits continue to hold a central place in etiological theories of substance use disorders (SUDs; e.g., Caspi et al., 1997; Cloninger, 1987a; Galen, Henderson, & Whitman, 1997; Howard, Kivlahan, & Walker, 1997; Sher & Trull, 1994; Sher, Trull, Bartholow, & Vieth, 1999; Tarter, 1988; Wood, Vinson, & Sher, 2001). However, relatively few systematic efforts have been made to predict clinically meaningful SUD diagnoses using multidimensional, validated systems of personality.

Over the past half century, a number of influential approaches have been developed for specifying the number and nature of domains of personality. From these, three dominant models have emerged: (1) the Big Five factor model (e.g., Costa & McCrae, 1992, 1995; Digman, 1990; Goldberg, 1982, 1990; John, 1990; Wiggins & Trapnell, 1997), (2) the Alternative Five factor model (e.g., Zuckerman, Kuhlman, Joireman, Teta, & Kraft, 1993), and (3) the Big Three factor model (e.g., Buss & Plomin, 1984; Cloninger, 1987a, 1987b; H. J. Eysenck, 1947, 1967, 1981, 1990; H. J. Eysenck & Eysenck, 1975; S. B. G. Eysenck, Eysenck, & Barrett, 1985; Tellegen, 1985). All of these models have received empirical support and are considered to have strong potential for systematically organizing the findings on personality and substance abuse (e.g., see Martin & Sher, 1994; Sher & Trull, 1994). This chapter focuses on two of the most prominent Big Three models—the personality systems of Cloninger (e.g., 1987a, 1987b) and Eysenck (e.g., H. J. Eysenck & Eysenck, 1975; S. B. G. Eysenck et al., 1985)—because both focus on the underlying neurobiological bases of personality that have implications for learning and psychopathology.

As it relates to substance abuse, Cloninger's model (e.g., Cloninger, 1987a, 1987b; Cloninger, Sigvardsson, Przybeck, & Svrakic, 1995; Cloninger, Svrakic, & Przybeck, 1993; Wills, Vaccaro, & McNamara, 1994) hypothesizes that brain systems of behavioral activation, behavioral inhibition, and behavioral maintenance will relate to heritable (i.e., genetic) dimensions of personality, labeled novelty seeking (NS), harm avoidance (HA), and reward dependence (RD). Table 12.1 displays the component traits related to these dimensions, which are assessed via the Tridimensional Personality Questionnaire (TPQ; Cloninger, 1987c). In recent revisions to the theory (e.g., Cloninger et al., 1993), Cloninger proposed a fourth basic dimension labeled persistence (PS; originally subsumed under RD) and added three character traits assumed to develop in adulthood (see Cloninger & Svrakic, 1997). Cloninger proposed that specific patterns of extreme scores on the original three dimensions, coupled with environmental factors, relate to predictable brain–behavior relationships that predispose affected individuals toward alcohol dependence (see Cloninger, 1987a). A large number of studies have concluded that high NS consistently predicts alcohol and other substance abuse and problems (e.g., Battaglia, Przybeck, Bellodi, & Cloninger, 1996; Cloninger et al., 1995; Galen et al., 1997; Heath et al., 1997; Howard et al., 1997; Sher, Wood, Crews, & Vandiver, 1995; Wills et al., 1994). NS also is highly correlated with impulsive sensation seeking (e.g., Zuckerman & Cloninger, 1996), a measure that shows strong relationships with substance abuse (see Zuckerman, 1994). Some

TABLE 12.1. Personality Traits Included in Cloninger's and
Eysenck's Big Three Personality Systems

Trait	Description
Eysenck	
Neuroticism	Anxious, depressed, guilt feelings, tense, irrational, shy, moody, emotional
Extraversion	Sociable, lively, active, assertive, sensation seeking, carefree, dominant, surgent
Psychoticism	Aggressive, cold, egocentric, impersonal, impulsive, antisocial, creative, tough-minded
Cloninger	
Harm avoidance	Cautious, apprehensive, fatigable, inhibited, sensitive to punishment
Reward dependence	Ambitious, sympathetic, warm, industrious, sentimental, persistent, moody
Novelty seeking	Impulsive, excitable, exploratory, quick-tempered, fickle, extravagant, disinhibited

evidence also suggests a potentially important role for HA in predicting alcohol dependence (Sher et al., 1995).

Eysenck's (e.g., H. J. Eysenck & Eysenck, 1975; S. B. G. Eysenck et al., 1985) model is composed of three broad dimensions, including introversion–extraversion (E), neuroticism (N), and psychoticism (P), assessed using the Eysenck Personality Questionnaire (EPQ; H. J. Eysenck & Eysenck, 1975) or the revised version (EPQ-R; H. J. Eysenck, 1988). Table 12.1 displays the traits related to these dimensions. In their study of personality dimensions, Zuckerman et al. (1988) concluded that the EPQ was an excellent marker for the three-factor models they examined. Like Cloninger's (1987a) model, components of Eysenck's model have been linked with substance abuse. Specifically, high scores on P and N have been associated with alcohol abuse (e.g., S. B. G. Eysenck & Eysenck, 1977; Heath et al., 1997; Kilbey, Downey, & Breslau, 1998), other substance use and abuse, or both (S. B. G. Eysenck & Eysenck, 1977; O'Boyle & Barratt, 1993; Rosenthal, Edwards, Ackerman, Knott, & Rosenthal, 1990; Zuckerman, 1993).

Although dimensions of both Cloninger's (e.g., 1987a, 1987b) and Eysenck's (e.g., H. J. Eysenck & Eysenck, 1975; S. B. G. Eysenck et al., 1985) systems have a hypothesized temperamental basis and both have been shown to relate to substance use and abuse, research indicates that the two systems are not simply alternative descriptions of the same dimensions of personality (Heath, Cloninger, & Martin, 1994; Sher et al., 1995; Zuckerman & Cloninger, 1996). Hence, it is useful to compare the two systems with respect to their correlations with SUDs.

Despite a multitude of studies of the personality correlates of alcohol and other substance use (see Sher et al., 1999), several shortcomings in this literature have left many unanswered questions. First, the majority of the studies in this area have investigated only concurrent (i.e., cross-sectional) substance involvement and have not examined prospective relations. Such study designs cannot resolve the issue of whether personality factors are antecedents to or consequences of problematic substance involvement (e.g., McGue, Slutske, & Iacono, 1999; Sher et al., 1999).

Prospective research designs allow the direct modeling of temporal relations. However, third-variable alternative explanations can still make the findings from many existing prospective studies difficult to interpret. For example, in some prospective studies (e.g., Krueger, Caspi, Moffitt, Silva, & McGee, 1996), researchers have not modeled the influence of baseline SUD diagnoses on the relationship between personality measured at baseline and later SUDs. Failure to account for the influence of existing or previous SUDs (i.e., autoregressivity) can artifically inflate prospective relations between personality variables and SUDs (see Nathan, 1988). Accounting for the influence of previous substance abuse can provide stronger evidence of the etiologic relevance of specific personality variables.

On a related note, when modeling the relations between personality and specific substance abuse variables, it is important to examine the specificity of personality effects by statistically controlling for the influence of other concurrent substance abuse. That is, the personality correlates of alcohol abuse, for example, may be partially mediated by other drug or tobacco dependence. By statistically controlling for the effects of such other substance use and abuse, the relations between aspects of personality and specific substance abuse patterns become more clear (e.g., Chassin, Pitts, DeLucia, & Todd, 1999; McGue et al., 1999).

An additional limitation of most work to date has been the tendency to focus on a single SUD category, thus restricting the generalizability of findings. For example, in another recent prospective study, Caspi et al. (1997) examined the influence of personality on subsequent diagnosis of alcohol dependence but did not include other drugs and tobacco. This approach makes it difficult to distinguish whether correlates were specific to alcohol use disorders or reflected more generalized addictive propensities—a limitation noted by Caspi et al.

In addition, many studies in this literature (e.g., Galen et al., 1997; Rosenthal et al., 1990; Shedler & Block, 1990; Wills et al., 1994) have examined personality correlates of substance use or abuse but not diagnoses of SUDs as assessed via structured diagnostic interview. Studies examining use or abuse may suggest dimensions of temperament that relate to the onset of alcohol or other drug involvement, but they do not directly speak to those aspects of personality that may foreshadow more serious and longer-lasting problems with substance abuse. Moreover, among studies that have examined personality correlates of clinically relevant SUD diagnoses, many have used clinical samples (e.g., Battaglia et al., 1996; Schaefer, Sobieraj, & Hollyfield, 1987), some containing individuals with multiple diagnoses (e.g., Gallucci, 1997; Nixon & Parsons, 1990). As discussed elsewhere (Sher et al., 1999), the use of patients in treatment likely oversamples individuals with the most severe problems (i.e., those who have the most frequent or lengthy treatments; Cohen & Cohen, 1984) and often includes individuals with comorbid psychopathology. Furthermore, samples in residential treatment facilities may exhibit different personality characteristics (e.g., lower extraversion, higher neuroticism, or both) merely because of the treatment environment (H. J. Eysenck & Gudjonsson, 1989). When nonclinical samples are used, they frequently are based on convenience or are not systematically ascertained, thus limiting their generalizability.

A final limitation in this literature is that researchers have used a wide variety of constructs to measure personality or behavior tendencies, many of which do not represent broad descriptions of temperament dimensions. For example, researchers have used individual profiles from the Minnestoa Multiphasic Personality Inventory (MMPI) (e.g., Gallucci, 1997; Jaffe & Archer, 1987), measures of sensation seeking and impulse expression (e.g., Ball, Carroll, Babor, & Rounsaville, 1995; see also Brennan, Walfish, & AuBuchon, 1986), impulsivity (along with other dimensions) assessed via observer ratings of behavior (e.g., Harvey, Stokes, Lord, & Pogge, 1996; Mâsse & Tremblay, 1997), measures of passive-aggressive personality (e.g., Flett & Hewitt, 1995), measures of internalizing–externalizing behavior (e.g., Mezzich et al., 1993), measures of ego control and subjective distress (e.g., Shedler & Block, 1990), and measures of augmentation–reduction (e.g., see Ludwig, Caine, & Wikler, 1977), to name a few. Studies using measures based on multidimensional systems of personality may be better able to account for differences among individuals in that findings can be referenced to a well-mapped factor structure and related to the larger personality literature.

A major goal of this work was to examine the role of personality in predicting SUDs, using multidimensional personality systems and standardized clinically relevant diagnostic criteria. Another goal of the study was to model these relationships both cross-sectionally and prospectively (over 7 years) to test the long-term predictive utility of personality constructs. This approach is useful in that variables that predict both current (i.e., cross-sectional) and subsequent (i.e., prospective) substance use disorders arguably can be considered the most important or diagnostic personality predictors. Further, our prospective models were constructed to account for the influence of year 1 (baseline) SUD diagnoses and sex in order to statistically control autoregressivity and gender differences. In addition, to test the specificity of personality effects on SUDs, we controlled for other concurrent SUD diagnoses in both our cross-sectional and prospective models.

Our review of the literature indicates that traits related to impulsivity–behavioral disinhibition are most strongly and consistently associated with substance use and abuse problems (e.g., Battaglia et al., 1996; Cloninger et al., 1995; Galen et al., 1997; Heath et al., 1997; Howard et al., 1997; Kilbey et al., 1998; O'Boyle & Barratt, 1993; Sher et al., 1995; Tarter, 1988; Wills et al., 1994; Zuckerman, 1993). As such, we anticipated that TPQ-NS and EPQ-P would emerge as the most consistent predictors of SUD diagnoses, both cross-sectionally and prospectively. The literature linking neuroticism–negative emotionality and substance abuse is somewhat less compelling (e.g., Sher & Trull, 1994; Sher et al., 1999) but still suggests a positive relationship. Therefore, we expected both TPQ-HA and EPQ-N to be positively related to SUDs. Extraversion–sociability has been less consistently related to substance use and abuse (see Sher et al., 1999). Hence, no specific hypotheses were made concerning the utility of EPQ-E in predicting SUDs. Finally, Cloninger proposed that depending on alcoholism typology (Cloninger, 1987a), reward dependence may exhibit either a positive or a negative association with substance abuse. Because of the young age of our sample (i.e., most relevant for early onset of problems), we anticipated that RD would be negatively related to SUDs.

METHOD

Participants and Procedure

Baseline Screening

An extended description of participant ascertainment and recruitment is provided in Sher et al. (1991) and is briefly reviewed here. All incoming first-time freshmen ($N = 3,944$) at a large Midwestern university were contacted as potential participants in a research study. Approximately 80% ($N = 3,156$) agreed to take part, and those students were screened for the presence of alcoholism in biological parents using versions of the Short Michigan Alcoholism Screening Test (SMAST; Selzer, Vinokur, & van Rooijen, 1975) adapted for assessing alcoholism in biological fathers (F-SMAST) and biological mothers (M-SMAST; Crews & Sher, 1992). Approximately 26% ($n = 808$) of those screened were tentatively classified as either family history positive (FH+) or family history negative (FH–) on the basis of their adapted SMAST scores (the remainder had SMAST scores that did not clearly identify them as either FH+ or FH–, and they were not assessed further). Attempts were then made to administer portions of the Family History–Research Diagnostic Criteria interview (FH-RDC; Endicott, Andreasen, & Spitzer, 1978) to all potential FH+ ($n = 373$); interviews were completed with 97% of them ($n = 362$). A random sample of FH– was also targeted for FH-RDC interviews ($n = 435$) and interviews were completed with 95% of them ($n = 413$). Participants whose biological fathers met both F-SMAST and FH-RDC criteria for alcoholism were classified as FH+, and participants whose first-degree relatives did not meet either F-SMAST or FH-RDC for alcoholism, drug abuse, or antisocial personality disorder, and whose second-degree relatives did not meet FH-RDC criteria for alcohol or drug abuse, were classified as FH–. Participants whose biological mothers but not fathers were alcoholic were not retained for further study ($n = 20$) because of a very low base rate. Participants also were excluded because of inconsistency between adapted SMAST scores and FH-RDC interviews ($n = 154$) and because of concern for possible SUD and antisocial personality disorder in control relatives of our FH– participants ($n = 33$). The sample targeted for further study ($n = 489$) was composed of roughly equal numbers of male and female FH+ and FH– participants (*n* ranging from 113 to 134). The mean age of this sample (at screening) was 18.2 years and 94% of participants were white.

Present Study Sample

Participants were assessed at baseline (year 1), at three subsequent yearly intervals (years 2, 3, and 4), and again 3 years later at year 7. (At baseline, a neuropsychological test battery was also administered.) At each assessment, a trained interviewer who was unaware of participants' family history status administered several sections of the Diagnostic Interview Schedule (DIS). DIS Version III-A (DIS-III-A; Robins, Helzer, Croughan, Williams, & Spitzer, 1985) was used for assessment at baseline and year 2, and DIS-III-R (Robins, Helzer, Cottler, & Goldring, 1989) was used at years 3, 4, and 7. All interviews were cross-edited by a second independent interviewer (also unaware of participants' family history classification) and then reviewed by the interview supervisor. Participants whose interview data were deemed incomplete or unclear during the editing process were recontacted by telephone for further information. In addition to the DIS at each year, participants completed a questionnaire battery containing measures of personality traits, and alcohol, tobacco, and drug consumption patterns, among other measures. For each annual assessment in which they took part, participants received either course credit (if enrolled in introductory psychology) or were paid $25 (at years 1–4) or $75 (at year 7), plus additional stipends for travel to the testing location. The mean age of the sample at year 7 was 24.5 years.

Although efforts were made to assess all participants from the initial baseline sample (*N* = 489) at each year of the study, not all participants were retained. By year 7, individuals who refused further participation (*n* = 29), whom we were unable to locate (*n* = 2), or who were deceased (*n* = 1) were no longer in the data set. The remaining sample size at year 7, therefore, was 457 (93% of participants targeted for follow-up). Although attempts were made to complete all assessments in person, it was not possible to do so in all cases, primarily because of participants' relocation out of the area. These participants were mailed the interview package and completed the interview by telephone. By year 7, we assessed 27% of participants in this way.

Measures

Personality

Tridimensional Personality Questionnaire (TPQ). The 98-item TPQ was developed by Cloninger (1987c) to measure three basic personality dimensions—novelty seeking (TPQ-NS), harm avoidance (TPQ-HA), and reward dependence (TPQ-RD)—hypothesized to be related to alcoholism and personality disorders. For the current analyses, TPQ was partitioned into four scales: TPQ-NS, TPQ-

HA, persistence (TPQ-PS; originally subscale 2 of TPQ-RD), and social sensitivity (TPQ-SS; composed of the original TPQ-RD subscales except PS). Previous studies in which the factor structure of TPQ has been discussed (e.g., Cloninger, Przybeck, & Svrakic, 1991; Heath et al., 1994; Sher et al., 1995) indicate that the persistence subscale of the Reward Dependence scale does not load on any of the factors associated with the other TPQ subscales and, as such, should be considered a separate factor. Coefficient alphas for TPQ scales were .85 for TPQ-HA, .80 for TPQ-NS, .75 for TPQ-SS, and .60 for TPQ-PS. TPQ was administered only at baseline.

Eysenck Personality Questionnaire (EPQ). EPQ (H.J. Eysenck & Eysenck, 1975) consists of 90 items designed to assess the personality traits of extraversion (EPQ-E), neuroticism (EPQ-N), and psychoticism (EPQ-P). A Lie scale is also included in the instrument to measure dissimulation. In previous research, the temporal stability of EPQ over 1 month has been good, with reliability coefficients ranging from .83 to .90. EPQ was administered at each wave of data collection, but the current report focuses only on EPQ data collected at baseline.

Responses to one item from the EPQ-P scale ("Would you take drugs which may have strange or dangerous effects?") were not considered during scoring because this question inquires directly about drug use. Its inclusion in the scoring could artificially inflate the magnitude of the relationship between the EPQ-P scale score and drug and alcohol diagnoses due to criterion contamination (e.g., see Darkes, Greenbaum, & Goldman, 1998). In the current sample, coefficient alphas for EPQ scales were .83 for EPQ-E, .63 for EPQ-P, and .85 for EPQ-N, consistent with previous work (e.g., H. J. Eysenck & Eysenck, 1975).

Substance Use Disorder Diagnoses

Diagnostic measures of alcohol-, drug- and tobacco-related difficulties were collected during the interview appointments at each year using the DIS. In order to maintain consistency across all years of data collection, *DSM-III* diagnostic criteria were used throughout.* For the purposes of the present analyses, three broad diagnostic categories of specific SUDs were examined at both baseline and year 7 (scored for occurrence in the past 12 months): *DSM-III* alcohol use disorder (AUD; alcohol abuse or dependence), *DSM-III* drug use disorder (DUD; drug abuse or dependence), and *DSM-III* tobacco dependence (TD). Alcohol use disorder was partitioned into both broad-band diagnoses (AUD) and narrow-band diagnoses (alcohol dependence, or AD). In addition, a superordinate diagnosis of substance use disorder (SUD-any) was defined as the presence of an AUD, DUD, or TD. Table 12.2 shows the numbers of participants with or without each SUD diagno-

---

*Note that the *DSM-III* criteria for alcohol dependence require evidence of physical dependence and are thus more stringent than the criteria used in the most recent versions of the manual (*DSM-III-R* and *DSM-IV*). In unpublished analyses using data from years

TABLE 12.2. Numbers of Participants Diagnosed at Year 1 and Year 7 as a Function Type of Substance Use Disorder

Temporal Pattern	Diagnoses				
	SUD-Any	AUD	AD	DUD	TD
Not diagnosed at either year	268	322	410	407	369
	(58%)	(70%)	(90%)	(90%)	(81%)
Diagnosed at year 1 only	61	62	20	26	17
	(13%)	(14%)	(4%)	(5%)	(4%)
Diagnosed at year 7 only	46	27	18	17	42
	(10%)	(6%)	(4%)	(4%)	(9%)
Diagnosed at both years 1 and 7	82	46	9	7	29
	(18%)	(10%)	(2%)	(1%)	(6%)
Stability coefficient	$r = .44$	$r = .40$	$r = .28$	$r = .20$	$r = .44$

Note. Each column represents the total year 7 sample ($N = 457$). Numbers in parentheses represent percentages of the total within columns. Diagnoses were made according to the Diagnostic Interview Schedule and *DSM-III* 12-month criteria. SUD-any = any substance use disorder, AUD = alcohol use disorder; AD = alcohol dependence; DUD = drug use disorder, TD = tobacco dependence.

sis at years 1 and 7 and includes stability coefficients (calculated as product-moment correlations).

RESULTS

We present the results of our cross-sectional analyses first, followed by our prospective analyses. Each table in which the results of the hierarchical logistic regression analyses are displayed includes values of c for corresponding steps. The c index (which ranges from 0.5 to 1.0) assesses the relationship between actual diagnosis and predicted probability of diagnosis and represents an index of fit in logistic regression.[†] Although a number of other methods for assessing model fit are available, we present the c statistic because it may be thought of as corresponding to the area under a receiver-operating characteristic (ROC) curve (Hanley & McNeil, 1982), which has been described as a useful tool for assessing diagnostic performance (e.g., Hsiao, Bartko, & Potter, 1989; Murphy et al., 1987; see also Trull & Sher, 1994).

At year 1, two participants did not provide complete EPQ data and two others did not provide complete TPQ data. As such, sample sizes for the baseline cross-sectional analyses ranged from 485 to 489, and sample sizes for prospective analyses ranged from 451 to 457.

3, 4, and 7, we have found that most cases of *DSM-III-R* dependence would be classified as abuse using *DIS-DSM-III* diagnoses.

[†]All logistic regression coefficients were produced using SAS Proc Logistic (SAS Institute, 1990), and all independent variables were standardized prior to analyses (Aiken & West, 1991).

Cross-Sectional Analyses at Baseline

Bivariate Associations

To examine the comparability of the two systems of personality description, we correlated EPQ scales with those of TPQ (see Table 12.3). The strongest associations appear to represent similar assessment of two global dimensions. First, consistent with existing data suggesting that novelty seeking and psychoticism are indicators of a broad impulsivity–disinhibition factor (e.g., Zuckerman & Cloninger, 1996), TPQ-NS and EPQ-P show a moderate, positive association. Second, TPQ-HA and EPQ-N are strongly associated, indicating that both may represent negative emotionality. However, the significant association between TPQ-HA and EPQ-E indicates that TPQ-HA is factorially complex when viewed from the perspective of EPQ. Examination of other correlations in the matrix reveals several small to moderate associations between EPQ and TPQ scales, indicating varying degrees of construct overlap.

Bivariate product-moment correlations between EPQ and TPQ scales and SUD diagnoses are presented in Table 12.4. As predicted, those dimensions most clearly related to impulsivity–disinhibition (i.e., EPQ-P and TPQ-NS) showed the strongest and most consistent associations with the diagnoses we examined. In addition, EPQ-N was consistently and positively related to all SUD diagnoses. It is interesting to note that although TPQ-HA and EPQ-N both appear to represent negative emotionality, and although the two scales were strongly associated in this sample (see Table 12.3), only EPQ-N showed any association with SUD diagnoses in this analysis. Also consistent with our hypotheses based on Cloninger's (1987a) early-onset alcoholism typology, TPQ-PS and TPQ-SS were both nega-

TABLE 12.3. Cross-Sectional Bivariate Associations
Between EPQ and TPQ Scales

Scale	TPQ Scale				EPQ Scale		
	HA	NS	SS	PS	E	N	P
TPQ							
NS	−.15**	—					
SS	−.02	.07	—				
PS	−.13*	−.26**	.07	—			
EPQ							
E	−.49**	.30**	.25**	.15**	—		
N	.52**	.14*	−.06	.02	−.13*	—	
P	−.08	.34**	−.31**	−.11*	.00	.17**	—

Note. N ranges from 487 to 489 for correlations. TPQ = Tridimensional Personality Questionnaire; EPQ = Eysenck Personality Questionnaire. For TPQ scales, HA = harm avoidance, NS = novelty seeking, SS = social sensitivity, PS = persistence (see text). For EPQ scales, E = extraversion, N = neuroticism, P = psychoticism.
*p < .01; **p < .001.

TABLE 12.4. Bivariate Associations Between TPQ and EPQ Scale Scores and Substance Use Disorder Diagnoses, Cross-Sectionally and Prospectively

Year 1 Personality	Year 1 Diagnosis					Year 7 Diagnosis				
	SUD-Any	AUD	AD	DUD	TD	SUD-Any	AUD	AD	DUD	TD
TPQ										
HA	.05	.01	.08	.02	.07	.05	.03	-.02	.02	.08
NS	.31**	.30**	.13**	.15**	.21**	.28*	.14*	.10*	.14*	.21*
SS	-.18**	-.15**	-.06	-.05	-.04	-.10*	-.10*	-.08	-.08	-.06
PS	-.19**	-.14**	-.06	-.08	-.13**	-.14*	-.07	-.07	-.10*	-.14*
EPQ										
N	.24**	.22**	.17**	.16**	.15**	.17*	.13*	.12*	.10*	.14*
E	.07	.12**	-.02	-.03	.05	.01	.05	.00	-.01	-.02
P	.31**	.34**	.19**	.17**	.16**	.25*	.23*	.25*	.16*	.06

Note. N ranges from 487 to 489 for cross-sectional correlations. N ranges from 451 to 457 for prospective correlations. Reported associations are point biserial coefficients. All diagnoses were made according to the Diagnostic Interview Schedule and *DSM-III* 12-month criteria. Tridimensional Personality Questionnaire (TPQ) scales: HA = harm avoidance; NS = novelty seeking; SS = social sensitivity; PS = persistence. Eysenck Personality Questionnaire (EPQ) scales: N = neuroticism; E = extraversion; P = psychoticism. Diagnoses: AUD = alcohol abuse, dependence, or both; AD = alcohol dependence; DUD = drug abuse, dependence, or both; TD = tobacco dependence; SUD-any = any substance use disorder.
* $p < .05$; ** $p < .001$.

tively associated with SUD diagnoses. EPQ-E showed only a small but reliable association with AUD.

Regression Models Relating Personality Scales and SUD Diagnoses

In order to examine the unique effects of each scale in predicting each disorder, we constructed several hierarchical logistic regression models. Although we were not interested in sex as a predictor of SUDs, sex was included in the first step of each model as a covariate to control for its effects.*

Table 12.5 presents the results of two logistic regression analyses in which SUD diagnoses were predicted from EPQ and TPQ scale main effects.[†] For both systems, the addition of the personality constructs resulted in a significant increment in model fit ($p < .05$) for each of the SUDs examined. Further, EPQ-P and EPQ-N were positive cross-sectional predictors of all SUD diagnoses. In addition, EPQ-E was significantly related to AUD but not the narrow-band AD diagnosis. As shown in the bottom section of Table 12.5, TPQ-NS emerged as a consistent, significant associate of each disorder. In addition, TPQ-HA was significantly related to the narrow-band AD diagnosis but not AUD. The negative relationship between TPQ-SS and SUD-any suggests that individuals with a particularly low sensitivity for social approval may be more likely to obtain an SUD diagnosis.

---

*In addition, no specific hypotheses involving family history of alcoholism were made in this study. Previous analyses using much of the same sample reported here (Sher et al., 1991, 1995) indicated that variations in adult temperament may mediate the effects of family history on substance use and abuse. Thus, family history was not included in our primary models so that the size of any personality–SUD relations could be better estimated. However, it is also possible that personality traits may moderate family history effects (Rogosch, Chassin, & Sher, 1990). Furthermore, family history was an important component of the sampling framework for this study, and as such its exclusion could have implications for our results. Therefore, we included family history main effects and interactions with personality scales in a separate set of regression models identical to those we report. The nature of our results was unchanged in these analyses. That is, we found no evidence of moderation by family history and the personality–SUD relations in these analyses were essentially the same as those we report.

[†]In both models presented in Table 12.5, a third step was included in which interactions of scales were considered. However, including interaction terms in the present data set did not lead to a significant change in chi-square for any of the diagnoses for either the EPQ or TPQ analyses, indicating that the majority of the unique variance in diagnoses was accounted for by the main effect terms. As such, no interactions are presented in the table. The same is true for the analogous prospective analyses presented in Table 12.6. In all cases where interactions among scale scores were examined, main effect terms were centered prior to construction of cross-products (Aiken & West, 1991). In addition, quadratic cross-product terms were entered into all models containing interaction terms to control for potentially spurious moderator effects (Lubinski & Humphreys, 1990). Although a three-way interaction involving RD, HA, and NS related to substance use was reported by Wills et al. (1994) and may be implied in Cloninger's (1987b) theory, no such relationship was apparent in our data for any of the diagnoses we examined.

TABLE 12.5. Baseline Cross-Sectional Logistic Regression Analyses Predicting Substance Use Disorder Diagnoses from EPQ and TPQ Scales Separately

	Year 1 Diagnosis														
	SUD-Any			AUD			AD			DUD			TD		
Year 1 Predictor	$\Delta\chi^2$	c	Std. Est.	$\Delta\chi^2$	c	Std. Est.	$\Delta\chi^2$	c	Std. Est.	$\Delta\chi^2$	c	Std. Est.	$\Delta\chi^2$	c	Std. Est.
Model Using EPQ Scales															
Step 1: Covariate	18.3*	.60		22.9*	.63		.23	.52		.10	.51		.90	.54	
Sex			−.21*			−.27*			.02			.03			.14
Step 2: EPQ Scales	66.0*	.76		71.1*	.80		24.9*	.73		20.0*	.69		22.3*	.68	
Psychoticism			.30*			.33*			.29*			.24*			.24*
Extraversion			.14*			.24*			−.02			−.04			.10
Neuroticism			.31*			.32*			.31*			.26*			.22*
Model Using TPQ Scales															
Step 1: Covariate	18.3*	.60		22.9*	.63		.23	.52		.10	.51		.90	.54	
Sex			−.21*			−.29*			−.03			.03			.12
Step 2: TPQ Scales	72.9*	.76		57.1*	.77		16.2*	.72		20.4*	.70		31.7*	.73	
Harm avoidance			.15*			.11			.23*			.09			.16
Novelty seeking			.43*			.44*			.35*			.33*			.39*
Social sensitivity			−.18*			−.12			−.14			−.14			−.14
Persistence			−.11			−.06			.00			−.06			−.12

Note. All coefficients are taken from the second step in each analysis. The c statistic relates to model fit in logistic regression (see text). For EPQ analyses, Step 2 $\Delta\chi^2$ $df = 3$; for TPQ analyses, Step 2 $\Delta\chi^2$ $df = 4$. For both analyses, Step 1 χ^2 $df = 1$. All diagnoses were made according to the Diagnostic Interview Schedule and *DSM-III* 12-month criteria. Sex was coded 1 = female, 0 = male. EPQ = Eysenck Personality Questionnaire; TPQ = Tridimensional Personality Questionnaire; AUD = alcohol abuse, dependence, or both; AD = alcohol dependence; DUD = drug use disorder; TD = tobacco dependence; SUD-any = any substance use disorder. Std. Est. = standardized logistic regression coefficient.
* $p < .05$.

161

As a more conservative strategy, we examined the specificity of personality trait effects on AUD, AD, DUD, and TD by including other concurrent SUD diagnoses as covariates (along with sex) in the first step of logistic regression analyses similar to those presented in Table 12.5.* These analyses demonstrate the unique effects of EPQ and TPQ scale scores on specific SUD diagnoses over the effects of other SUD diagnoses. In predicting AUD, the effects of all three EPQ scales remained significant (standard estimates .25–.30, $p < .05$), as did TPQ-NS (standard estimate = .40, $p < .05$), when controlling for the effects of DUD and TD. Similarly for AD, the effects of EPQ-P, EPQ-N, and TPQ-NS remained significant (standard estimates = .22, .25, and .26, respectively, $p < .05$) while controlling for the effects of DUD and TD. On the other hand, in predicting DUD, the effects of EPQ-P, EPQ-N, and TPQ-NS were all reduced to nonsignificance (standard estimates = .13, .15, and .17, respectively) when the effects of AUD and TD were modeled. For TD, the effects of EPQ-P and TPQ-NS remained significant (standard estimates = .16 and .30, respectively, $p < .05$) when controlling for AUD and DUD, and although the size of the EPQ-N effect was comparable with that of EPQ-P, it did not reach statistical significance (standard estimate = .16, $p < .07$). Thus, in general it appears that EPQ-P, EPQ-N, and TPQ-NS are robust cross-sectional correlates of most SUD diagnoses even when controlling for potential comorbidity with other concurrent SUDs. However, associations with DUD were reduced when the effects of TD and AUD were simultaneously modeled.

Prospective Analyses: Baseline to Year 7

Bivariate Associations

Table 12.4 presents product-moment correlations between baseline EPQ and TPQ scales and year 7 SUD diagnoses. As shown in the table, the pattern of significant prospective associations is highly similar to that found with the cross-sectional analyses at year 1. In general, TPQ-NS, EPQ-P, and EPQ-N were all consistent and positive correlates of later SUD diagnoses, whereas TPQ-SS and TPQ-PS were negatively associated with diagnoses.

Predicting Year 7 SUD Diagnoses From Year 1 Personality

We constructed a series of prospective, hierarchical regression models analogous to the cross-sectional models presented in Table 12.5. To control for autoregressivity in our outcome variables (see stability coefficients in Table 12.2), year 1 diagnosis was entered into each model in the first step as a covariate, along with sex. The results of these analyses are presented in Table 12.6. As expected, receiving an

---

*In examining the specificity of personality trait effects on DUD and TD, we covaried the broad-band AUD diagnosis and not the narrow-band AD diagnosis because the former encompasses the latter. Similarly, in examining specific prediction of AUD, we did not control for AD, and vice versa.

TABLE 12.6. Prospective Analyses Predicting Substance Use Disorder Diagnoses from EPQ and TPQ Scales

	SUD-Any			AUD			AD			DUD			TD		
Year 1 Predictor	$\Delta\chi^2$	c	Std. Est.	$\Delta\chi^2$	c	Std. Est.	$\Delta\chi^2$	c	Std. Est.	$\Delta\chi^2$	c	Std. Est.	$\Delta\chi^2$	c	Std. Est.
Model Using EPQ Scales															
Step 1: Covariates	93.2*	.76		75.5*	.77		27.4*	.73		21.7*	.74		66.6*	.73	
Baseline diagnosis			.45*			.41*			.27*			.24*			.46*
Sex			−.17*			−.28*			−.29*			−.40*			−.18*
Step 2: EPQ Scales	8.0	.78		5.4	.79		15.0*	.84		5.7	.80		4.8	.75	
Psychoticism			.13*			.12			.33*			.15			−.07
Extraversion			.00			.07			.09			.05			−.06
Neuroticism			.10			.10			.14			.18			.14
Model Using TPQ Scales															
Step 1: Covariates	93.2*	.76		75.5*	.77		27.4*	.73		21.7*	.74		66.6*	.73	
Baseline diagnosis			.42*			.44*			.31*			.20*			.42*
Sex			−.22*			−.31*			−.30*			−.43*			−.17
Step 2: TPQ Scales	19.9*	.79		2.9	.78		4.7	.76		13.6*	.81		14.2*	.79	
Harm avoidance			.10			.08			−.09			.14			.15
Novelty seeking			.28*			.10			.15			.35*			.25*
Social sensitivity			−.01			.01			−.08			−.07			−.01
Persistence			−.05			−.03			−.15			−.16			−.09

Note. All coefficients are taken from the second step in each analysis. The c statistic relates to model fit in logistic regression (see text). For EPQ analyses, Step 2 $\Delta\chi^2$ $df = 3$; for TPQ analyses, Step 2 $\Delta\chi^2$ $df = 4$. For both analyses, Step 1 χ^2 $df = 2$. All diagnoses were made according to the Diagnostic Interview Schedule and *DSM-III* 12-month criteria. Sex was coded 1 = female, 2 = male. EPQ = Eysenck Personality Questionnaire; TPQ = Tridimensional Personality Questionnaire; AUD = alcohol abuse, dependence, or both; AD = alcohol dependence; DUD = drug use disorder; TD = tobacco dependence; SUD-any = any substance use disorder. Std. Est. = standardized logistic regression coefficient.

* $p < .05$.

SUD diagnosis at baseline consistently predicted diagnosing at year 7. In addition, and consistent with the findings of nationally based epidemiological studies (e.g., Harford & Grant, 1994; Warner, Kessler, Hughes, Anthony, & Nelson, 1995), men were significantly more likely to receive each diagnosis at year 7 than were women.

Of greater interest in Table 12.6 is the prospective prediction of diagnoses by baseline EPQ and TPQ scales. Similar to the cross-sectional analyses, EPQ-P and TPQ-NS emerged as the most important scales in predicting later substance abuse problems. Specifically, high baseline scores on EPQ-P were predictive of later alcohol dependence, whereas high baseline scores on TPQ-NS predicted later drug use disorder and tobacco dependence. No other personality scales emerged as significant prospective predictors of SUD diagnoses in these analyses where baseline diagnosis was statistically controlled.*

As with our cross-sectional models, we examined the specificity of personality predictors of AUD, AD, DUD, and TD by including other concurrent SUD diagnoses as covariates (along with sex and baseline diagnoses) in the first step of logistic regression analyses similar to those presented in Table 12.6. EPQ-P remained a significant predictor of AD (standard estimate = .30, $p < .05$) when controlling for the effects of DUD and TD. In addition, TPQ-NS significantly predicted DUD (standard estimate = .29, $p < .05$) when controlling for AUD and TD, and it significantly predicted TD (standard estimate = .21, $p < .05$) when controlling for AUD and DUD. Hence, controlling for other concurrent SUD diagnoses had little impact on the prospective prediction of specific SUD diagnoses by EPQ-P and TPQ-NS, indicating that these scales are fairly robust in predicting later problems with alcohol, and other drugs and tobacco, respectively.

DISCUSSION

The primary goal advanced for this study was to examine the nature of cross-sectional and prospective relations among well-defined systems of personality and interview-derived SUD diagnoses. Several important findings related to this goal emerged in our analyses. Within each personality system, traits that relate most clearly to disinhibition or behavioral undercontrol (i.e., TPQ-NS and EPQ-P) were the most consistent predictors of SUDs, both cross-sectionally and prospectively. This finding is generally consistent with previous work linking antisociality–disinhibition with alcohol involvement, drug involvement, or both (e.g., Bates &

---

*As a less stringent test of prospective prediction, we constructed an additional set of models in which baseline diagnoses were not included as covariates. In these models, EPQ-P, EPQ-N, and TPQ-NS all emerged as strong predictors of each diagnosis, and TPQ-HA was important in predicting TD and AUD. Hence, although neuroticism and harm avoidance do not appear to be important prospective predictors in our other models, researchers may wish to consider their influence as potentially important.

Labouvie, 1995; Caspi et al., 1997; McGue et al., 1999; Schuckit, 1998; Sher et al., 1995). In the cross-sectional analyses using multiple predictors, both TPQ-NS and EPQ-P provided very robust prediction of all of the SUDs we examined. However, using a conservative approach, prospective prediction was very limited with both personality systems when baseline diagnoses were modeled. Nevertheless, individuals with high baseline scores on either TPQ-NS or EPQ-P were more likely than their lower-scoring peers to later receive an SUD diagnosis. Even when the effects of other concurrent SUD diagnoses were statistically controlled, EPQ-P and TPQ-NS showed significant cross-sectional relations to all SUD diagnoses other than DUD. Furthermore, prospective models controlling for other concurrent SUDs similarly showed that EPQ-P remained a significant factor in predicting later AD, and TPQ-NS reliably predicted later problems with other drugs and tobacco.

In addition, traits related to negative emotionality were reliable correlates of SUD diagnoses cross-sectionally. Specifically, EPQ-N demonstrated significant small to moderate correlations as well as moderate logistic regression coefficients with each of the outcomes we examined. Controlling for the effects of other concurrent SUDs did not eliminate these effects for AUD and AD—a finding similar to those of McGue et al. (1999). TPQ-HA was a less important predictor overall and was primarily related to AD. Prospectively, scales assessing negative emotionality did not demonstrate robust prediction of SUD diagnoses when autoregressivity was controlled. However, TPQ-HA and EPQ-N did emerge as significant prospective predictors using less conservative models (see footnote on p. 162). Because controlling for autoregression eliminated prospective prediction from traits related to negative emotionality, the interpretation of these data is ambiguous. More specifically, our findings are consistent both with the perspective that negative emotionality is a consequence of SUDs and that negative emotionality is causally related to SUDs (but long-term effects are mediated by autoregression of diagnosis). More extensive statistical modeling of the association between alcohol use disorders and anxiety disorders (Kushner, Sher, & Erickson, 1998) also provides evidence consistent with both perspectives.

Extraversion, also identified in the literature as a potentially important correlate of SUDs (e.g., see Sher et al., 1999), was a reliable cross-sectional predictor of AUD and a weak but reliable predictor of the superordinate SUD-any category. However, it did not relate to any SUD diagnoses prospectively. Thus, we must conclude that the support for an Extraversion-SUD link is weak at best and most implicated with respect to (broad-band) alcohol use disorders. Presumably, highly sociable individuals might be at high risk for developing drinking problems primarily because they seek out situations where alcohol consumption is embedded in the social context. Perhaps one reason why no prospective effect of EPQ-E was found in this study is because the social context of drinking changes dramatically between the freshman year in college and 6 years later (see Sher, Bartholow, & Nanda, in press).

EPQ and TPQ appeared to be differentially sensitive to specific diagnoses in our data. In all of the prospective models we reported, the personality system assessed by EPQ, and specifically the dimension of personality measured by the P scale, added significantly to the prediction of a diagnosis of alcohol dependence even when the variance from several other factors (i.e., baseline diagnosis, concurrent SUD diagnosis, sex) was modeled. However, Eysenck's (e.g., H. J. Eysenck & Eysenck, 1975; S. B. G. Eysenck et al., 1985) system does not appear to make any unique contribution in prospectively predicting other diagnoses, such as tobacco and drug abuse or dependence.

On the other hand, the findings from all of our prospective models indicate that Cloninger's (1987a, 1987b) system of personality contains unique and important predictors of both tobacco and drug abuse and dependence but does not appear to reliably predict alcohol abuse or dependence over 7 years. Specifically, it appears that the dimension of personality tapped by the NS scale should be considered an extremely important personality factor in determining which late adolescents or young adults may be at risk for developing problems with tobacco and other drugs by the time they reach their mid-20s. This finding is entirely consistent with prior behavioral genetic research (Heath, Madden, Slutske, & Martin, 1995), which shows that novelty seeking, but not psychoticism, is an important personality predictor of smoking behavior among Australian twins.

These patterns of findings may speak to the issue of where the two systems are similar and where they are unique, as discussed by others (e.g., Heath et al., 1994; Sher et al., 1995; Zuckerman & Cloninger, 1996). Heath et al. argued that the two systems are not merely alternative descriptions of the same dimensions of personality. It is not yet obvious whether differences across EPQ and TPQ represent gaps in the constructs used within each system or psychometric limitations of the individual scales.

Our hypothesis that traits related to behavioral undercontrol are most relevant for predicting addictive phenomena was supported by the data linking NS and P to later SUDs. That these results were still obtained after controlling for baseline diagnoses provides strong evidence against the hypothesis that these personality–SUD relations are spurious. However, the exact meaning of these findings requires further clarification.

There appears to be noticeable inconsistency across forms of SUD, which may be attributable to important differences in the constructs assessed by NS and P. Some recent evidence bears on these potential differences. For example, although in our previous conjoint factor analysis (Sher et al., 1995) we found that P loaded strongly on an NS factor, substantial cross-loadings also were evident with TPQ-SS. This finding is consistent with the Big Five factor interpretation of P (e.g., Costa & McCrae, 1995), which suggests both an agreeableness and a conscientiousness component. In contrast, NS appears to be more reflective of impulsivity and sensation seeking (Zuckerman & Cloninger, 1996). Furthermore, behavioral genetic research indicates that NS may be a more heritable dimension than P (Heath et al., 1994; Zuckerman, 1994) and that the underlying coherence of P is not genetically based (Heath & Martin, 1990). Thus, it is not surprising that although NS and P were moderately correlated in the present study, the correlation is far from unity and the patterns of correlations with external criteria differ.

However, even if seeming differences in SUD correlates of NS and P could be detailed, the etiological significance of obtained personality correlates must be examined in the context of specific motivational processes. As we have discussed elsewhere (Sher et al., 1999; Sher & Trull, 1994), personality constructs are probably best viewed as quite distal to drug use and abuse, and several alternative models relating behavioral undercontrol can be considered. For example, the psychobiological underpinnings of behavioral control could conceivably represent a vulnerability to the disinhibiting (McDougall, 1929), hypnotic (H. J. Eysenck, 1957), or stress-reducing (Sher, 1987) effects of sedative drugs. Alternatively, facets of behavioral undercontrol such as sensation seeking could relate to reward seeking (Cooper, Frone, Russell, & Mudar, 1995) and consequent use of drugs to enhance experience. Evaluation of specific mechanisms mediating personality effects is beyond the scope of this chapter. Nevertheless, it is important to emphasize that correlations between traits and behaviors represent mere associations and do not provide an accounting of etiological process. It may be best to direct research efforts toward placing aspects of temperament within the context of larger, more comprehensive psychosocial models (see Cooper et al., 1995; Sher, 1991; Sher et al., 1999).

The use of a large mixed-gender sample, multidimensional personality systems, structured diagnostic interviews, and lengthy follow-up intervals are important strengths of this research. Moreover, by controlling for baseline associations, other concurrent diagnoses, and sex differences, we were able to provide a more stringent test of the etiologic relevance of temperament than has typically been examined. Nonetheless, some limitations of the present study should be noted.

Although the sample was systematically ascertained using a known sampling frame (all first-time freshmen at a large university), college enrollment requires a degree of academic success in secondary school and, consequently, certain aspects of educational achievement and its correlates (e.g., conduct problems, lower intelligence) may be underrepresented in this sample. Also, all forms of SUD are relatively prevalent in young adulthood, suggesting that perhaps substance involvement is more related to developmental and social factors associated with this stage of life as opposed to stable individual differences. Thus, it is possible that stronger or even different personality correlates would be evident in older samples. Further follow-up of the sample will provide additional opportunities to observe possible changes in SUD–personality relations.

It should be noted that because the age of onset of many substance-related problems may predate college enrollment (Warner et al., 1995), and given the high prevalence of SUD diagnoses in our baseline data, the prospective personality–SUD relations we report may indicate both persistence of diagnoses and onset of new diagnoses, rather than purely onset. Finally, all of the data reported in this chapter are based on self-reports and the diagnostic data derived from structured interviews. Consequently, various self-report biases could influence the levels of both predictor and criterion variables and represent a "third variable" confound affecting the magnitude of personality–SUD correlations. However, any such effects should be minimized in all prospective analyses, because the bias would need to be maintained over 6 years. When baseline diagnoses are statistically controlled, effects of such a confound should be effectively eliminated. It is for these reasons that we have greatest confidence in our prospective analyses that control for baseline diagnosis. However, such highly conservative prospective analyses can fail to detect genuine causal effects and care must be taken not to equate negative findings in these analyses with the lack of an effect, especially because less conservative cross-sectional and prospective (excluding baseline control) models do show patterns of hypothesized relations.

Despite potential limitations, the current study represents an important advance in the search for personality correlates and predictors of SUDs. Several weaknesses in the extant literature have been addressed in this study and our findings suggest that the systems of Cloninger (e.g., 1987a, 1987b) and Eysenck (e.g., H. J. Eysenck & Eysenck, 1975; S. B. G. Eysenck et al., 1985) provide unique predictions of problems with alcohol and other drugs. These results provide further evidence of the etiologic relevance of traits related to behavioral undercontrol for SUDs. Future research could profitably extend these findings to other developmental periods and further explicate the potential mediational processes by which personality dimensions influence SUDs.

REFERENCES

1. Aiken LS, West SG. *Multiple Regression: Testing and Interpreting Interactions.* Newbury Park, CA: Sage; 1991.
2. American Psychiatric Association. *Diagnostic and Statistical Manual of Mental Disorders, Third Edition.* Washington, DC: Author; 1980.
3. American Psychiatric Association. *Diagnostic and Statistical Manual of Mental Disorders, Third Edition Revised.* Washington, DC: Author; 1987.
4. American Psychiatric Association. *Diagnostic and Statistical Manual of Mental Disorders, Fourth Edition.* Washington, DC: Author; 1994.
5. Ball SA, Carroll KM, Babor TF, Rounsaville BJ. Subtypes of cocaine abusers: support for a Type A–Type B distinction. *Journal of Consulting and Clinical Psychology* 1995;63:115–124.
6. Bates ME, Labouvie EW. Personality-environment constellations and alcohol use: a process-oriented study of intraindividual change during adolescence. *Psychology of Addictive Behaviors* 1995;9:23–35.
7. Battaglia M, Przybeck TR, Bellodi L, Cloninger CR. Temperament dimensions explain the comorbidity of psychiatric disorders. *Comprehensive Psychiatry* 1996;37:292–298.
8. Brennan AF, Walfish S, AuBuchon P. Alcohol use and abuse in college students: I. A review of individual and personality correlates. *International Journal of the Addictions* 1986;21:449–474.
9. Buss AH, Plomin R. *Temperament: Early developing personality traits.* Hillsdale, NJ: Erlbaum; 1984.
10. Caspi A, Begg D, Dickson N, Harrington H, Langley J, Moffitt TE, Silva PA. Person-

ality differences predict health-risk behaviors in young adulthood: evidence from a longitudinal study. *Journal of Personality and Social Psychology* 1997;73:1052–1063.

11. Chassin L, Pitts SC, DeLucia C, Todd M. A longitudinal study of children of alcoholics: predicting young adult substance use disorders, anxiety, and depression. *Journal of Abnormal Psychology* 1999;108:106–119.

12. Cloninger CR. Neurogenetic adaptive mechanisms in alcoholism. *Science* 1987a;236:410–416.

13. Cloninger CR. A systematic method for clinical description and classification of personality variants. *Archives of General Psychiatry* 1987b;44:573–588.

14. Cloninger CR. *Tridimensional Personality Questionnaire, Version 4.* Unpublished manuscript; 1987c.

15. Cloninger CR, Przybeck T, Svrakic DM. The Tridimensional Personality Questionnaire: U.S. normative data. *Psychological Reports* 1991;69:1047–1057.

16. Cloninger CR, Sigvardsson S, Przybeck T, Svrakic DMM. Personality antecedents of alcoholism in a national area probability sample. *European Archives of Psychiatry and Clinical Neuroscience* 1995;245:239–244.

17. Cloninger CR, Svrakic, DM. Integrative psychobiological approach to psychiatric assessment and treatment. *Psychiatry: Interpersonal and Biological Processes* 1997;60:120–141.

18. Cloninger CR, Svrakic DM, Przybeck T. A psychobiological model of temperament and character. *Archives of General Psychiatry* 1993;50:975–990.

19. Cohen P, Cohen J. The clinician's illusion. *Archives of General Psychiatry* 1984;41:1178–1182.

20. Cooper ML, Frone MR, Russell M, Mudar P. Drinking to regulate positive and negative emotions: a motivational model of alcohol use. *Journal of Personality and Social Psychology* 1995;69:990–1005.

21. Costa PT, Jr, McCrae RR. *Revised NEO Personality Inventory (NEO-PI-R) and NEO Five-Factor Inventory (NEO-FFI) Professional Manual.* Odessa, FL: Psychological Assessment Resources; 1992.

22. Costa PT, Jr, McCrae RR. Primary traits of Eysenck's P-E-N system: Three- and five-factor solutions. *Journal of Personality and Social Psychology* 1995;69:308–317.

23. Crews TM, Sher KJ. Using adapted short MASTs for assessing parental alcoholism: reliability and validity. *Alcoholism: Clinical and Experimental Research* 1992;16:576–584.

24. Darkes J, Greenbaum PE, Goldman MS. Sensation seeking-disinhibition and alcohol use: exploring issues of criterion contamination. *Psychological Assessment* 1998;10:71–76.

25. Digman JM. Personality structure: emergence of the five-factor model. *Annual Review of Psychology* 1990;41:417–440.

26. Endicott J, Andreasen N, Spitzer RL. *Family History—Research Diagnostic Criteria (FH-RDC).* Washington, DC: National Institute of Mental Health; 1978.

27. Eysenck HJ. *Dimensions of personality.* New York: Praeger; 1947.

28. Eysenck HJ. Drugs and personality I: theory and methodology. *Journal of Mental Science* 1957;103:119–131.

29. Eysenck HJ. *The Biological Basis of Personality.* Springfield, IL: Charles C Thomas; 1967.

30. Eysenck HJ. General features of the model. In: Eysenck, HJ, ed. *A Model for Personality.* New York: Springer-Verlag; 1981, pp 1–37.

31. Eysenck HJ. *Eysenck Personality Questionnaire-Revised.* San Diego, CA: Educational and Industrial Testing Services; 1988.

32. Eysenck HJ. Genetic and environmental contributions to individual differences: the three major dimensions of personality. *Journal of Personality* 1990;58:245–261.

33. Eysenck HJ, Eysenck SBG. *Manual of the Eysenck Personality Questionnaire.* San Diego, CA: Educational and Industrial Testing Services; 1975.

34. Eysenck HJ, Gudjonsson GH. *The Cause and Cures of Criminality.* New York: Plenum; 1989.

35. Eysenck SBG, Eysenck HJ. The place of impulsiveness in a dimensional system of personality description. *British Journal of Social and Clinical Psychology* 1977;16:57–68.

36. Eysenck SBG, Eysenck HJ, Barrett P. A revised version of the psychoticism scale. *Personality and Individual Differences* 1985;6;21–29.

37. Flett GL, Hewitt PL. Criterion validity and psychometric properties of the Affect Intensity Measure in a psychiatric sample. *Personality and Individual Differences* 1995;19:585–591.

38. Galen LW, Henderson MJ, Whitman RD. The utility of novelty seeking, harm avoidance, and expectancy in the prediction of drinking. *Addictive Behaviors* 1992;22:93–106.

39. Gallucci NT. On the identification of patterns of substance abuse with the MMPI-A. *Psychological Assessment* 1997;9:224–232.

40. Goldberg LR. From Ace to Zombie: some explorations in the language of personality. In: Spielberger CD, Butcher, JN, eds. *Advances in Personality Assessment,* vol. 1. Hillsdale, NJ: Erlbaum; 1982, pp 203–234.

41. Goldberg LR. An alternative "description of personality": the Big-Five factor structure. *Journal of Personality and Social Psychology* 1990;59:1216–1229.

42. Hanley JA, McNeil BJ. The meaning and use of the area under a receiver operating characteristic (ROC) curve. *Radiology* 1982;143:29–36.

43. Harford TC, Grant BF. Prevalence and population validity of *DSM-III-R* alcohol abuse and dependence: the 1989 National Longitudinal Survey on Youth. *Journal of Substance Abuse* 1994;6:37–44.

44. Harvey PD, Stokes JL, Lord J, Pogge DL. Neurocognitive and personality assessment of adolescent substance abusers: a multidimensional approach. *Assessment* 1996;3:241–253.

45. Heath AC, Bucholz KK, Madden PAF, Dinwiddie SH, Slutske WS, Bierut LJ, Stratham DJ, Dunne MP, Whitfield JB, Martin NG. Genetic and environmental contributions to alcohol dependence risk in a national twin sample: consistency of findings in women and men. *Psychological Medicine* 1997;27:1381–1396.

46. Heath AC, Cloninger CR, Martin NG. Testing a model of the genetic structure of personality: a comparison of the personality systems of Cloninger and Eysenck. *Journal of Personality and Social Psychology* 1994;66:762–775.

47. Heath AC, Madden PAF, Slutske WS, Martin NG. Personality and the inheritance of smoking behavior: a genetic perspective. *Behavior Genetics* 1995;25:103–117.

48. Heath AC, Martin NG. Psychoticism as a dimension of personality: a multivariate genetic test of Eysenck and Eysenck's psychoticism construct. *Journal of Personality and Social Psychology* 1990;58:111–121.

49. Howard MO, Kivlahan D, Walker RD. Cloninger's tridimensional theory of personality and psychopathology: applications to substance use disorders. *Journal of Studies on Alcohol* 1997;58:48–66.

50. Hsiao JK, Bartko JJ, Potter WZ. Diagnosing diagnoses: receiver operating characteristic methods and psychiatry. *Archives of General Psychiatry* 1989;46:664–667.

51. Jaffe LT, Archer RP. The prediction of drug use among college students from MMPI, MCMI, and sensation seeking scales. *Journal of Personality Assessment* 1987;51:243–253.

52. John OP. The "Big-Five" factor taxonomy: dimensions of personality in the natural language and in questionnaires. In: Pervin LA, ed. *Handbook of Personality: Theory and Research.* New York: Guilford; 1990, pp 66–100.

53. Kilbey MM, Downey K, Breslau N. Predicting the emergence and persistence of alcohol dependence in young adults: the role of expectancy and other risk factors. *Experimental and Clinical Psychopharmacology* 1998;6:149–156.

54. Krueger RF, Caspi A, Moffitt TE, Silva PA, McGee R. Personality traits are differentially linked to mental disorders: a multitrait-multidiagnosis study of an adolescent birth cohort. *Journal of Abnormal Psychology* 1996;105:299–312.

55. Kushner MG, Sher KJ, Erickson DJ. Prospective analysis of the relation between DSM-III anxiety disorders and alcohol use disorders. *American Journal of Psychiatry* 1999;156:723–732.

56. Lubinski,D, Humphreys LG. Assessing spurious "moderator effects": illustrated substantively with the hypothesized ("synergistic") relation between spatial and mathematical ability. *Psychological Bulletin* 1990;107:385–393.

57. Ludwig AM, Caine RB, Wikler A. Stimulus intensity modulation and alcohol consumption. *Journal of Studies on Alcohol* 1977;38:2049–2056.

58. Martin ED, Sher KJ. Family history of alcoholism, alcohol use disorders, and the Five-Factor model of personality. *Journal of Studies on Alcohol* 1994;55:81–90.

59. Mâsse LC, Tremblay RE. Behavior of boys in kindergarten and onset of substance use during adolescence. *Archives of General Psychiatry* 1997;54:62–68.

60. McDougall W. The chemical theory of temperament applied to introversion and extroversion. *Journal of Abnormal and Social Psychology* 1929;24:293–309.

61. McGue M, Slutske W, Iacono WG. Personality and substance use disorders. II. Alcoholism versus drug use disorders. *Journal of Consulting and Clinical Psychology* 1999;67:394–404.

62. Mezzich A, Tarter R, Kirisci L, Clark D, Buckstein O, Martin C. Subtypes of early age onset alcoholism. *Alcoholism, Clinical and Experimental Research* 1993;17:767–770.

63. Murphy JM, Berwick DM, Weinstein MC, Borus JF, Budman SH, Klerman G. L. Performance of screening and diagnostic tests: application of a receiver operating characteristic analysis. *Archives of General Psychiatry* 1987;44:550–555.

64. Nathan PE.. The addictive personality is the behavior of the addict. *Journal of Consulting and Clinical Psychology* 1988;56:183–188.

65. Nixon SJ, Parsons OA. Application of the Tridimensional Personality Questionnaire to a population of alcoholics and other substance abusers. *Alcoholism, Clinical and Experimental Research* 1990;14:513–517.

66. O'Boyle M, Barratt ES. Impulsivity and *DSM-III-R* personality disorders. *Personality and Individual Differences* 1993;14:609–611.

67. Robins LN, Helzer JE, Cottler L, Goldring E. *NIMH Diagnostic Interview Schedule, Version III Revised.* Washington, DC: Public Health Service; 1989.

68. Robins LN, Helzer JE, Croughan J, Williams JBW, Spitzer RL. *NIMH Diagnostic Interview Schedule, Version III-A.* Washington, DC: Public Health Service; 1985.

70. Rogosch F, Chassin L, Sher KJ. Personality variables as mediators and moderators of family history risk for alcoholism: conceptual and methodological issues. *Journal of Studies on Alcohol* 1990;51:310–318.

71. Rosenthal TL, Edwards NB, Ackerman BJ, Knott DH, Rosenthal RH. Substance abuse patterns reveal contrasting personality traits. *Journal of Substance Abuse* 1990;2:255–263.

72. SAS Institute. *SAS/STAT User's Guide, Version 6, Fourth Edition.* Cary, NC; 1989.

73. Schaefer MR, Sobieraj K, Hollyfield RL. Severity of alcohol dependence and its relationship to additional psychiatric symptoms in alcoholic inpatients. *American Journal of Drug and Alcohol Abuse* 1987;13:435–447.

74. Schuckit MA. Biological, psychological, and environmental predictors of the alcoholism risk: a longitudinal study. *Journal of Studies on Alcohol* 1998;59:485–494.

75. Selzer M, Vinokur A, van Rooijen L. A self-administered Short Michigan Alcohol-

ism Screening Test (SMAST). *Journal of Studies on Alcohol* 1975;36:117–126.

76. Shedler J, Block J. Adolescent drug use and psychological health. *American Psychologist* 1990;45:612–630.

77. Sher KJ. Stress response dampening. In: Blaine HT, Leonard KE, eds. *Psychological Theories of Drinking and Alcoholism*. New York: Guilford; 1987.

78. Sher KJ. *Children of Alcoholics: A Critical Appraisal of Theory and Research*. Chicago: University of Chicago Press; 1991.

79. Sher KJ, Bartholow BD, Nanda S. Short- and long-term effects of fraternity and sorority membership on heavy drinking: a social norms perspective. *Psychology of Addictive Behaviors*, 2001.

80. Sher KJ, Trull TJ. Personality and disinhibitory psychopathology: alcoholism and antisocial personality disorder. *Journal of Abnormal Psychology* 1994;103:92–102.

81. Sher KJ, Trull TJ, Bartholow BD, Vieth A. Personality and alcoholism: issues, methods, and etiological processes. In: Leonard K, Blaine H, eds. *Psychological Theories of Drinking and Alcoholism, Second Edition*. New York: Guilford; 1999, pp 54–105.

82. Sher KJ, Walitzer KS, Wood PK, Brent EE. Characteristics of children of alcoholics: putative risk factors, substance use and abuse, and psychopathology. *Journal of Abnormal Psychology* 1991;100:427–448.

83. Sher KJ, Wood MD, Crews TM, Vandiver PA. The Tridimensional Personality Questionnaire: reliability and validity studies and derivation of a short form. *Psychological Assessment* 1995;7:195–208.

84. Tarter RE. Are there inherited behavioral traits that predispose to substance abuse? *Journal of Consulting and Clinical Psychology* 1988;56:189–196.

85. Tellegen A. Structures of mood and personality and their relevance to assessing anxiety with an emphasis on self-report. In: Tuma AH, Maser JD, eds. *Anxiety and the Anxiety Disorders*. Hillsdale, NJ: Erlbaum; 1985, pp 681–706.

86. Trull TJ, Sher KJ. Relationship between the Five-Factor model of personality and Axis 1 disorders in a nonclinical sample. *Journal of Abnormal Psychology* 1994;103:350–360.

87. Warner LA, Kessler RC, Hughes M, Anthony JC, Nelson, CB. Prevalence and correlates of drug use and dependence in the United States: results from the National Comorbidity Survey. *Archives of General Psychiatry* 1995;52:219–229.

88. Wiggins JS, Trapnell PD. Personality structure: the return of the Big Five. In: Hogan R, Johnson J, Briggs S, eds. *Handbook of Personality Psychology*. New York: Academic Press; 1997, pp 737–765.

89. Wills TA, Vaccaro D, McNamara G. Novelty seeking, risk taking, and related constructs as predictors of adolescent substance use: an application of Cloninger's theory. *Journal of Substance Abuse* 1994;6:1–20.

90. Wood MD, Vinson DC, Sher KJ. Alcohol use and misuse. In: Baum A, Revenson T, Singer J, eds. *Handbook of Health Psychology*. Hillsdale, NJ: Erlbaum; in press.

91. Zuckerman M. P-impulsive sensation seeking and its behavioral, psychophysiological biochemical correlates. *Neuropsychobiology* 1993;28:30–36.

92. Zuckerman M. *Behavioral Expressions and Biosocial Bases of Sensation Seeking*. New York: Cambridge University Press; 1994.

93. Zuckerman M, Cloninger CR. Relationships between Cloninger's, Zuckerman's, and Eysenck's dimensions of personality. *Personality and Individual Differences* 1996;21:283–285.

94. Zuckerman M, Kuhlman DM, Camac C. What lies beyond E and N? Factor analyses of scales believed to measure basic dimensions of personality. *Journal of Personality and Social Psychology* 1988;54:96–107.

95. Zuckerman M, Kuhlman DM, Joireman J, Teta P, Kraft M. A comparison of three structural models for personality: the big three, the big five, and the alternative five. *Journal of Personality and Social Psychology* 1993;67:757–768.

Permission Acknowledgments

The following chapters were previously published. Permission to reprint is gratefully acknowledged here.

Compton WM III, Cottler LB, Phelps DL, Ben Abdallah A, Spitznagel EL. Psychiatric disorders among drug-dependent subjects: are they primary or secondary? *Am J Addict* 2000;9(2):126–34. © 2000 American Academy of Addiction Psychiatry. Reprinted by permission of Brunner-Routledge and Taylor & Francis.

Drake RE, Essock SM, Shaner A, Carey KB, Minkoff K, Kola L, Lynde D, Osher FC, Clark RE, Rickards L. Implementing dual-diagnosis services for clients with severe mental illness. *Psychiatr Serv* 2001;52(4):469–76. Review. © 2001 American Psychiatric Association. Reprinted with permission.

Franken IH, Hendriks VM. Screening and diagnosis of anxiety and mood disorders in substance abuse patients. *Am J Addict* 2001;10(1):30–9. © 2000 American Academy of Addiction Psychiatry. Reprinted by permission of Brunner-Routledge and Taylor & Francis.

Jacobsen LK, Southwick SM, Kosten TR. Substance use disorders in patients with posttraumatic stress disorder: a review of the literature. *Am J Psychiatry* 2001;158(8):1184–90. Review. © 2001 American Psychiatric Association. Reprinted with permission.

Kendler KS, Karkowski LM, Neale MC, Prescott CA. Illicit psychoactive substance use, heavy use, abuse, and dependence in a U.S. population-based sample of male twins. *Arch Gen Psychiatry* 2000;57(3):261–269. © 2000 American Medical Association

Martino S, Carroll KM, O'Malley SS, Rounsaville BJ. Motivational interviewing with psychiatrically ill substance abusing patients. *Am J Addict* 2000;9(1):88–91. © 2000 American Academy of Addiction Psychiatry. Reprinted by permission of Brunner-Routledge and Taylor & Francis.

McCann BS, Simpson TL, Ries R, Roy-Byrne P. Reliability and validity of screening instruments for drug and alcohol abuse in adults seeking evaluation for attention-deficit/hyperactivity disorder. *Am J Addict* 2000;9(1):1–9. © 2000 American Academy of Addiction Psychiatry. Reprinted by permission of Brunner-Routledge and Taylor & Francis.

McGrath PJ, Nunes EV, Quitkin FM. Current concepts in the treatment of depression in alcohol-dependent patients. *Psychiatr Clin North Am* 2000;23(4):695-711, V. Review. © 2000 W.B. Saunders Company. Reprinted by permission.

Salyers MP, Mueser KT. Social functioning, psychopathology, and medication side effects in relation to substance use and abuse in schizophrenia. *Schizophr Res* 2001;48(1):109–123. © 2001 Elsevier Science. Reprinted with permission. Reprinted by permission of Brunner-Routledge and Taylor & Francis.

Sher KJ, Bartholow BD, Wood MD. Personality and substance use disorders: a prospective study. *J Consult Clin Psychol* 2000;68(5):818–829. © 2000 American Psychological Association. Reprinted with permission.

Toneatto T, Negrete JC, Calderwood K. Diagnostic subgroups within a sample of comorbid substance abusers: correlates and characteristics. *Am J Addict* 2000;9(3):253–64. © 2000 American Academy of Addiction Psychiatry. Reprinted by permission of Brunner-Routledge and Taylor & Francis.

Weiss RD, Kolodziej ME, Najavits LM, Greenfield SF, Fucito LM. Utilization of psychosocial treatments by patients diagnosed with bipolar disorder and substance dependence. *Am J Addict* 2000;9(4):314–320. © 2000 American Academy of Addiction Psychiatry. Reprinted by permission of Brunner-Routledge and Taylor & Francis.

About the American Academy of Addiction Psychiatry

The American Academy of Addiction Psychiatry is a professional membership organization with approximately 1,000 members in the United States and around the world. The membership consists of psychiatrists who work with addiction in their practices, faculty at various academic institutions, nonpsychiatrist professionals who are making a contribution to the field of addiction psychiatry, and residents and medical students.

The American Academy of Addiction Psychiatry was founded in 1985

- To promote accessibility to highest-quality treatment for all who need it,
- To promote excellence in clinical practice in addiction psychiatry,
- To educate the public and influence public policy regarding addictive illness,
- To provide continuing education for addiction professionals,
- To disseminate new information in the field of addiction psychiatry, and
- To encourage research on the etiology, prevention, identification, and treatment of the addictions.

The Academy sponsors various scientific meetings, including an Annual Scientific Meeting and Symposium, a Review Course on Addiction Psychiatry, and symposia and workshops on timely clinical, educational, and research topics in the addiction field.

The American Journal on Addictions, a leading clinical journal listed in Index Medicus and many other databases, is the official journal of AAAP. The journal serves as a forum from which today's leading clinicians gain rapid access to advances in current treatment methods, original peer-reviewed research, and improved clinical outcome.

For more information about AAAP activities or to request a membership packet, call 913-262-6161, e-mail info@aaap.org, or visit the AAAP Web site, at www.aaap.org

Index